About this map: Locations are approximate and not to scale.
This illustration captures the spirit of the journey rather than geographic precision.

An Adventure Log

A CHRONICLE OF CLIMBING, RUNNING, AND BIKING

An Adventure Log

A CHRONICLE OF CLIMBING, RUNNING, AND BIKING

JIM DOTI

An Adventure Log, A Chronicle of Climbing, Running, and Biking
Published by Fern Press
fern-press.com

Library of Congress Control Number: 2025917385

ISBN 979-8-218-76217-9

Second Printing

Printed in the United States of America

DEDICATION

To the memory of our fellow adventurer extraordinaire,
John Stephen Dahlem

Author's Note

All proceeds from the sale of this book will be donated to the Chapman University
Dahlem-Doti-Struppa Climbing Wall and Mountaineering Alcove.

CONTENTS

CLIMBING

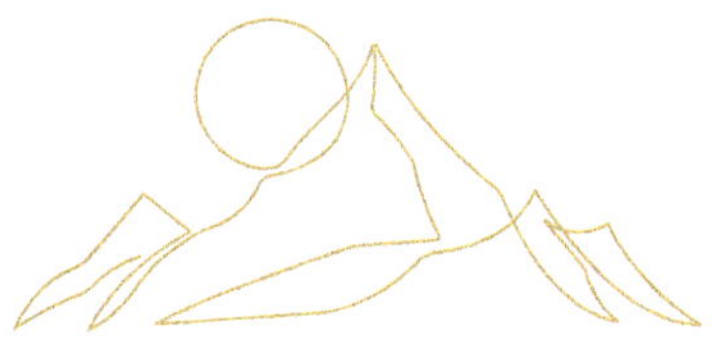

*The ranges heaved up all round them; they met mountain air,
with its life-giving holy pureness. They entered
the open secrecy of the heights.*

—Mary Renault

A NOTE BY JIM DOTI

SUMMITING a mountain – be it the 5,689-foot Santiago Peak in Orange County, California, or the 29,032-foot Mount Everest in the Himalayas – is not the real purpose of mountain climbing. Such a view by the editor of this adventure log and contributor to many of its articles may strike one as surprising. That may be, but it also focuses attention on that aspect of climbing that defines its real meaning and special allure.

That special allure can be found in the articles on climbing in Part I of this adventure log. To aid in that discovery, be on the lookout for the sights, sounds, and smells that make each of our climbing experiences less a test of endurance and more an adventure in living. Be particularly mindful of the colorful cast of characters we meet along the way.

In my account, for example, of climbing Mount Rainier with my son, Adam, I hope you'll be able to imagine the smell of John and Tammi Bratholm's Special "Pizza with the Works" as well as be impressed with how we integrated that pizza in our climb. My wife Lynne's log of climbing a small peak turns out to be a big experience with Cindy – our Santiago Mountain Shepherd. It also shows that one doesn't have to go to the ends of the world to find adventure. It can often be discovered close to one's backyard.

Reaching the summit of Mount Kilimanjaro, as recounted in "Climbing Kili Pole-Pole," wasn't half as much fun as singing and eating ugali with our porters. In "Ascending Mount Aconcagua," I learned how simple encouragement from our lead guide, Eric Murphy, like "You can do it," can become a powerful stimulant. Eric's admonition to us not to be intimidated by the summit looming in the distance but rather focus on all the mini-goals along the way was a critically important leadership strategy for me. I often think about that strategy whenever I'm confronted by a challenging task.

My account of "Scaling Mount Elbrus" provides evidence that it's actually possible to communicate with the dead, even Russian greats like Dostoevsky and Tchaikovsky.

"Climbing Antarctica's Highest Peak" taught me how my comparative advantage in knowing how to treat blisters helped compensate for being my climbing team's laggard. My article, "Anatomy of a Denali Summit Bid," and my son Adam's follow-up, "Summiting Denali," are more about the rite of passage between father and son than they are about summitting a mountain.

The two articles about climbing Carstensz Pyramid (Puncak Jaya) by me and the other by Scott Chapman show how the same climb can evoke contrasting memories on the part of different climbers. Daniele Struppa's experience climbing the "Turquoise Goddess… Mount Cho Oyu" beautifully captures the trade-offs between climbing and one's career and even one's love life. One other thing: The scene of Daniele seeing Japanese tourists on a terrace as he closed in on the summit of the arête is a great example of how climbing is a never-ending wellspring of surprises.

Ryan Dahlem's account of summiting Everest with his Dad beautifully explains how such a feat pales in comparison to how that feat can bond a father and son as well as climbers to their sherpas. Ryan's concluding thoughts about Everest's legacy, I believe, say it all: "The summit was never just a place. It was a moment in time that represented a larger journey and an enduring bond between a father and son."

The authors of these articles all have day jobs. Somehow, some way, they carved out enough time to experience and then record their adventures, pushing against the boundaries that often constrain the range of life's offerings. Their joie de vivre mirrors that of Hunter S. Thompson when he famously wrote:

Life should not be a journey to the grave with the intention of arriving safely in a pretty and well-preserved body, but rather to skid in broadside in a cloud of smoke, thoroughly used up, totally worn out, and loudly proclaiming, "Wow! What a ride!"

Mt. Rainier Beckons

Jim Doti

IN 2002, my 28-year-old son, Adam, called me and said, "Let's do Mt. Rainier." Last summer, Adam and I scaled Mt. Whitney and had a terrific time doing it. But Mt. Rainier is different. It has glaciers, crevasses and avalanches. More to the point – people die there.

But Adam caught me at a weak moment. A respite from everyday life to courageously battle the elements and conquer a snow and ice-covered peak sounded like the stuff of a great adventure. Already, I could imagine myself standing on top, victoriously waving my ice ax high in the air. Besides, it would be a terrific way of getting into shape. So I agreed to go, not quite sure what I was getting myself into.

That became a bit clearer when I received in the mail my first information from our guide service, Rainier Mountaineering, Inc. (RMI). In addition to requiring that I sign all my rights away in an "Acknowledgement of Risk" form, the accompanying literature was not quite as inviting as a Club Med brochure. This is what it said:

Mt. Rainier is considered to be one of the toughest endurance climbs in the lower 48 states. Mt. Rainier, at 14,410 feet, is the most extensively glaciated volcanic peak in the continental United States. It is NOT an easy climb. Significant elements of risk in mountaineering, such as avalanches, ice falls, rock falls, crevasse falls, inclement weather, high winds, and severe cold, can be managed but not eliminated. The two-day climb is an eighteen-mile round trip, with an elevation gain and loss of 18,000 vertical feet. On summit day, be prepared to climb for 12 to 18 hours while carrying a backpack.

Mountaineering is a physically demanding sport and conditioning is the single most important way you can help ensure a safe and successful climb. Remember, you cannot over train for this trip! Be in the best shape of your life!

So began the most intense conditioning to which I've ever subjected my body. In addition to my usual training like running, weight-lifting, and Nordic Track, I added walking around with a backpack weighted down with 60 pounds of cat food, a task that was particularly challenging for me since I weigh about 130 pounds.

To give you an idea of how challenging, I don't think I'll ever forget an early experience I had on a practice walk with my wife, Lynne, and our dog, Cindy. (Named "Cindy" because her big brown eyes and a mole on the right side of her mouth gave her an uncanny resemblance to Cindy Crawford.)

As is her wont, Cindy (the dog, that is, not the model) took a dump on the side of the walking path. As I leaned over to blue bag her business, the weight of the backpack caused me to topple over on my back. I never gave much thought to how a turtle feels on its back, but during the next few moments, as I struggled to right myself, I had a pretty good idea. Thankfully, Lynne was able to help me up, at least after her hysterical laughter ran its course.

As recounted in the next article, the three of us also climbed Santiago Peak ("Saddleback" to us locals). At an altitude gain of 4,000 feet, rising from about 1,700 feet to 5,700 feet, it isn't much of a practice run, but it sure is a beautiful trail with its abundance of waterfalls, streams, and oak trees right here in Orange County, California. There's also an element of danger. With 60 pounds of cat food on my back, I suspect I was being stalked by every mountain lion in close proximity.

When we finally made it to the top of Santiago Peak for a spectacular 360° view of the haze and smog that enveloped Orange County, I was particularly proud of Cindy. At 10 years old, I like to think that she is the oldest dog to have made it to the summit. If you're wondering what this powerful dog's breed is, I should tell you that Cindy's a mutt we adopted on what we were told would be her last day at the pound. To impress my friends who own exotic dogs, I've invented a breed name for Cindy. She will be the first and last "Santiago Mountain Shepard" to ever roam the face of the world.

About a month before our Rainier trip, I decided to go for a practice climb on Mt. Whitney, along with Adam and his fiancée, Brenda. Our plan was to climb from the Whitney Portal at 8,500 feet to the Trailside campsite at around 12,000 feet and spend the night before going on to the summit at 14,494 feet. The only problem was that Adam and Brenda decided to stay at a lower base camp. Since I wanted a head start in going for the summit, I decided to go on alone to Trailside.

Normally, in the summer, this camp is like the spaceport Mos Eisley in *Star Wars*, so I fully expected to have the company of plenty of similarly deranged fellow climbers. Not so. As I approached the campsite late in the day, I realized

Brenda and Adam near base camp

I was the only one there. This meant I'd have to camp alone – well, not quite all alone. We were warned that bears were just coming out of hibernation and were likely to be very hungry. As I lay there in my sleeping bag, I suspected every rustle of wind against my tent was the sound of bear claws tenderly sizing up what might be inside that was good to eat. Needless to say, I didn't get much sleep that night.

I wanted to test my mettle in snow and found plenty of it. So much, in fact, that without the crampons, ice axes and other special gear we would be renting at Mt. Rainier, I couldn't quite get to the top of Mt. Whitney. But it was a great training climb, and I had just enough time to recover fully before our attempt at Mt. Rainier. Adam and I met in Seattle and headed to Ashford to meet the RMI group.

Breathing Lessons

One of the great advantages of being on an RMI expedition is that everyone is expected to attend a one-day climbing school before making a summit attempt on Mt. Rainier. So my son, Adam, and I became students again and learned the basics of ice/glacier climbing with crampons and the techniques of climbing on a rope team. We were told an altitude gain of around 9,000 feet from the base to the summit of Rainier is like walking up the Empire State Building almost eight times.

If that wasn't bad enough, we were reminded that we would have to do it carrying heavy packs while continually ascending into thinner air.

Because of the lower air pressure at high altitudes, every breath of air we take in at the summit of Rainier results in 40 percent less oxygen than at sea level. It's the thin air and lack of oxygen that sometimes lead to acute mountain sickness (AMS) or the more serious and potentially fatal high-altitude cerebral edema (HACE). Because of these maladies, we needed to climb as efficiently as possible, and that meant learning how to maximize our oxygen intake by a technique called "pressure breathing." This involves sucking air in and then exhaling as if you're blowing out a hundred candles.

To climb most efficiently, we also had to learn how to do the rest step. This technique essentially involves shifting one's body weight to the resting forward leg when it is in a vertical position and then raising the trailing leg to the next step while keeping it as close to the ground as possible. Sounds complicated, but after you get in the groove, it's easy to see why RMI believes this is the most efficient way to climb.

We also learned and were rigorously tested on safety techniques, the most important of which was quickly getting into an anchor position to save a roped teammate who may have fallen. When you hear that teammate yell "falling," you're supposed to immediately drop to the ground, plant your ax into the snow about an inch away from your face, and desperately hold on at all costs.

Practicing my ice ax in the snow to "self-arrest"

Only the week before, three experienced climbers had died on Mount Rainier, and thus, our safety lessons took on heightened importance.

Although only about half of those who attempt Mt. Rainier make it to the summit, we learned the ratio is lower in May and June because of erratic weather patterns and particularly high winds. Mt. Rainier's microclimate mirrors Himalayan climbing conditions, albeit at a much lower altitude, which is why it is often used as a training ground for those preparing to summit Mt. Everest.

Beginning the Climb

When our big day finally arrived to start our bid for the summit, the weather at the 5400-foot base seemed pleasant enough, but we knew anything could be happening on top. That first day involved a seemingly relentless, slogging,

Me and Adam bringing up the rear

five-and-a-half-hour climb to Camp Muir at 10,000 feet. When we arrived late in the afternoon and got settled in our unheated, three-level bunkhouse, I quickly recognized the accuracy of Bruce Barcott's description of Camp Muir in his wonderful book, *The Measure of a Mountain: Beauty and Terror on Mount Rainier:*

Muir is a micro soviet of cranky, tired, nauseous, scared, anxious, angry, cold, and often-paranoid human beings whose brains are not receiving as much oxygen as they should. They smell bad. Since walking in plastic climbing boots is awkward and taxing, the main activity at Camp Muir is sitting.

Me and Adam at the 10,000 ft crest at Camp Muir

I should also add eating. Since our next day's climb would involve 12 to 18 hours of climbing, we needed to work on some serious carbo-loading. Rather than consume the freeze-dried stuff that some people generously, but I might add inaccurately, call food, Adam and I decided the best source of carbohydrates is pizza.

Since Camp Muir is not the kind of place with a Pizza Hut around, we needed to plan for this in advance. The previous night, the proprietor of Ashford's general store told us there was a pizza place about a half-hour drive away in the town of Eatonville. When we got there, we found that the pizza place was actually named the "Pizza Place." From the front, it looked like somebody's garage. But as my mother often told me, don't go by appearances. It turned out that the "Pizza Place" rated near the top of pizza places I've known and loved. The owners, John and Tammi Bratholm, are Rat Pack aficionados and have plastered the walls of the Pizza Place with photos of Frank, Dino and Sammy. As Dino could be heard in the background singing "That's Amore," Adam and I wolfed down John and Tammi's "Special with the Works" that included as toppings: sausage, prosciutto, meatballs, artichoke, pepper, onion, asparagus and spinach. After we ate our fill, Tammi took our leftover slices and carefully wrapped them in aluminum foil and sealed plastic bags so that the pizza could be easily transported in our backpacks.

In Camp Muir, we ceremoniously unwrapped the pizza and dug in. I felt the jealous eyes of all our climbing mates on us as they sullenly ate their boil-in-a-bag versions of beef stroganoff and Hungarian goulash.

When we finished eating, at around 7:00 p.m., our lead guide, Matt Farmer, told us we needed to get in our sleeping bags and get some sleep before his wake-up call in about six hours at 1:00 a.m. Leaving at that ungodly time of the morning is called an "Alpine Ascent" and is necessary in order to reach the summit while the snow is still firm and makes it possible to climb down the mountain the same day. Matt then supplied us with earplugs so we wouldn't be disturbed by our bunkmates' sleeping sounds.

Lead guide Matt Farmer is in the middle

In spite of the earplugs, the cacophony of snores, wheezes, grunts, and groans came through loud and clear. And since the earplugs made my head feel like it was ready to explode, I took them out and resigned myself to staring all night at the ceiling (I had a top bunk) while listening to my bunkmates' symphonic interpretations.

Ascent into a Blizzard

At 1:00, Matt came into the bunkhouse to tell us it was a "go" for attempting the summit, but he was worried that the weather "looked squirrely out there."

Adding to his worries was the fact that two more climbers (not RMI-related) had been killed the previous day. They were blown off a ridge and fell down a steep part of Ingraham Glacier – the very glacier we'd be negotiating in a few hours.

With that on our minds, when we got outside to start putting on our crampons, it was a beautiful evening with stars all aglow, and while the temperature was in the teens, it didn't seem too cold.

And it wasn't as dark as I expected, either. When we took our first steps, I not only felt good but marveled at the surrealistic sight of our three separate teams of four walking in unison across the Cowlitz Glacier. The sight of an ant-like line of headlamps on the helmets of all my rope partners and the other two roped teams ahead reminded me of the seven dwarfs. I felt like singing, "Hi-ho, hi-ho, it's off to work we go." Bruce Barcott described those first steps on the Cowlitz Glacier beautifully:

> *There are few more thrilling moments in life than the first steps of a summit day... Even the satisfaction of topping out cannot match it. Under a brilliant moon, you step onto a shadowy glacier, matching your rope partners step for step, your heart pumping equal parts apprehension and adrenaline to the ends of your fingers and toes, and all you hear is the sound of your boots shattering thousands of crystals.*

Unfortunately for me, I heard more than the sound of boots. The sound of wind began to grow. Every so often, unsettling gusts of wind would rip through the glacier, making it difficult to continue our trek. But continue we did, and quickly too, since we were warned that the Cowlitz Glacier is a rock slide area, a warning that was shown to be well-founded by the presence of large rocks all around us.

As we proceeded up the steep Cathedral Gap leading to the Ingraham Glacier, the wind steadily picked up and began to howl. Maintaining our balance proved increasingly difficult in the rocky crags of the gap. Hobbling over rocks and stones, our crampons created sparks that flashed through the night.

When we arrived at the Ingraham Flats at around 11,500 feet, the wind increased to about 50 MPH with gusts hitting 70 MPH. At that point, all we could do was protect our eyes and faces from air-born snow and ice crystals by turning our helmets directly into the wind. Our training paid off as we planted our axes in the snow and held on for dear life. As I peeked out, I saw my son and his rope mate in anchor positions, holding onto a teammate between them who had fallen off the trail.

While hunkering down in the middle of this blizzard, the likes of which this native of the Windy City had never experienced before, I asked myself how

I ever got into this predicament. The British climber George Mallory justified his ill-fated attempts to summit Mt. Everest by saying, "Because it is there." A friend of the famous psychologist Carl Jung had another rationale for the allure of climbing. He told Jung of a dream he had where when reaching the top, "my happiness and elation are so great that I feel I could mount right up into space."

I didn't quite see it that way. In the ghastly situation I found myself, my hopes were centered not on the happiness and elation of reaching the top, but on the safety and security of reaching the bottom. My hopes came closer to realization as I saw our lead guide, Matt Farmer, circle his hands in the air, indicating a retreat from this living Hell.

After two hours of retreat, we tromped into the friendly confines of our bunkhouse at Camp Muir. We all, I'm sure, shared the same bittersweet feelings. While we were happy to be out of a howling blizzard, we hadn't accomplished our goal to "bag" the summit. Matt did the best he could to boost our spirits by telling us we gave it our all and, more importantly, made it back safely. He said, "Rainier will be there when you want to try again."

Sunk Costs

Our final descent from Camp Muir to Paradise gave me an opportunity to pass on to my son, Adam, one of the great laws of life: The law of sunk costs, one of the most practical and useful economic laws out there.

Matt told us we would need only one quart of water each to get down. But Adam and I had two quarts each. Since no water is readily available at Muir, it must be made by melting snow using very expensive, short supplies of propane gas. Obviously, water is a very precious commodity at 10,000 feet. As a result, we were all told to be very careful in our use of water.

My response, though, in hearing we needed only one quart of water to make it to the bottom, was to immediately begin dumping my extra quart into the snow. Adam was aghast at my wastefulness and ranted over my profligacy. But why should I add weight to my pack when that water, at anything near sea level, was of no real value? When Adam demonstrated that the tremendous costs of producing the water justified schlepping it down, I was able to illustrate the law of sunk costs. That is, the costs of producing water at 10,000 feet have no relevance in determining the value of water at a different time and location. In other words, when it comes to costs, forget about the past and look to the future.

All of this led me to a different conclusion about why climbers strive for the mountaintop. I don't think Mallory or Jung's friend had it right. I see mountain climbing as something akin to the purpose of education. That purpose revolves around the search for truth.

A former professor at Chapman University by the name of Quintin DeYoung described that search for truth as follows:

The vision dims… I grow weary. I am old and tired now… Will you seize and grasp my flickering flame? Oh!… Love truth! Seek knowledge! Not because I implore you. But seek your knowledge and truth for its own sake. Try it! Test it! You may find, as I have found, there is no truth… only the quest. But if you find the truth, please spare me. Don't let me know. While I breathe, I prefer to seek.

Striving for the mountaintop, I think, is like the search for truth. It's not the allure of the summit but rather the allure of the quest.

It's about getting in shape by carrying a heavy backpack around the neighborhood and local hills with my dog, Cindy, close at my side. It's camping alone at 12,000 feet under the stars while imagining what it's like to be grasped by the claws of a hungry bear. It's learning the techniques of rope climbing and anchoring. It's being caught in a brutal blizzard the likes of which I've never encountered before. It's about having an opportunity to impart the law of sunk costs on an unsuspecting soul. Most important, it's about setting goals and striving to accomplish them.

P.S. About a month later, an opportunity came along for me to make another attempt on Rainier. This time, I made it to the top. How was it, you ask? I believe Professor DeYoung was right on: "There is no truth… only the quest."

At the summit of Mt. Ranier on my second attempt

Climbing Santiago Peak

Lynne Doti

THE guidebook said it would take 7 hours, so Jim and I left at 8 a.m. and had a nice breakfast at IHOP. Our Chapman University colleague and friend, Raymond Sfeir, enjoyed his pancakes, noting he'd had nothing more than water in the morning for many years, presumably one reason for his rail-thin frame. I got Swedish rather than the German pancakes I ordered, but Jim thought that was for the best as he associates lingonberries with Roald Amundsen's successful expedition to the South Pole. We only planned to hike to the top of Santiago Peak, which, at about 6,000 ft, is the highest point in Orange County, California.

After our pancakes, we drove to Trabuco Canyon Road. We had hiked this area before, but it was in far worse shape than we remembered, riddled with potholes and massive puddles of indeterminate depth. It took 20 minutes to negotiate 3 miles to the parking area. "I wonder why they don't pave this," said Jim, missing the point of the rural thing.

The day was lovely and sunny, with some haze to cut the heat. We strolled by rustic cabins, marveling that the people living in them negotiated the dirt road routinely. The large trees along the swift-flowing stream cast deep shade. It was lovely, and we decided to take the mile detour to Holy Jim Falls. Only in OC would a 12-foot tall, 2-foot wide waterfall be a tourist attraction!

We got back to the cutoff and began up the switchbacks, looping between the green, damp, and fern-clad side to the desert, dry, and chaparral side of the hills as we rose. When Raymond and I turned back at a switchback, our dog, Cindy, would stop walking, looking down at Jim below and at Raymond and me walking up the trail. She would stay in place until Jim reached the turn where she was, always keeping him in her sight. Then she would speed up and catch up to Raymond and me. She did this at every long switchback, keeping all of us in her sight at all times. Jim occasionally reported on the altitude, using his oversized, over-bred watch. The distant but loud sound of rushing water and the pine trees dotting the shady side of the hills made it seem pleasantly alpine.

Jim and Raymond at the trailhead

We stopped for lunch at about 2 p.m., where the trail meets a dirt road. Cindy remembered the spots where there were water puddles the last time on the mountain. She seemed puzzled that this year they had dried up. So she gave up and settled down to beg for some of our lunch. I was prepared for this, however, and offered her some dog food we brought with us. She wasn't interested. A woman came with her large golden retriever and sat on a rock to read. Her dog and Cindy sniffed, then set off to run aimlessly together. However, after they returned and the woman offered both dogs some people food, a truly vicious fight ensued. I set off to retrieve Cindy as the woman frantically tried to separate the two dogs. I dragged Cindy off, assuring her that she had won. She was happy. I leashed her and she resumed begging for bits of turkey sandwich.

The road continues to the top but is rocky, gutted, and steep. We were getting tired and spread out. Cindy didn't like this, but she was tired, too. Instead of shepherding us, she resorted to waiting patiently for the straggler. I grew dazed and walked for I don't know how long, not noticing my surroundings or how long I had been out of contact with everyone else. I sat to have a snack and Raymond soon caught up to me. Jim and Cindy came just a short time later, and we all refueled.

It was definitely getting more difficult to move my legs. When a vista opened of the 15 freeway and its attendant development, I took a long break. At least we were above the brown air that blanketed the valley below.

People started passing us, coming down from the top - with snowballs!

"There is snow on top?" we asked incredulously. Soon, we found ourselves, warm in thin shirts, walking on a deep bed of slushy snow. It was only in areas protected from the sun, of course, but there was a remarkable amount left, considering the last precipitation was about 10 days ago.

We made it to the various towers that marked the top of the peak. Raymond stretched precariously on a large log and feigned sleep. Later, he joined Jim and me in wondering what the sign on the door of a tiny concrete building meant: "Space Available: Call 714 635-3953." Space for what? Who would want space at the top of Santiago Peak for an 8 X 10 feet building?

Jim said, "Let's go before our bodies freeze up." I got up but inquired, "What does that mean, exactly?" My legs seemed to like sitting down. He assured me that sitting would only lead to more pain in the end. So I shouldered my backpack and started down. Only after the towers were above us did I realize that I had not taken any pictures of us at the top.

The downward trip was a forced march, mostly silent people just putting

Jim and me at Holy Jim Falls

one foot in front of the other. Cindy seemed to be favoring her right front paw and clearly no longer cared if we straggled or kept in close formation. We gradually began to realize that it was getting dark. The distant sound of rushing water only reminded us that at the bottom, there were seven or eight difficult crossings of the rushing stream, which had not been easy even in the bright light of day. Then, there was the drive on the dirt road to come after we made it to the car.

It soon got very dark, but there was a sliver of moon to give us faint light where the trees left gaps. I slightly wrenched my ankle on an unexpected drop. We made our way very slowly, losing count of the stream crossings and wondering before each crossing if the path continued on the other side.

The first light we saw, car or house not determined, was a very welcome

Raymond, Jim and Cindy near the summit

sight, and passing the gate that marked the difference between trail and road gave us confidence. As it turned out, the most difficult stream crossing was yet to come, and Raymond terrified us by walking along the top of a small dam to avoid the water spilling across the road. Soon after that, we turned into a clearing and discovered we were standing in the parking lot.

Once in the car, we prepared ourselves for the final challenge: driving our car through the 4.3-mile dirt road before the paved highway. It was a horrible ride in spite of very careful driving by Jim. We were jerked violently by potholes, and we crawled around massive ponds. There was a particularly bad spot that had spawned a detour sign. A Jeep was sunk halfway into a pond and several trucks had collected nearby, trying to rescue the vehicle. We were able to squeeze by. Jim said, "You had better enjoy this ride while you can because we are never coming this way again."

Climbing Kili Pole-Pole

Jim Doti

From my log, August 1 – 16, 2003:

August 1

After arriving in Nairobi, my wife, Lynne and I met our tour bus to start our 5-hour trip south to Arusha, Tanzania near the foothills of Mt. Kilimanjaro. The bus was crammed, from young children in uniforms to an Arab with two wives and three kids, to an Australian couple. We saw giraffes and antelopes along the way. I missed a lot of the scenery since I was half-conscious from jetlag. We arrived in Arusha at 7:30 p.m.

August 2

We were picked up at 9:00 a.m. and taken to the tour office for a briefing. I told the tour official about my concerns about climbing Kilimanjaro and dealing with its peak elevation of 19,341 feet. When he asked about my climbing experience and told him I climbed Mt. Rainier, he said, "Don't worry. Kili will be a piece of cake."

Later that day, Adam finally arrived to join us, and we all ate a big Chinese dinner. The entertainment included local acrobats. They reminded me of old acts on the Ed Sullivan Show.

August 10

Following a traditional "Jambo Jambo" greeting from our team leader and six porters (Africa's version of sherpas), Adam and I started our 6-day Kili climb following the popular Machame route. It was a 7-hour climb to Machame Camp at 9,800 feet. It started out in a dry riverbed that goes through a rainforest. True to its name, heavy rain soon flooded the dry bed and turned it into a raging river.

What started out as an idyllic trek through a forest of trees filled with exotic birds and screeching monkeys turned into a tough slog through what seemed like quicksand. When we finally made it to our camp, we along with all of our gear were soaked. It took us a day to dry everything out.

Here comes the flood

August 12

Compared to our first day's slog in a torrential downpour, our climb to Shira Camp at 12,700 feet was "a piece of cake."

It took us five hours to make it to camp. On the way, we enjoyed incredible views of the valley below us. At camp, a wonderful multi-course dinner prepared by our porter chef, Daniel, awaited us.

Drying out

Our lead guide, God Bless

Chef Daniel serving us rice

Even our tents were already set up. A Kili climb with porters is more like a pleasant stay at a nice resort. The porters did the heavy lifting by carrying all of our camp gear. All that was left for us to carry were light day packs. It's easy to get spoiled on a climb like this.

Our tent with Kili in the background

August 13

Our hike to Barranca camp at 13,000 feet was pretty effortless. After a nice lunch, we continued our 4-hour hike – not climb - to our camp. It's interesting that only a few days ago, we were in what seemed like a tropical jungle, and now the terrain looks more like a desert. I've been taking Diamox to prepare for the altitude gain to Barafu camp at 15,300 feet. Up to now, the highest I've climbed is the summit of Mt. Whitney at 14,500 feet.

Here I am taking my Diamox

August 14

After a bountiful breakfast, the climb to Barafu was steeper and rockier than any of the terrain we'd experienced so far. It wasn't really difficult, especially carrying only day packs, but I was definitely breathing harder. Our guide, whose name is "God Bless," kept telling me, "pole-pole" which translates to slowly-slowly.

As Adam and I were eating our dinner, we heard singing going on in the porter's tent. We peaked in and asked God Bless if we could join them. They not only were willing to have us as a company, but they also seemed to enjoy having us share in their festivities. As they taught us enough Swahili to join them in the singing, they shared with us their native dish of ugali, a simple dish similar to polenta made from cornmeal and water. The way we ate it was to grab a handful of ugali from a common pot and form it into a ball, like making a meatball. Then you punch a hole into the ball with your thumb and fill it with various ingredients like spinach or potato. I don't know if it was the altitude or the camaraderie we shared, but our ugali experience will go down as one of my all-time favorite dining experiences.

August 16

After a short hike to high camp at around 16,000 feet, we had a light dinner and took a short nap in preparation for an early start at midnight for our summit attempt.

At midnight, we put on headlamps. Now starts the serious climbing through scree and steep terrain. While I'm breathing deeply, I have no problems with the altitude, even though I stopped taking Diamox a few days

High camp

Adam and me on the summit

ago. I didn't like the tingly feeling I had in the tips of my fingers, a common symptom of Diamox. Seems like I'm one of the lucky ones who can handle the altitude, at least at 19,000 feet.

As we approached the summit following a zig-zag trail, we reached "Uhuru Peak" at the 19,500-foot summit. We arrived at the peak to witness a glorious sunset while looking out at nearby peaks as well as the Rebmann and Furtwangler glaciers.

While the snows of Kilimanjaro had receded from what we had seen in photos, we saw what was left. It probably won't be long before even that disappears.

After taking the obligatory photos at the historic sign at the Uhuru Peak summit, we started our long 6-hour climb down to the Millennium camp at around 12,250 feet. That climb down the mountain turned out to be a lot more challenging than we expected. The terrain was akin to the desert planet Tatooine at the outer rim of the Star Wars galaxy.

Our Tatooine on Kili

Adam with his bandana

The winds traveling through our Kilimanjaro "desert" lifted clouds of fine sand that soon caked our noses and made breathing difficult. We improvised by wrapping bandanas around our noses and mouths. While that got us through the worst of it, we would have been better prepared if we had brought face masks with us.

After a deep sleep, Adam and I joined our team for the final trek back to the Mweka Camp at 10,000 feet. Lynne and our safari guide extraordinaire, Martin Matei, were there to join us for a final breakfast.

As Adam and I drove back to our hotel with Lynne and Martin, we were already beginning to strategize about our next climbing adventure. Now that we had knocked off our first of the Seven Summits, we began to set our sights on a much tougher challenge than Kili – making it to the top of the 22,837 summit of Mt. Aconcagua in Argentina.

Our last Kili breakfast

Ascending Mt. Aconcagua

Jim Doti

I wake up gasping for breath. This has become a nightly occurrence since ascending to an altitude of over 16,000 feet, not that its familiarity makes it any less horrifying.

After 10 or so heaving gasps, I feel my life returning – as well as the sudden urge to urinate. My hand gropes around inside my sleeping bag to find a bottle wrapped with duct tape. The tape serves a critically important function: to distinguish a pee bottle from all the water bottles stashed inside my sleeping bag to prevent them from freezing. While I'm thankful that I don't have to venture outside to relieve myself in gale-force winds and a temperature 20 degrees below zero, the task of crawling out of a sleeping bag inside our tent at an altitude of 20,500 feet to kneel and urinate in a pee-bottle while sandwiched between my son, Adam, and our tent partner, Laura, is not a pleasant undertaking.

Finished, I close the cap of my pee-bottle as tightly as I can and place it back inside the sleeping bag, down near my feet for warmth. I fluff up the make-shift pillow formed from my down jacket and try to get back to sleep. I'm physically exhausted after the day's climb, but the thin air and the fierce winds loudly snapping the sides of our tent make it difficult to sleep.

Thoughts drifting, I realize that if the raging storm outside clears by morning, tomorrow will finally be our summit day. After three weeks of climbing, our team will venture out of the relative safety and security of our tents to attempt a summit of Mt. Aconcagua. Named "Kon-Kawa" or "Snowy Mountain" by the Ayamara Indians who lived in the Andes near Argentina's Province of Mendoza, the summit of Aconcagua stands at almost 23,000 feet, making it not only the highest peak in the Western Hemisphere but also the highest outside of Central Asia.

Before I fall asleep, I take out my Moleskine notebook to record my daily log. What follows are the entries I kept during our summit attempt of Mt. Aconcagua.

Adding an entry in my Moleskine notebook

From my log, January 9 – 28, 2005:

January 9 - This morning, after flying for nearly 15 hours, Adam and I arrived in Santiago, Chile feeling excited, but also somewhat anxious about our climb of Mt. Aconcagua. Six months ago, Adam called me and asked, "Hey, how about bagging another mountain?" Sounded great at the time. Now, we wonder what we've gotten ourselves into. Together we've climbed Mt. Whitney, Mt. Rainier, and Mt. Kilimanjaro, but at 23,000 feet and with a reputation for severe winds and intense cold, Mt. Aconcagua is in a different class.

Adam doing his gear check

When we went to check in for our short, 45-minute connecting flight from Santiago to Mendoza, Argentina, I was told that something was wrong with my plane ticket. No one in the entire airport seemed to know exactly what the trouble was or what to do about it. All the passengers were seated for the flight, including Adam, who had quickly abandoned me back at the gate. At the last minute, I was allowed to board the plane, probably because the guy in charge felt sorry for me. When I finally took my seat, feelings of elation were mixed with some anxiety over the ominous beginnings of our odyssey.

Soon after we arrived at the Hotel Nutibarra in Mendoza, our lead guide, Eric Murphy, and assistant guide, Joey Stock, checked out our equipment in the hotel parking lot. This check is critically important. Finding out you forgot gloves, crampons or an ice ax when you're high on the mountain is not good.

Adam and I met our five fellow climbers. We all eyed each other from head to foot, no doubt searching for any weak links in the team. I had instant respect for the only female team member, Laura Ross, a physical fitness professional and triathlete from Florida, who didn't seem to mind going on a climb with eight males.

After a fabulous dinner of the well-known Argentinean beef and wine from the Napa-like region of Mendoza, we're back in our hotel room watching the only TV channel available – MTV. Adam tells me MTV is more "advanced" here since viewers are able to vote for one of two music videos they want to see next. The running tab of votes shown on the screen must be pretty humiliating to the loser. Just now, Destiny's Child beat out Britney Spears… poor Britney. Inexplicably, the dialogue of the show switches from English to Spanish, putting Adam in a foul mood.

Logging off at 10:30 p.m.

January 10

Today, we took a long van ride to the Penitentes ski area at an elevation of 8,600 ft. It was dusty and looked pretty barren.

Most of my fellow male team members, wisely anticipating the next three weeks without a shower, sported buzz haircuts. It was too late to see a barber, so I used small scissors to cut my hair as close to my scalp as I could. Looks a bit choppy, but all in all, not bad. Since all my uncles were barbers, I must have it in my genes.

January 11

This morning I took my last shower for the next three weeks. Tried to enjoy and relish every moment of it. My Spanish is improving. All on my own, I figured out that the foil packet with "A condicionador" printed on it is conditioner. Helping me figure that out was the other Spanish on the packet: "Reductione de Friz."

We all hopped into the van for the half-hour ride to the trailhead of the Vacas Valley route, where we began our three-day, 30-mile trek to Base Camp. The trailhead is at an altitude of 8,000 feet. While longer than the more commonly used Normal Route, the less traveled Vacas Valley route is more scenic. And with fewer climbers on this route, the lower campsites are much cleaner and quieter.

We have mules helping carry the heavy stuff to Base Camp. They're packed with our tents and all the other equipment we'd need higher up on the mountain, like ice axes and crampons. So all we needed to carry in our packs to Base Camp weighed only 40-pounds or so. Since my physical conditioning for the climb had progressed up to carrying a 65-pound backpack on steep inclines, this seemed pretty light – at first. After climbing for about two or three hours in the 90-degree heat, the weight of my pack seemed to grow exponentially and I began to feel like I was on a chain gang. It's ironic, considering the cold and wind that Aconcagua is so well known for, that it's the intense heat that is wearing me out.

The heel of my left foot hurts. It turns out that the lightweight hiking shoes I brought for the first part of the climb are not nearly sturdy enough for this rocky trail. After soaking my feet in a stream (boy, did that feel good!), I put pads and moleskin on my developing blisters. It's a bit discouraging that we're not even at Base Camp, and I'm already feeling hurt and tired. Adam seems fine except for his griping about the heat.

Working on the blisters

After almost six hours of climbing, I drag myself into our first camp, Pampa de Leñas at 9,400 feet, at least 10 minutes behind everyone else. Looks like I may be the weak link on the team.

Setting up our tents involved threading long metal rods through the nylon fabric and then anchoring the tent cords with heavy rocks. Not too difficult, but it seems like it'd be impossible to do in gale-force winds and extreme cold higher up.

After drinking some steaming hot chocolate, I felt my strength and spirit slowly returning. It's funny how everything around us that we typically ignore back home takes on more clarity when living under the stars. I saw shades of darkness over the horizon. I smelled the pine needles in the wind and could almost taste the sage in the air. And as I looked up at the star-filled sky, I saw the Southern Cross for the first time in my life.

January 12

After a breakfast of cereal and canned fruit, we set out for our second camp, Ref. Casa de Piedra, at 10,600 feet. Although we ascended only 1,200 feet, it was a long, eight-hour march.

Setting out for Ref. Casa de Piedra

For a while, I listened to my new Rio Forge MP-3 player. With its 512K internal memory and a 1G chip, I had room to store 25 CDs of my favorite music as well as three books I downloaded from Audible.com. Unfortunately, the book I'm listening to is a little boring, and I wasn't in the mood for music. So I had plenty of time to think.

In fact, I was thinking about why people climb mountains. When we took our first rest break, it gave me an opportunity to share with my teammates an economic theory about mountain climbing that I'd been noodling around in my head.

I explained that mountain climbers and other adventurers know they must give up most of the basic creature comforts of life to do what they do. But they also realize that when they return to civilization, all the things the ordinary folk take for granted – like hot water, clean toilets and a cushy bed – will yield a great deal more pleasure to them as adventure seekers than to those who find fulfillment in the hum-drum of daily life.

I then presented an example to nail the point: "Back home, when I get up in the morning and take a shower, I hardly think about it. I just go through the motions. But when I get home after experiencing more than three weeks without a shower and stand under that beautiful spray of water, I will experience a burst of 'utils' like you wouldn't believe. Utils, by the way, is a term economists use to measure and compare different levels of pleasure or happiness."

Our assistant guide, Joey, who has a penchant for new words, suggested that this burst of utils from that shower be called "utiliphic." But other than Joey, who listened carefully to my theorizing, the other members of the team, including Adam, eyed me suspiciously. Maybe I'd better keep my trail thoughts to myself.

We got our first view of Aconcagua's east face just before reaching camp. It looks majestic, beautiful, stunning… and impossible to climb. Realizing our shock at seeing this intimidating summit looming in the distance, Eric pulled us together and told us in no uncertain terms, "Don't look at that. I want you guys to concentrate on getting past that next hill in front of you, then the next ridge line, then crossing the next river. If you can tackle those mini-goals, you'll reach that summit." He concluded with a statement I often think about: "It's amazing how taking little steps will add up to one giant step as long as you keep moving forward."

Dinner tonight was stew – no meat, but lots of beans. Adam (first name alphabetically) had KP duty.

The camp toilet is awful – just a hole in the ground in an open-doored, ramshackle enclosure. All the people queuing up can see you do your thing. It seems even worse given that the toilet at our first camp was the best I've ever used in a backpacking environment. That one even had a porcelain seat! Adam is constipated, so I gave him a laxative out of my bag of tricks. But given the status of the latrine, he should consider himself lucky.

First look at Mt. Aconcagua in all its scary glory

January 13

We started out today at 8:00 a.m., right after breakfast. Almost immediately, we crossed two shallow rivers. Not really a problem, except for the fact that all my blister protection came off in the water, and I'm beginning to run low on the special blister pads I brought.

Walking on bolder-strewn paths

Much of the time, we no longer walked on trails but on long, bolder-strewn paths. So now my ankles are beginning to bother me. The ankle I twisted yesterday really hurts.

Thankfully, it's cooler at our higher elevation. Unfortunately, the wind is beginning to kick up with gusts of 30 to 40 miles per hour.

When we finally arrived at our Base Camp at Plaza Argentina at 13,700 feet, the mules were there waiting for us. It was already cold, even though it was only 4:00 in the afternoon. A park ranger is stationed here throughout the short climbing season and is in radio contact with climbing teams at higher camps. "Permanent" tents, including a Quonset-like mess hall, are already in place at Base Camp. What a relief not to have to set up our tents, especially in this wind.

A "permanent" tent at Base Camp Plaza Argentina

The pee bottles we use in our tents at night are highly valued. Since we're drinking a minimum of five liters a day to prevent dehydration, we'd be getting out of the tent all night long if we didn't have them. The only problem is that we each have only one pee bottle, one liter in size. Adam had to get up twice last night to empty his bottle. I think he may have set the Guinness Book of Records for the most volume of any single urination – one liter!!

Ah… to be young again.

January 14
Slept fitfully last night. I woke up in the middle of the night, gasping for breath. The sudden feeling of drowning caused by irregular breathing and

hyperventilation, known as Cheyne-Stokes Syndrome, is a common malady at higher altitudes.

I was glad that today was an acclimatization day at Base Camp, so we were able to sleep late. Acclimatization is all about allowing your body to adapt slowly to the increasingly thinner air. To do this, we try to limit our altitude gains on any single day to less than 2,500 feet. We also have an acclimatization day several times a week, when we stay active at camp rather than progressing on up the mountain.

Staying active today involved going down to the river bed to wash our clothes, namely the same underwear I'd worn for the last four days.

In the afternoon, the mules left us. From now on, we'll do all the carrying. I can hardly walk around Base Camp without getting seriously winded, so I don't know how I'm going to carry a backpack that weighs 50 pounds or more. And when I gaze up toward the top of Aconcagua, it looks unclimbable. I need to keep thinking: "One day at a time."

January 15

Today was the first of two carries up to Camp 1 at 15,500 feet. The double carries keep the weight of our packs down and also help in the acclimatization process.

We took food, fuel and other team provisions to our next camp site and cached (deposited) them under rocks and boulders. We returned to Base Camp for the night, and will go back up tomorrow with a second load of food, fuel and our tents.

For me, today's carry was brutal. The thin air made my pack feel even heavier than its actual weight. The grades were steep, and we passed through long stretches where there were large boulders in our path. Trying to "skip" over these boulders with heavy packs was agony.

The blisters covering the heel and sole of my left foot made the going even worse. Thankfully, Joey had a special kind of glue to help keep the moleskin on my foot. Without that covering, I don't know how I could have made it back to Base Camp. As it was, I hobbled into camp at least a half hour behind everyone else.

Tonight, I had a heart-to-heart talk with our lead guide, Eric Murphy. I told him I didn't think I could make it with all my hurting and lagging behind. I pointed out that this is the third try for our teammate, Kurt Gusinde, to summit Aconcagua. Here is a guy who prepared and planned every detail of the climb so that this time he'd make it to the top. Just watching him is a lesson in how planning is so important in reaching one's goals. Yet, if I have to be helped down from a higher altitude, the chances of the team summiting would be jeopardized.

Brutal carry to Camp 1 at 15,500 feet

Thinking about turning back or continuing the climb

After explaining all this and droning on about my aches and pains, Eric looked me in the eye and, pointing his index finger close to my face, said, "You can do it." As I now record that line in this log, I realize how trite it sounds. But something about the look in his eye and that pointing finger convinced me that Eric really meant it. He believes in me.

Eric went on to say that he's been watching me and likes the way I'm pacing myself. PACING! What I thought was "lagging," he considers "pacing."

Damn the blisters! … Damn the thin air! … Damn the heavy packs! … I'm going to follow this guy wherever he leads me.

January 16
Today was our second carry to Camp 1. I don't know if it was my little talk with Eric or what, but I felt better today. Instead of holding up the rear, I arrived at camp with everyone else. With all the glue Joey gave me, my moleskin and bandages are holding up, so my blisters don't hurt as much.

Adam and I adopted a team member, Laura, to share our tent. As we continue our ascent, we'll reduce the number of tents to save on weight and have fewer tents to set up at each camp. I volunteered to be the first of the three-person tents since I'm the smallest guy on the team.

When I complained about the trouble I have breathing at night, Laura gave me a saline solution that helps lubricate nasal passages in dry conditions. I don't know if it's Laura's saline solution or maybe the new falling snow that's increasing the humidity, but whatever, I can breathe through my nose again. Hopefully, I'll sleep better tonight.

January 17
Another acclimatization day. We took a short hike up the stretch we'll be covering on our way to Camp 2 at 17,600 feet tomorrow. I'm feeling stronger. Tonight we had vegetable soup, followed by couscous with tuna and tons of garlic. We're all smelling so bad that the garlic on everyone's breath is like perfume to us.

January 18
The eight-hour trek on our first carry to Camp 2 at 17,600 feet was a nightmare. The worst part of it was near the beginning when we had to go through a steep stretch of sharp, cone-like spikes of snow and ice that are called the "penitentes." The name comes from the fact that these three-to twelve-feet tall cones resemble rows of repenting monks. The only way to negotiate the dark, narrow and claustrophobic passageways is by gripping the cones tightly and then jumping to the next cone, trying not to fall into the deep gullies between them.

This was particularly difficult for me because of my shorter stride. After one jump, I wrapped my arms around a penitente and grasped it tightly while I caught my breath. I looked to the side and saw a climber from another team doing pretty much the same thing. In a thick, British accent he said, "I've never been through anything like these bloody penitentes."

When I finally made it out of this frozen hell, my elation was tempered by the realization that I'd have to go through all this again in a second carry. All the

Negotiating the "penitentes"

confidence I'd built up the last few days disappeared. There was no way I could enter the "bloody penitentes" again. I convinced myself in no uncertain terms that I had to quit. "You can do it" wouldn't work this time.

As it turned out, Eric was also troubled by the penitentes. He told us that getting through the penitentes was much harder today than he'd ever experienced before, so tomorrow, we would go by a different route. So my quitting was put off, at least for now.

Curiously, Adam loved the whole penitentes experience and found it a great adventure.

By the time we made it to our Camp 2 site, it was getting windy and cold. We quickly cached our gear and started to make our way back down to Camp 1. Just above the penitentes was a steep slope of loose rocks and pebbles, called "scree," that gave way like sand as we climbed down. When we positioned our plastic climbing boots at a certain angle, we could "ski" down these slopes. One "run" was every bit as "utiliphic" as a great ski slope.

Again, I crossed paths with the English guy who remarked, "This scree is as soft as potty." I asked, "Do you mean putty?" He replied, "No, I mean potty!"

As I write, it's night and we're in our tent and sleeping bags. Adam and Laura are laughing about our experiences. While they laugh, I groan and tell them that this is definitely – without equivocation – the last mountain I will ever climb. To make the point more dramatic, I borrowed indiscriminately from the great Nez Perce Chief Joseph, "When we get off this mountain, from where the sun there sets, I will climb no more forever."

January 19

As Eric promised, on today's second carry to Camp 2, we bypassed what has become known by all of us on the team as the "bloody penitentes." We arrived at camp beat after an elevation gain of more than 2,000 feet.

One of our team members seems to have a bad case of altitude sickness. The rest of us are in pretty good shape, although some members of the team are experiencing headaches, nose bleeds and the runs. Having diarrhea is never fun, but having it on a mountain is serious business, especially because it worsens the dehydrating effects of higher altitude. There is another problem with diarrhea, more annoying than the impact on one's health. Let me explain.

Alpine Ascents is an environmentally concerned climbing outfit. In fact, that was one of the major reasons Adam and I chose to climb with them. Their philosophy is to leave the mountain as you found it. That means packing out everything we pack in … so we use "Wag Bags" to dispose of our solid waste. The bags are like blue bags for dogs but more sophisticated. Inside the bag is a plastic sheet with a funnel in which a chemical agent is present and activated with a little snow, water or urine. You do your thing, hoping to hit the funnel target – tough to do, especially in an extreme wind.

When you've completed your business, you fold the bag and place it under a rock for reuse – up to three times! On the way down the mountain, we will pick up all of our fully used and stored bags and put them in our backpacks. We'll dispose of them at Base Camp in a special receptacle that will be removed off the mountain by helicopter.

A "Wag Bag"

I've used blue bags for my dog, Cindy, so I know what it's like carrying bagged doggy-do. I only wish Cindy were here on the mountain to pick up after me for a change.

I'd better quit writing now before my altitude-induced fantasies become even more delusional.

January 20

We lost a team member today. He was really sick last night. By morning, his face was visibly swollen. It was important to get him off the mountain while he could still walk. Joey started down with him, and they were met partway by an Alpine Ascents guide who had come up from Base Camp. This guide will take him back to Base Camp, where he will be evacuated by helicopter or mule, depending on his condition.

Now we're down to six climbers and, when Joey returns, two guides.

We did our first carry to Camp 3 at 19,200 feet today. By the time we got back to Camp 2, it was freezing outside, with wind gusts over 50 miles per hour. Good thing our return to Camp 2 meant we didn't have to put up our tents.

We ate dinner, and just after we got back into our tents, I was summoned from the Oval Office (my teammates have gotten into the habit of calling me El Presidente and referring to my tent as the Oval Office) to give feedback on an argument they were having about, believe it or not, the global economy.

El Presidente gives a lecture on the global economy

I don't know how they got into it at an altitude of 17,600 feet, but for some strange reason the topic of outsourcing captured their attention. Funny, but earlier today I noticed that my Eddie Bauer water bottle (I used one for a pee-bottle, too) had stamped on it in small print "Made in China," and in larger print "Made with Lexan by GE."

I pointed out to my teammates that Eddie Bauer evidently found a manufacturer in China that could produce the thermo-plastic extruded bottles more cheaply than U.S. manufacturers. But to meet Eddie Bauer's specs for heat, sturdiness, etc., the Chinese company had to buy the high-tech, plastic pellets used in the manufacture of the bottles from GE in the U.S. My guess was that for an Eddie Bauer bottle that retails for $10, most of the revenue would pay for GE's plastic pellets and Eddie Bauer's marketing services. Very little would go to the Chinese manufacturer engaged in a low-tech, low-margin, commodity-like business.

Ergo, we shouldn't be afraid of outsourcing, as long as we hold the technological edge.

As I lectured on, I noticed that my teammates were not as attentive to my pearls of economic wisdom as they were to the weather that had suddenly turned nasty again. So as they drifted back to the safety of their tents, I headed back to the Oval Office clutching my Eddie Bauer bottle.

January 21

Our second carry to Camp 3 was a killer, not so much because of the climb, but because Adam and I came in leading the group. As a result, Eric gave us a terrible campsite because he evidently felt we had the strength to do the physical work required to remove rocks from the pad where the tent would be placed as well as rebuild the rock wall protective screen. At an altitude of 19,200 (almost as high as Kilimanjaro) any physical work is exhausting, but it's especially tough moving heavy boulders around.

For supper, we had soup with carrots and onions, followed by a potato broth with what Eric said were strips of Argentinean "Spam."

I'm trying to eat as much as I can, but I've lost my appetite in the thin air. I have to force down food and liquids to keep me going. Metabolism isn't efficient at high altitudes, so you have to eat even more to get your body to absorb the nutrients it needs for all this exertion and cold, windy weather. Thankfully, I have a secret weapon. When candy bars, trail mix, and hardtack were being distributed for our lunches and snacks, I noticed a round log that looked like a roll of salami. A closer look revealed it was a roll of crushed fig. All of a sudden, I remembered my dad telling me when I was just a kid that all anyone needs to survive is not bread and wine but figs and wine. Dad passed away almost 25 years ago, but it seemed like he was out there somewhere telling me to take that fig roll that no one else wanted. When I pulled that fig roll out of my pack today, everyone laughed at the way the crushed fruit oozed out of its plastic casing. Our teammate, Matt Franklin, who is always making everyone laugh, said, "It looks like potty – not putty!"

Well, they could laugh all they wanted. They could eat their Snickers. They could eat their Oreos. They could eat their jerky. Dad and I could laugh back, for I was eating from the staff of life.

January 22
I woke up this morning at Camp 3, happy it was another acclimatization day. We had a great breakfast of scrambled eggs (from dried eggs) and bacon. Although I like my bacon crisp, the virtually uncooked bacon we ate tasted great.

Happy to have an acclimatization day

On our acclimatization hike, we went uphill for about an hour to see the Polish Glacier, which is close to a magnificent ice wall and sharply plunging cliff. What an incredible vista and view!

Near the Polish Glacier, we ran into a climbing team heading down. One of the climbers I met on that team who had successfully summited was John Dahlem, who lives in Huntington Beach, CA. We had a lot in common since he was a fellow educator who had taught history and served as a principal at several Orange County high schools. The short conversation we had before he went down and I went up was the beginning of a beautiful friendship.

Looking up at the Polish Glacier

Ominous reminder of where we are: Near the bottom of the glacier is a cross memorializing a climber killed in a fall.

After dinner, Joey asked me for a new word he could think about tonight. I suggested the economic term "equilibrium." This led to a discussion about the value of the dollar and oil prices. I'd like to write what we discussed, but at this altitude, I've already forgotten.

High camp at 20,600 feet

January 23

Long, agonizing traverse to Camp 4, or High Camp, at 20,600 feet. We had to set up four tents in a cold, raging blizzard. It would be bad enough doing this under any conditions, but at this altitude, it was pure misery.

Hard to eat... Hard to breathe... Hard to sleep... Tomorrow… Summit day!

January 24

We woke to Eric's 6:00 a.m. call. The winds had calmed, and the sky was clear. It was a "go."

In spite of all our talk and preparations for summit day, there was general pandemonium in camp. Like the Three Stooges, Adam, Laura, and I scurried around in tight quarters, trying to get ready. While Eric and Joey were trying to get us to eat oatmeal and down as much liquid as possible, we were fussing around and looking for all our clothing and equipment.

We left at 7:30 a.m., an ice ax and one climbing pole in hand. Eric placed us in two groups, with Adam, Laura, Matt, and me in the advance team. Will Prittie, a highly skilled climber who has ascended Mt. Everest three times, joined our team from Base Camp. So we had a ratio of six climbers to three guides.

We could feel the lack of atmospheric pressure in our gasping for air. After a long and relentless upward climb, we hit Independencia Hut, supposedly the highest man-made structure on earth. It looked to me, however, to be little more than a large dog house in an advanced state of disrepair.

We then entered a very windy, long traverse. We had to scramble to

Independencia Hut

The dreaded Canaleta

negotiate several steep, rocky areas on what is called the West Face.

At about 12:00 noon, I ate from my fig roll before we hit the dreaded Canaleta, a scree-filled, rocky stretch that is the most challenging segment of an Aconcagua climb. We took off our snow crampons to negotiate the loose scree and steep grades.

The frustrating part was that the summit was now in our sight, and it looked so tantalizingly close. But after all our strenuous efforts in such rarified air, it appeared we weren't getting any closer. I counted as many as ten gasps for air as I made each step.

In the loose scree, it seemed that for every step forward I lost a half step sliding back down. Particularly nerve-wracking was dodging the falling rocks knocked loose by the climbers above us. Each time a rock gave way under my foot, I looked down in dread hoping it wouldn't hit a climber below.

Just when I felt my body could take no more, I realized that I was beyond the Canaleta and had literally stumbled upon Summit Ridge.

At 4:00 p.m., Eric walked on the summit toward the well-known cross that marks Aconcagua's peak. Adam and I followed him. Although the wind gusts were 30 to 40 miles per hour and the temperature was -15° F, the magnificent view of the Andes Mountains, including several 20,000 feet plus peaks, was exhilarating. Especially striking was the South Face of Aconcagua, which is thought to be one of the great mountain faces in the world.

We all took lots of photos, including one of Adam and me holding a

Chapman University pennant. Since Himalayan climbs are rare at this time of year, we realized we might be the highest humans standing on earth.

But it wasn't that, nor was it the view, that struck me most. Most rewarding for me was the fact that I hadn't given up. Pushing myself to the limit of my endurance led to an epiphany of sorts. In many ways, it was a spiritual awakening, not in a religious sense, but in the way Aconcagua revealed through self-discovery that the spirit can transcend physical boundaries.

Eric then gathered us around for group photos. He must be very proud

Resting at Summit Ridge

Me and Adam on the summit of Mt. Aconcagua

that six of the seven climbers who started on this team actually summited. This high rate compares to an overall average of about 50 percent for all climbers attempting this mountain. Eric then asked Adam, Matt, and me to lead the team back to High Camp. I kept up with Adam and Matt through Canaleta but then ran out of steam and was the last to arrive at camp around 8:00 p.m.

One member of our team, Frank Thomas, was hurting badly with fatigue and symptoms of altitude sickness. We all had to admire and be inspired by him for making it to the top in spite of his condition.

Too tired to celebrate our summit success, we skipped dinner so we could

Our proud climbing team at the summit

A well-earned sleep after summiting

crawl back into our tents, our little homes that provided us with warmth, comfort and sleep.

January 25

Another difficult carry today, though now we are going downhill. Cognizant of the fact that most accidents occur on the descent, we trekked downhill carefully from High Camp with the goal of reaching Base Camp, a descent of almost 7,000 feet, by the end of the day. Moving downhill, our feet took a different sort of pounding, with our toes rather than our heels taking the most abuse.

We struggled with even more weight, adding to our packs the cached goods (and Wag Bags!!) left at the various camps we'd created along the way. By the time we got to Base Camp at around 8:00 in the evening, we were carrying 70 pounds in our packs. In two consecutive days, we went from an altitude of 20,600 feet up to almost 23,000 feet and then back down to 14,000 feet.

Frank, who was hurting badly, valiantly struggled into Base Camp on his

Adam's backpack

own and immediately sought out medical care. Just watching him carry on makes us all feel proud that he's on our team. Looks like Frank will be OK, but he'll require a mule ride out and a lot of rest and fluids to counteract the effects of dehydration.

Along the way today, it seemed that all anyone could talk about was the beer that awaited us at Base Camp. I was getting more and more excited myself, even though I don't much care for beer. Maybe all the hype worked since the Chilean bock beer we had tonight was incredibly good. But maybe it was the indescribably delicious hamburgers that accompanied the beer. Whatever, our appetites had returned.

The high point of the day for me, besides the beer and hamburgers, was skiing down the scree-filled "ski runs" between Camp 2 and Camp 1.

January 26

I write this log in our tent during a rest day at Base Camp. I sold some of my gear to the locals for about $100. I could have sold almost all I had, but most of my gear has a tender place in my heart. In addition, I still need my sleeping bag for the two-day trek out of Base Camp.

The reason the "market" is so hot is that Argentina has a 40 percent tariff on imported goods and services. Nothing like a tax to create a hot black market.

We have another celebration – a pizza dinner, no less. I don't know how Eric and Joey made pizza for eight ravenous climbers with one small burner at an altitude of 14,000 feet, but somehow, they did. Mixing up a type of Bisquick dough and topping it with cheese, hearts of palm, white asparagus, salami, and sardines, they created about the best pizza I've ever had… and I've had the best.

January 27

Joey dishing out the pizza

Me and Adam back at base camp

Long, gruesome descent from Base Camp to Pampa de Laños (our first campsite). Started at around 8:00 a.m., I was last to come in at around 7:00 p.m. – 11 hours of trekking downhill. Several rushing stream crossings we negotiated by hopping over widely scattered boulders freaked me out. I kept thinking that if I fell into one of these torrents, I'd end up in Buenos Aires.

This was our last campsite before marching out tomorrow. There was a

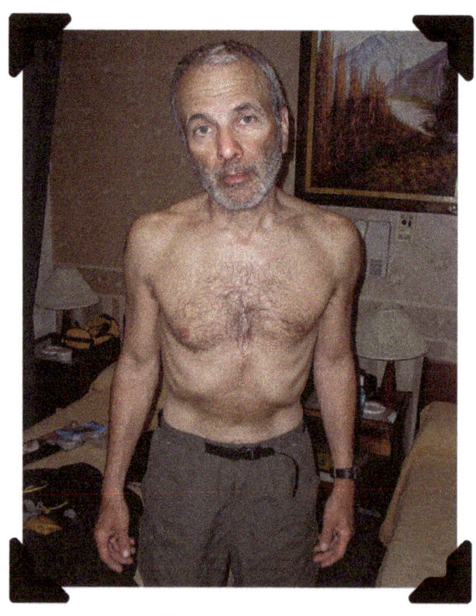

Here I am sans a few pounds back at our hostel

solar-heated bag of water that I used to take my first shower in 16 days. The water was still pretty cold and there wasn't much of it, but ohhhh... what a heavenly, utiliphic feeling!

January 28

Left camp at 7:45 a.m. Eric challenged us to a "Vacas Valley Race." Only Adam and I joined in. I passed Eric early in the race downhill when his pants fell off as he ran. He's lost so much weight, as all of us have, that he had to tie a rope around his pants to keep them up. After leading for the first half, I took a wrong turn in a river valley, and that's where Adam and Eric passed me up. I was never able to recover. Eric won, about a minute ahead of Adam, and Adam about a minute ahead of me.

We knew we'd reached civilization when the van driver waiting for us at the trail head, in celebratory fashion, handed each of us a tepid can of Coke.

As we gulped down our Cokes, we all traded stories about the trip. I reminded everyone of my promise: "From where the sun now stands, I will climb no more forever."

Two Weeks Later

A call from Adam: "Dad, Alpine Ascents has just posted on its website next year's scheduled climbs of Mt. Elbrus – the highest mountain in Europe. Come on, let's bag another mountain. Should I sign us up?"
... Hmmm.

Scaling Mt. Elbrus

Jim Doti

I. The Artists' Necropolis

Luxuriating in the many comforts of business class, we chomped on cashews (not peanuts) and washed them down with Lufthansa cordials (not Cokes) that we found oh-so soothing. My son, Adam – the computer expert, had somehow figured out a complex but legal way to get free upgrades from our coach fares. As he proudly related his online stratagems, I drifted off to sleep. No better sleeping aid than interminable monologues about navigating the bowels of the World Wide Web.

Landing at St. Petersburg's airport, we were met by our climbing guide, Vern Tejas. He would lead us – we hoped – to the top of Mt. Elbrus, the highest mountain in Europe and, therefore, one of the infamous "Seven Summits" (the highest mountain on each continent). Vern is one of the world's truly great climbers. Not only has he scaled Mt. Everest seven times, he is legendary for the first solo winter climb of Mt. McKinley (Denali) and the first solo ascent of Mt. Vinson in Antartica.

Vern's muscles bulged. When he shook my hands, I tried not to wince at the firmness of his grip. I also noticed Vern's probing eyes doing a quick scan, assessing my chances of staying out of trouble on the climb.

We checked in at our hotel and had a few days to tour St. Petersburg and see the sights. These included the usual visits to cathedrals, landmarks, and museums. It was late July, the height of the tourist season, but we stoically jostled through the crowds and frenzied tour groups, telling ourselves it was good conditioning for the climb.

One of our sightseeing stops was the Hermitage. The famed museum has no air conditioning, and I couldn't help but wonder about the effects of the open windows on the priceless artworks on display. Moreover, I was amazed by the lack of security. So it was not surprising to me when the next day's news included a report about a major theft of artwork from the Hermitage.

On our last day in St. Petersburg, Adam and I decided to take an early morning jog. Not a good idea. Pollution from Communist-era Skodas made the air oppressive and heavy, and negotiating through the teeming throngs on their way to work was pretty much impossible. We were relieved to see ahead of us a park that offered a respite from this asphalt jungle. But it wasn't a park. It turned out to be "The Artists' Necropolis," the last resting place for some of Russia's greatest musicians, artists and literary heroes. As we walked along the cemetery's winding paths, the early-morning fog started to rise, revealing a large monument. There before us was a bust of Fyodor Dostoevsky.

Gazing at Dostoevsky's countenance, memories of the Russian literature course I took in college flooded my mind. It seemed like I spent half of the course trying to figure out the plot points of The Brothers Karamazov, the Dostoevsky novel Sigmund Freud described as "the most magnificent novel ever written." Sadly, all I could remember about the novel was a desperate but futile attempt on my part to make sense of the Grand Inquisitor's seemingly endless and indecipherable monologue.

Just across from Dostoevsky's grave site, I noticed an imposing sculpture towering over the rest. Inspecting it revealed a bust of Peter Ilyich Tchaikovsky. Behind him, an angel supported a cross while also inexplicably holding a sword. A second angel, poised in front of the master, appeared to be studying one of his scores.

Tchaikovsky's Gravesite

Adam and I sat on a nearby bench and gazed at Tchaikovsky's gravesite. Suddenly, remembering I had my iPod with me, I scanned my music library to find the "Violin Concerto in D Major." I listened to the somber and evocative notes, with Tchaikovsky as my neighbor, and fell into a contemplative mood. As my thoughts were stirred and given special nuance by Tchaikovsky's music, I was reminded of a quote from one of my favorite writers, Pico Iyer: "All the great journeys are, like love, about being carried out of yourself."

II. The Flight

It wasn't long after my reverie in "The Artists' Necropolis" that I was reminded of the rest of Iyer's quote: "… journeys are… about being carried out of yourself and deposited in the midst of terror and wonder." The terror and wonder, in our case, was flying the unfriendly skies of Aeroflot.

We knew our flight from St. Petersburg to Mineral Vody in the southernmost reaches of the Caucasus Mountain range would not be ordinary as soon as we entered the plane. As steam wafted along the floor, I was reminded of a scene out of "The Towering Inferno" when an office worker asked, "Do you smell smoke?"

Our concerns about whether the haze came from steam or smoke were quickly forgotten when we realized that the unairconditioned plane was insanely hot. Sweat poured off us as the plane sat on the tarmac with the sun beating down on its metal hull. I was reminded of a book I once read about ancient torture devices that described how victims who were forced into a huge hollow metal bull met their demise. As the sun baked the poor souls inside, their cries could be heard coming through the tips of the metal horns to the delight, I imagine, of some sadistic potentate. Sitting inside that plane, I felt a new-found sympathy for those wretched creatures that I now considered kindred spirits.

Making our imprisonment even worse were the giant horseflies that buzzed around inside the plane, evidently hitching a ride to Mineral Vody. Attendants passed fly swatters around to deal with the problem.

Finally, as the engines revved up, the plane shuddered with a mind-shattering vibration. I fumbled with inoperable seat belts, eventually giving up when I noticed that some people were standing as we started to take off.

I've read and heard that all living creatures are endowed with some kind of adrenaline-related, mind-numbing painkiller. Maybe that's why, in my disoriented state, I didn't feel any more pain when an Aeroflot flight attendant asked in halting English, "Would you like a creamed fish sandwich?"

III. Meeting Nikolai

We met our local climbing ace, Nikolai, as our van deposited us near the base of Mt. Elbrus in the Baksun Valley. Nikolai was a short, bow-legged man of about

70 years old with a weathered countenance and amazingly muscled arms and legs. Our team captain, Vern Tejas, had warned us not to be put off by Nikolai's brusque manner and told us how lucky we were to have such an experienced Russian climber as part of the team. So as we lumbered out of the van, we were not too startled at hearing Nikolai shouting orders like some overbearing drill sergeant. His English consisted of only a few words, but he got his point across by pointing and shouting commands like "Carry here… Not there, HERE!… Take this… Not that, THIS!… MOVE, MOVE, MOVE!"

Nikolai

Having never served in the military, Nikolai's command and control demeanor was particularly disconcerting to me. But after a few practice climbs, I grew to respect his leadership and incredible climbing ability. On one climb designed to help us with rescue techniques and cutting traverses in deep snow on steep inclines, I marveled as Nikolai led the way charging through knee-deep snow on what looked like a 50-degree slope. Although he really isn't that much older than me, I began to look up to Nikolai, not unlike the way I idolized and feared some of my coaches in high school.

At a higher camp, I had a real shock when I couldn't find one of my gators – a protective "sleeve" that wraps around one's ankles and keeps your boots dry – essential equipment, especially higher up. But my panic was more directly related to what Nikolai would do to me when he became aware of my ineptitude. My relief was palpable when I found the missing gator Velcroed to my backpack.

As we slogged upward for seven hours one day from an altitude of 12,000 feet to 15,000 feet, we all started to complain about the weight of our packs. That seemed to set Nikolai off. He yelled at us, "You Americans bunch of babies. You bring much water, drink all day, pee all day. You carry fancy packs and complain. No wonder we Russians win the war for you."

A teammate of ours, Dave McCrane, had a great rejoinder to that one: "Yeah, Nikolai, but didn't we win the Cold War because of all that fancy equipment?"

To Nikolai's credit, he laughed heartily and said, "Ya, Ya, you right!"

IV. The Barrels and Latrines

In contrast to other campsites where we pitched our tents, our campsite at 13,000 feet offered the luxury of living inside one of several large fuel tanks. Lined up side-by-side and secured together by heavy cables, the tanks formed a "residential development" commonly referred to as "The Barrels." The expression evoked in me memories of a scene from one of my favorite novels by Steinbeck, *Sweet Thursday*, a sequel of sorts to *Canary Row*.

In *Sweet Thursday*, the character Suzie takes up lodging in an old, unused, and empty boiler. The advantages Suzie explained for living there mirrored the benefits I perceived from bunking in The Barrels: "... it is absolutely rainproof; it is cozy; and it has wonderful ventilation. By adjusting the damper and fire door, you can have as much ventilation as you like."

The Barrells

The only drawback at the Barrels was the camp latrine. First off, technical climbing skills were needed to get there. The path included one particularly steep, rocky stretch that brought to mind photos I've seen of the "Hillary Step," the last tough barrier before reaching the peak of Mt. Everest.

The infamous camp latrine

As if the trip to the latrine wasn't bad enough, even more disconcerting were the multi-sensory experiences that awaited us there. The latrine jutted halfway off the edge of a cliff. In addition to instilling a fear of tipping off the edge of the mountain, it created a rather repugnant sort of "ventilation." Adam warned me that after he disposed of his toilet paper, an updraft blew it right back at him. Maybe that's why used toilet paper was strewn all over the floor.

But that's not all that was on the floor. One of my teammates came back from the latrine to report, "Hey, mates, watch out in there. There's a steaming turd on the floor." Instead of the usual round hole, there was a narrow slit – a Russian innovation to help keep the smell from rising. Unfortunately, it was evident that many people miss the slit and…

On my first late-night trip to the latrine, I attached my headlamp and made my way up the "Hillary Step." A guy in line ahead of me paused before proceeding into the latrine, and in a barely audible voice, it sounded at first like he was saying a prayer. Actually, he was a member of a British climbing team, and he was reciting aloud a stanza from Tennyson's *Charge of the Light Brigade*:

When it was my turn, I headed in, completed the business at hand as quickly and expeditiously as I could, and then turned to unlatch the latrine door. To my utter horror, I couldn't open the latch. Frantically, I juggled and jostled the latch but couldn't make it open. I was LOCKED IN! In spite of the bitter cold, I immediately started sweating bullets. While it was probably only a minute or so, it seemed like I was locked in for hours. Whatever time it actually took, it was undoubtedly the more terrifying moments of my life. When that latch finally seemed to magically open, I recalled another stanza from Tennyson's poem:

V. Summit Day

By the time summit day arrived, gastrointestinal problems had hit most of us. Several of our team members suffered so severely that they had to abandon the climb. The rest of the "From Russia with Love" team (name given to identify our cybercasts) started for the summit at 3:30 a.m. The skies were clear, but 40-knot winds lashed against our faces.

The first hurdle on our quest for the summit was putting on our crampons so we could climb what seemed like a near-vertical ice face. We then hit a long and steep traverse at about the 17,000-foot mark. The traverse turned into "the flats" as we entered the "saddle" between the upper and lower twin peaks of Mt. Elbrus.

Still lurking ahead of us was the most dangerous part of the climb: a long and very steep ledge only about one foot wide. Any slip off that ledge would prove deadly. It was too steep to self-arrest with an ax, and a free-fall would result in landing atop the massive, jagged rocks that awaited at the bottom of the wall. Too exhausted to face this new danger, several teammates gave up and started their trek back down the mountain. I, too, felt spent. Adam eyed me dubiously. Vern was obviously worried about me. He looked me closely in the eye and said, "You've done good, so it's okay if you want to head down. But only go up if you feel strong enough."

As I soaked in his words, I realized that our rest break seemed to give me a second wind. Moreover, we were able to cache the heavy stuff we wouldn't need on the final 500-foot push to the 18,510-foot summit, so our packs were blissfully lighter. For me, it was a go. While the wind remained brutal, the thin air was crystal clear. I could see every inch of that one-foot ledge as I firmly and carefully planted my crampons with each step forward on this "nearer my God to thee" portion of the climb. I don't recall being scared on that ledge. Maybe I'd run out of fear. More likely, I had faced down my fear by focusing all my mental and physical energies on getting to the top of the ledge. Each carefully planted step got me closer.

We finally arrived at the summit at around 11:00 a.m. Unlike most peaks, Mt. Elbrus has an obvious summit at the top of a small hill. As I stepped onto the top of that hill, Nikolai was there to greet me. He said, "Da, Jim, you did good, you did good."

Savoring the moment, I realized that was the first time Nikolai addressed me by my name.

Adam and me at the summit note my red nose guard

On the summit, we took photos and celebrated with members of a British climbing team. Planting the Chapman pennant that I had taken up to the top of Mt. Aconcagua, I felt tired, yes, but I also felt resilient. I felt giddy, but I also felt reflective. The words of a great marathoner, John J. Kelley, came to my mind – words that served as my mantra during tough marathons: "The things we do should consume us. If they don't, our lives won't have any meaning."

On the way down the mountain, I was feeling rather pleased with myself. It was a mood that proved short-lived. Just before reaching camp, a very tall and very pretty Russian climber approached our team. She bypassed my teammates

Group photo with the Chapman pennant

and, to my surprise, headed straight toward me. She stopped squarely in front of me and pointed to the red circular guard protecting my nose from the sun. With a heavy Russian accent, she said, "You funny – look like Bozo." That's odd, I thought. I didn't realize the Russians knew about Bozo.

My mood was dampened further when we were served the usual mush rather than a special celebratory dinner, which is often the norm after a successful summit attempt. Even Adam was off his high. As a mixture of beets, beans, and unidentifiable meat fragments was ladled into our waiting bowls, Adam whispered to me, "Oh, no, not more of that goulash crap."

But later in the evening terrible news arrived that made us realize how fortunate we were to be back at camp safe and sound. We learned four members of a Ukrainian climbing team had perished by falling off the same ledge we negotiated earlier that day. They made a catastrophic mistake of climbing roped together, so when one of the climbers slipped, the rest of the team was dragged down. No one could self-arrest, given the speed they must have fallen.

VI. Fatima

We descended to a ski village in the resort town of Azau, located in the beautiful Baskan Valley, an area that combines the cultures of Turkish, Georgian, Azerbaydzhani, and Russian people. It was here our team celebrated our safe return with lunch at one of the local bars that serve barbecued meat. As we were seated, I noticed a goat being slaughtered near a wood-burning barbecue.

Shashlik
(Spicy Grilled Goat Kebabs)

In a large bowl, combine:
- 2 lbs. trimmed boneless goat meat*
- 1 Cup white wine
- 1/2 Cup vegetable oil
- 1/3 Cup white vinegar
- 2 tsp. salt
- 1 tsp. crused chile flakes
- 1 tsp. fresly ground black pepper
- 6 whole (garlic) cloves
- 4 finely chopped large garlic cloves
- 2 dried crumbled bay leaves

Toss to coat meat well. Cover the bowl with plastic wrap and regfrigerate for 24 hours.

Build a medium-hot fire in an outdoor grill. Impale the goat cubes (along with any marinade that clings to them) on 6 long skewers, leaving only a slight space between the cubes. Discard any remaining marinade. Grill the kebobs over the fire, turning them occasionally, until cooked through, tender and lightly charred all over, about 14 minutes. Serves 4 to 6.

* lamb or pork can be subsitutied but it won't be real shashlik.

That goat, after being cubed, slathered in oil and garlic, and impaled on a metal skewer, proved to be our main course in a dish known to the locals as shashlik (see accompanying recipe above).

The night before, over another goulash dinner, our team had argued over which American franchise has the best hamburger. Turned out that hamburgers are a regional kind of thing. Adam and I pushed "In-N-Out," but the Texans were adamant about their "What-a-Burger" chain. The Floridians countered with their favorite son: "Cheeburger, Cheeburger."

Maybe it was the endless rounds of goulash, or maybe we were beginning to get homesick. Whatever it was, we all seemed to crave meat that actually looked like meat. Barbecued goat fits the bill. We dined on mass quantities of the stuff, and all suffered later from our overindulgence. But it was worth it. That shashlik made it one of the best meals I can recall. What makes that even more remarkable is that the Russian wine that accompanied our meal was about the worst wine I've ever had.

The rest of our time in Azau was spent hiking through beautiful meadows and canyons near the Chechyian border and going to homemade saunas that some of the Russian farmers devised in their barns to attract tourists. A sharper contrast of this experience to the spa services offered by posh places like the "St. Regis" could not be made.

We also shopped around the many stalls in the local markets where peasants hawked their wares, particularly the finely knitted apparel that seemed to be an Azau specialty. One stall displayed what appeared to be the best of the lot. Behind the many hats, scarves, and sweaters on display, I noticed a middle-aged woman with rosy red cheeks that complemented her red hair. When I asked her a few questions, she called over her teenage son, who spoke English. The prices of the beautiful work were so low that I didn't haggle, even though I consider myself one of the more accomplished hagglers around. I then described what I imagined in my dreams to be a perfect ski cap – one that was cardinal and gray (Chapman University colors), with ear flaps, a long tail, and Cyrillic letters spelling out "Mt. Elbrus" knitted into the front. Through her son, she said she would knit one for me, but it would take some time. Since our bus was leaving the next day at 5:00 p.m., I pressed her on her ability to get it done before our departure. She assured me she would.

The next day, I periodically dropped by her stall to check on her progress. She'd look up at me, smile, and then return to work to work on my hat. Every so often, she would get up and wrap her hands around my head to check my hat size. Finally, at 4:30 p.m., she finished the cap. It was the most beautiful ski cap I ever imagined. She tenderly placed it on my head and carefully inspected it. Like an artist completing a masterwork, she nodded to herself in a way that indicated her pleasure.

When I asked her how much I owed her, she said, "200 rubles" ($8). I happily gave her a 1,000 ruble note and gestured for her to keep it all. At first, she seemed confused, but then she realized I was giving her a "tip." She called her son over and asked him to explain to me that 200 rubles was fine. I argued for her to take the 1,000 rubles. As we haggled back and forth, I realized that this was the first time I ever used my haggling prowess to pay more than the stated price. I finally gave up when it came to mind that paying more might be perceived by her as a charity, or maybe it was something a true artist could not accept. Then we talked, mostly about our families. She laughed and hugged me when I proudly told her about my newly-born first grandchild, Parker. Then she told me her name. It was Fatima.

Fatima

As our team later filed into the waiting bus, I saw Fatima running toward us. She tenderly handed me a little red sweater and said, "For baby, for baby." She blew kisses at us as the bus drove away. As I gazed at her smiling face through the window, I knew I would never see Fatima again. I also knew I would never forget her.

VII. Lenin's Tomb

Before leaving Russia, we were able to spend a few days in Moscow to see the sights. We stayed at the Hotel Ukrainia, a monument to Soviet classicism built by German slave labor after WWII. From the looks of the place, it appeared that not much had been done with the hotel since the Germans left.

Hotel Ukrainia

The next day, a tour guide arrived and gave us a brief review of the churches, museums, and tourist traps in store for us. Having already visited these places, I repeated the same question I asked the last time I was in Moscow: "Will we get to see Lenin's tomb?"

I received the same response I got back then: "No, you don't want to go there. There's a two-hour wait, and there's no way to get around it."

But Adam and I had seen all the churches and museums we could take. So we decided to bail on the group tour and see Lenin or bust.

We questioned the wisdom of that decision when a sudden downpour hit just as we moved to the end of a seemingly endless line of people, all waiting to see the supposedly lifelike remains of the Father of Communism. Hawkers on the sidelines sold umbrellas at inflated prices. I gladly paid the market premium, reveling in the fact that so many budding Russian entrepreneurs were visible evidence that Lenin's legacy was rapidly diminishing. I sought to personally reinforce that message. Catching sight of the familiar McDonald's golden arches not too far away, I asked Adam to get a sack full of hamburgers and "Super Size" fries.

When he got back, we went up and down the line exuberantly handing out hamburgers and fries to anxiously waiting hands. As everyone chomped away, I felt satisfied that this ubiquitous symbol of capitalism's global outreach was reaching full flower right near Lenin's tomb in Red Square. I didn't think my actions were too disrespectful to Lenin since breaking bread together helped create a communal spirit. As we continued our wait, several women behind us told me they lived in Iran, and after their Moscow visit, they were going to California to visit a relative living in Placentia – a small town not far from Chapman University. They, along with others, broke through the language barrier by demonstrating the many features of their camera equipment, PDAs, iPods and other techie devices.

Our longest discussion took place with David Shimabukuro, an Asian graduate student working on his Ph.D. in earth and planetary science at U.C. Berkeley. David's dissertation topic involved studying the geological formation of the Southern Italian region of Calabria and Basilicata. Since my father was born in Basilicata, I found the theory David was testing of particular interest. His analysis of sedimentary rock, which he explained in some detail, suggests that Southern Italy was at one time attached to Northern Europe, while Northern Italy was once part of Africa.

How amazing but also emblematic of a new global order that I was in Red Square talking with an Asian student from California doing research in an area of Italy that was the home of my ancestors.

David then helped to resolve what had been a rather heated debate amongst members of our climbing team. The controversy involved whether Mt. Kosciusko, the highest mountain in Australia, is really one of the Seven Summits. Some people argue that Mt. Kosciusko is on the same tectonic plate as the higher Carstensz Pyramid, located in Indonesia. The difference is not trivial. While Kosciusko, at only 7,308 feet, is a walk-up, Carstensz Pyramid, at 16,023 feet, is a technical climb. Even worse, it's surrounded by militant rebels not known to be friendly to visiting climbers.

Good news! David told Adam and me that Australia is on a separate plate and, therefore, Mt. Kosciusko is definitely one of the Seven Summits. But before he could thoroughly defend that position, a Red Square guard told us it was time to enter Lenin's tomb. I looked at my watch and saw that we had been in line for exactly two hours.

To my amazement, I realized I'd rather continue waiting in line and carrying on with interesting banter than move on to see Communism's great leader. But move on, we did.

And what did I think of Lenin? His glass-enclosed tomb looked very much like Snow White's tomb in Disney's animated classic. But unlike Snow White, Lenin is definitely dead.

The entrance to Lenin's Tomb

Climbing Antarctica's Highest Peak

Jim Doti

From my log, January 7 – 22, 2009:

January 7 – Orange County

I leave for LAX with Lynne (my wife) for an 11 a.m. flight. As we hit the 22 freeway, I realize I've forgotten the Chapman University pennant I planned to bring to the top of Vinson Massif. It's the same pennant that my friend John Evans brought up on Mt. Kilimanjaro (Africa) and that my son, Adam, and I brought to the top of Mt. Elbrus (Europe) and Mt. Aconcagua (South America).

These are three of the Seven Summits – the highest mountains on each continent. A Mt. Vinson summit would make it four of the seven. My climbing buddies John and Ryan Dahlem took the same pennant to the top of Cho Oyu. Standing in the shadow of Mt. Everest, Cho Oyu is the sixth-highest mountain in the world. (They later would bring the pennant to the summit of Mt. Everest.)

So I simply had to go back and pick up the pennant. I frantically call my assistant, Dorothy Farol, to get it from our Leatherby Libraries, where it's on permanent display. She has it waiting for me at my office, where I retrieve it before we are back en route to LAX.

January 8 – Santiago, Chile

I get off the plane in Santiago when I hear, "Hi, Jim!" Turns out it's three neighbors of mine from Villa Park, two of whom have daughters at Chapman University. They are in Chile to watch a motocross race… small world.

A connecting flight brings me to Punta Arenas near the southern tip of Chile, where I sleep the afternoon away at the Hotel Tierra del Fuego. Not bad – good water pressure, comfortable bed, firm pillow. What more could one ask?

Oooh… that afternoon siesta felt good. Later is dinner and meeting my teammates:

- Alex Iscoe – Canada
- Dave Goehl – Virginia
- Rick Salter – Mexico

- Eduardo Martinez – Mexico
- Herbert Blauensteiner – Austria
- Y. Suzanna Derby – Connecticut
- Carlos Tejerina Vieyra – Argentina
- Alan Suen – Canada
- John Rudolf – Washington
- Ken Honig – California

Ken Honig's presence on the team is a complete surprise. I've known Ken, who hails from Newport Beach. Another pretty incredible "small world" experience.

If that isn't enough, John Rudolf, who operates a wealth management fund, Summit Capital, tells me his godson, Tyson Hauff, attends Chapman. John relates to the entire team how he dreamed of Tyson going to Notre Dame. Since none of his own children attended his alma mater, he worked on Tyson, taking him to Notre Dame football games to set his sights on fulfilling his godfather's dream. His fondest hopes of that happening were dashed when Tyson called to tell him he'd decided to attend a school in Southern California by the name of Chapman University. Tyson explained to John that Chapman has a better film program than Notre Dame… music to my ears.

Hotel Tierra del Fuego

January 9 – Puntas Arenas, Chile
Get word at breakfast that the huge Russian-built Illuyshin cargo plane may be ready to fly us to Patriot Hills, Antarctica today. After an equipment check to

make sure we have all of our essential climbing gear, our team attends a briefing given by the group that controls all Antarctic expeditions. It's basically a lecture about "leaving no trace" on the climb. That means leaving absolutely nothing on the mountain, including solid waste, which is brought back to base camp in personal "wag bags" to be flown off the continent. Only exception is designated "pee" holes where contents of "pee bottles" can be "deposited."

Our first briefing

Rest of the lecture is to warn us of all the challenges of a Vinson climb: Need to be on the watch for crevasses that evidently are all over the place. Main problem, though, is the intense cold and risk of frostbite. It's summertime in Antarctica now but temperatures can still be minus 50 degrees or colder (Fahrenheit and Celsius about the same at that level). Any noticeable wind at those extremes will produce windchill temperatures that can cause frostbite on exposed skin within minutes.

The gruesome photos of frostbitten hands, feet, and faces remind me of my third-grade religion classes, where Sister Mary Tomasina (aka sister Mary Gruesome) related graphic details about the hideous deaths suffered by Christian martyrs. I still have nightmares about her stories.

As the "briefing" drones on and on, my fellow climber, Rick Salter, nudges me. I turn to see him show me that he's missing three of his fingers. "Happened during a Denali climb," he whispers.

At 7:30 p.m. we get word, "No Illuyshin flights – too windy for a safe landing."

January 10 – Punta Arenas, Chile

In the morning, we hear there will be no flights out today either. I go for a six-mile run around town to get my blood flowing. I discover an incredible bakery with pastries to die for. Stuffing myself, I figure I need to add weight anyway for the pounds I'll shed while climbing. But then I feel too bloated to run anymore.

A special feature of Punta Arenas is all the dogs that roam around the town. Several of them accompany me on my runs.

In the afternoon, I read every article in an entire issue of Vanity Fair. First time I've ever done that. Feels kind of good to be so self-indulgent.

Great cell phone reception. Talk to Lynne before going to sleep.

The dogs of Punta Arenas

January 11 – Punta Arenas, Chile

Still heavy winds, so no flights for at least another 24 hours.

This waiting around may sound pretty horrible, but it could be worse. We hear another climbing team has been stuck in Patriot Hills for the last five days, waiting for the second leg of Antarctic flying – a Twin Otter aircraft flight to Base Camp. While they're holed up in tents battered by winds, I'm in a warm and cozy hotel, stuffing myself with pastries and great food and wine and enjoying bonding with my newly found dog companions.

January 12 – Punta Arenas, Chile

We get word a flight out tonight is possible. So now is a good time to recap my physical preparation for the trip.

After a marathon in early December and a triathlon the following week, I was ready to begin specific training for the climb. I started by carrying a backpack filled with 35 pounds of dog food. Each week I added a little more weight and steeper hills or higher inclines on my treadmill.

The training program for Vinson required that I build up to climbing 3,500 feet in three hours while carrying a 65-pound backpack. After recalling all the basic geometry I could muster, I figured out that if I walked an hour at an elevation of 10 degrees at a pace 26 (26 minutes per mile or about 2 MPH), then did another hour at 12 degrees at a pace of 33 and finally a third hour at 15 degrees (maximum elevation on my treadmill), I'd gain 3,500 feet. I finally accomplished that, but whoa, my aching back.

That's only part of it. A Vinson climb also requires pulling a heavily laden sled from 5,000 feet at base camp to 9,000 feet at Camp 2. Southern California obviously presents a challenge for practicing sled pulling in snow.

No problem. My friend, David Whiting, had improvised a system where pulling a cord attached to a chain that, in turn, is wrapped around a large tire simulates the feel of pulling a sled in the snow. My other climbing friend, John Dahlem, had already used David's system, so he loaned me his tire and chain.

That's me training at St. Peter's Canyon

The sight of me with a dog food-laden backpack, dragging a tire behind me around the hills of Peter's Canyon Regional Park with Lynne and my dog, Roxy, generates quips from hikers. Here's a sampling:

- "Hey, did ya know you snagged a tire?"
  (Many variations of that line.)
- "What's with the old guy and the tire?"
  (Overheard by Lynne.)
- "How about a ride on that tire?"
- "Shouldn't your dog be pulling that?"
- "Don't you know that's women's work?"

As our wait in Punta Arenas goes on into the afternoon, some of us visit the town's natural history museum. I get busted by a security guard for taking photos of shrunken heads, evidently a specialty of a certain Ecuadorean Indian tribe.

Back at the hotel, I get a call from our assistant guide, Garrett Madison, that our Illuyshin is finally cleared to leave for Antarctica. At 9 p.m., we're off in the big bird. Incredible aircraft. Smooth, five-hour flight to Patriot Hills.

Inside the cabin of the Illuyshin

It was pretty much laissez-faire on the flight. We even got a chance to sit in the copilot's seat. When I pointed out to our Russian pilot that all the gauges didn't seem to be working, he pulled out his cell phone to show me that was the only instrument he'd need.

Although it's 2 in the morning, it's bright and sunny outside. A little cold at minus 20 degrees, but after a five-hour flight, we make it to Patriot Hills. The

All gauges point to zero on the Illuyshin

Illuyshin has no brakes, so reverse thrusters are used about a mile on an ice field before we come to a stop.

We walk very carefully on slick ice for about a kilometer to Patriot Hills Camp. We're welcomed in a Quonset hut with a delicious beef stew, and then we're off to our two-person tents that are already set up for us. My tent partner is Suzanna Derby. She doesn't snore. Even better, we get along great.

January 13 – Patriot Hills, Antarctica

Woke up to a great pancake and bacon breakfast. Now we wait for the Twin Otter to fly us to Base Camp. Hope we won't have to wait here five days like the last team.

Shoot the breeze most of the day in the mess hall. John Rudolf tells our teammates that they should carry all his and my stuff on the climb since we're the two oldest members of the team. John's 60, while I'm the oldest at 62.

John adds, "Herbert (Blauensteiner) is pretty old (54), but since he's from Austria, he should carry his own gear. Climbing's in their blood. I'd guess that two minutes after Herbert was born, they sized him up for boots and crampons."

Our lead guide, Vern Tejas, joins the group. Vern's one of the great climbers of the world. He's the only person to climb all Seven Summits eight times, let alone the first solo winter ascent of Denali. My son, Adam, and I were really lucky to have him lead our Mt. Elbrus climb in Russia. This time, it wasn't luck. I chose this team because Vern was leading it.

Vern Tejas

The Twin Otter gets us to base camp

Mt. Vinson in the distance

Our luck holds. At 5:30 p.m., we're given clearance for the Twin Otter to fly us to base camp. It's a smooth, 90-minute flight. Weather is clear and crisp. My God, Antarctica is an amazing place – otherworldly and desolate but eerily beautiful.

We arrive and quickly set up our tents. I'm a little rusty, but Suzanna, who has been knocking one summit off after another in rapid-fire succession, shows me all the tricks.

Outside our tents, we can see the tip of Mt. Vinson above a crevace-laden glacier.

We're in our sleeping bags at 11:30. Twenty-four hours of daylight is hard to sleep through. Should have brought eye shades, but I improvise by covering my eyes with a balaclava (face mask).

January 14 – Vinson Base Camp

Overcast, but no wind, and fairly warm at minus 20 degrees.

Vern takes us through lessons in tying various knots needed during the climb. I've never been very good at knots. Can do them when shown, but 24 hours later, I'm all thumbs. Hope Suzanna will be around whenever I need a particular knot. She's pretty adept at it.

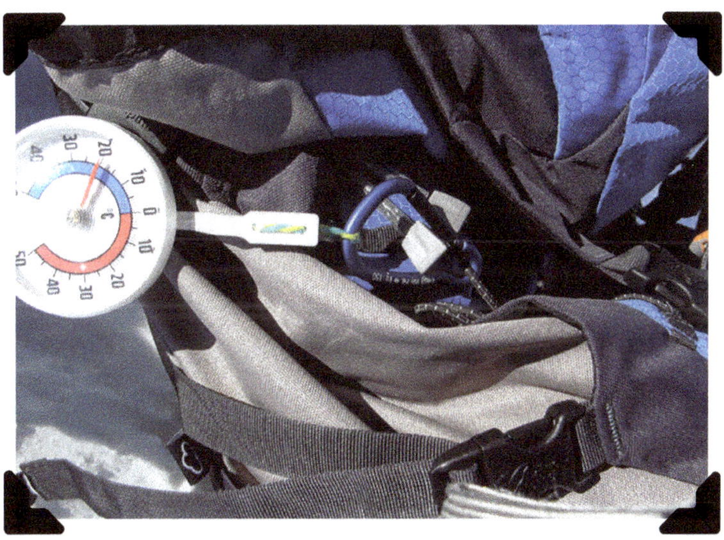

-20 degrees outside our tent

We left for Camp 1 at 4:15 p.m. Temperature still "warm" at around minus 20 degrees. It's not long before I'm sweating bullets from the exertion of carrying a heavy pack while pulling a full sled. Sweat is dangerous because if your body is damp and it suddenly turns cold, you freeze. So I started taking off layer after layer of clothing until I'm down to only three layers of underwear.

The team has been divided into two separate climbing groups. One group, led by Todd Passey, includes Rick, Eduardo, Carlos, Alan and Ken. Our group is led by Vern, with Garrett Madison as his assistant. It consists of Alex, John, Herbert, Dave, Suzanna and me. So with Vern and Garrett as our two expedition leaders, that's a total of eight on our team. And since our team has the only female, Dave Goehl comes up with the bright idea to identify ourselves in all cybercast reports to the outside world as "Lady and the Tramps." I can't help but think of Bruce Springsteen's lyric, "Tramps like us, baby we were born to run…"

When we make it to Camp 1, Vern asks the "Lady and the Tramps" whether we feel up to moving on to Camp 2. Everyone seems OK, except me. With all my sweating (How ironic is that in Antarctica?), I'm just beat. So Vern decides we'll set up Camp 1, get rested, and head for Camp 2 tomorrow. The team can only climb as fast as its slowest member. Guess that's me.

Setting up Camp 1

In our tent, I find Suzanna examining blisters on her heels and shins where her new boots are causing "hot spots." After feeling a little down for holding the group back here at Camp 1, I feel better that I can apply my advanced blister-control skills, developed after years of marathon running, to helping my tent mate. Thankfully, I brought liquid skin as well as various sorts of bandages. Problem is the freezing cold appears to impair the adhesiveness of the tape. Anyway, I do the best I can and hope it will hold up. Funny thing is Suzanna doesn't seem too concerned. If I had blisters like hers, I'd be calling for a helicopter rescue. That, would be a bit of a problem, though, since there are no helicopters or any other rescue vehicles up here.

Ready to offer my blister-control skills

January 15 – Camp 1

Left for Camp 2 fairly early after breakfast of rice porridge. It's pretty much like oatmeal but made out of rice. With cinnamon and big hunks of butter, it tastes like rice pudding. Maybe it's the eight-to-ten thousand calories we're burning each day, but whatever it is, the food we're eating up here tastes incredibly good.

Today I layer my clothes better to control my body temperature. I also transfer a lot of the weight from my backpack to my sled. With all the training I did pulling the "Whiting Tire," I find "man-hauling" easier than carrying a heavy pack.

I arrive at Camp 2 feeling a lot stronger than yesterday. The other team, led by Todd Passey, got ahead of our team yesterday, skipping Camp 1 and moving directly to Camp 2. They still seem pretty tired from the long haul and use all of today to rest. So maybe it was a good idea to hold up at Camp 1 and better acclimate. Only downside is that we had to set up our tents twice.

After dinner, we receive basic training in working an ascender – a small, hand-held device used in going up and down fixed lines. Tomorrow we'll ascent on a fixed line to help get us over a steep head wall so we can cache (store) provisions at High Camp. Then we'll descend back to Camp 2 and the next day carry more food and other supplies to High Camp.

Working an ascender on a fixed line that Vern set up for us to practice doesn't seem too difficult, at least on flat ground. But what about tomorrow, when we're on a steep slope? I'm worried about how I'm going to flick the various levers on the ascender while wearing heavy mittens. As much as I try, I just can't do it. I decide I'll wear only thin glove liners so that I'll be able to work my fingers. But that, of course, will increase the risk of cold or maybe even frostbitten hands.

I'm really anxious, scared and nervous, especially since I'll have to clamp and unclamp the ascender and carabineer (clip) on each of the twenty cutoff points on the 1200-meter-long line. Hard to figure how that will be possible on steep slopes, encumbered by a heavy pack and wearing only light glove liners in freezing cold weather. Thinking about that, I lay awake most of the night, unable to sleep.

Working an ascender

Getting up the headwall

January 16 – Camp 2

Now, the tough climbing begins. Strategy today is to get half of our food and gear from Camp 2 at 9,000 feet to High Camp at 13,000 feet.

Thankfully, weather is clear. It's cold at minus 30 degrees, but only light winds.

We leave our sleds at Camp 2. After a one-hour mild climb, we make it to the fixed lines on the headwall. In prior years, climbers took a gentler route up the headwall. That route was less steep but more dangerous because of crevasses. To avoid the crevasse danger, all climbers now are required to go up a steeper slope using the fixed line.

After all my worry about the ascender, it doesn't take long to get the hang of it. I place the fixed line between my legs, push the ascender forward and pull myself up while the ascender automatically grips the line.

Constantly using my fingers helps keep them from freezing. I find that it helps even more to grip one hand over the other on the ascender and rotate hands every minute or so. The hand warmers I popped in my gloves are a Godsend.

It took about three hours to finally make it to the top of the line. Incredible exertion, at least for me. To think, we'll have to go through all this again tomorrow. I keep repeating to myself my mantra: "Pain is temporary. Success is forever."

It's another two-hour ascent beyond the fixed lines before we make it to High Camp. After quickly caching (storing) our food and gear, we head down.

Waiting for our grub

I crawl into our tent feeling totally wasted but very, very hungry. Don't remember ever feeling so famished. So I manage to pull myself out for dinner.

Garrett's grilled chicken and elbow macaroni is easily the best dinner I've ever had. Alex downs four heaping bowls full and is proclaimed our team's "Joey Chestnut." Joey's the guy who won Nathon's Hot Dog Eating Contest by devouring 66 hotdogs and buns in 12 minutes, setting a new world record.

During dinner, I read to my teammates from Sir Robert Scott's log that the Englishman wrote during his 1911 race to the South Pole against Norway's Roald Amundsen. Today is the 98th anniversary of the very day that Scott and his team made it to the pole only to discover that Amundsen had beaten them by about a month.

January 16 - Camp 68. Height 9760. T. -23.5. The worst has happened, or nearly the worst. We marched well in the morning and covered 7½ miles. Noon sight showed us in Lat. 89 42' S., and we started off in high spirits in the afternoon, feeling that tomorrow would see us at our destination. About the second hour of the march Bowers' sharp eyes detected what he thought was a cairn… Half an hour later he detected a black speck ahead. Soon we knew that this could not be a natural snow feature. We marched on, found that it was a black flag tied to a sledgehammer; near by the remains of a camp; sledge tracks and ski tracks going and coming and the clear trace of dogs' paws—many dogs. This told us the whole story. The Norwegians have forestalled us and are first at the Pole. It is a terrible disappointment, and I am very sorry for my loyal companions.

Robert Falcon Scott Journals, *Scott's Last Expedition*, pages 375-376

Back in our tents, Suzanna tells me she hurt her knee on the trek back to camp. While she doesn't say so, I can tell she's really hurting. There's no stopping her, though. She points out it's all uphill now to the summit, and her knee only hurts on the downhill. I figure it best not to remind her that if we make it to the summit, it's a long downhill after that. Actually, Suzanna is right to concentrate on the next day rather than on what's happening later in the climb. Like running a marathon, climbing is not really a long race; it should be thought of as many short races tacked on to one another.

Thankfully, the bandages on her blisters are holding up pretty well, and the pain is tolerable. What a fighter! I don't think I've ever seen someone as focused and determined as she is to make it to the top of a mountain.

Scott and his team at the South Pole

January 17 – Camp 2

This morning, after getting out of my tent to go to breakfast, I am startled to see what looks like an insect flying in front of me. Since there's supposed to be no living creatures (except for us interlopers) in Antarctica, I'm totally amazed. But upon closer inspection, I realize it's only a feather from someone's down jacket or sleeping bag.

After breakfast, our second carry to High Camp seems easier despite a heavier pack and colder weather at minus 30 degrees. Maybe it's because now that I've had a day to figure out how to work the ascender, I'm not scared stiff anymore.

My confidence in the line is especially apparent at its steepest section near the top. Rather than holding on for dear life and grimacing with every move, as I was yesterday, I find myself having a conversation with John, who is just behind me on the line.

> Me: My wife is writing a business history of the U.S. based on entrepreneurs. It looks at how entrepreneurs, like Marconi and Edison, affected history more than politics or high finance.
> John: Just read a great book on Marconi.
> Me: Let me guess – *Thunderbolt* by Eric Larsen, right?
> John: Yeah. I loved it as well as his other book, *The Devil in the White City*.
> Me: Yeah, me too. In fact, I recommended both as summer reading to our Chapman students.

John and me getting near High Camp

Building snow walls around our tents

From there, we somehow got into a discussion of religion and theology. But now I can't recall that part of our chat. The altitude is probably starting to get to me.

When we arrive at High Camp, the weather turns ugly. We need to build V-shaped snow walls to protect our tents from the wind. We dig blocks out of the snow, and using a carpenter's saw, cut them into bricks for the walls and a seating area for our mess tent.

Cold. Cold. Cold! Hard to function in this kind of weather.

After our tents are set up and protected, we finally relax a bit in our sleeping bags.

Suzanna and I talk about how we miss our families back home. Then we get into all the creature comforts of life that we're missing more and more. This is only our sixth day living in a tent, and the prospect of a warm bath is looking better and better. I'm wearing the same three thermal layers of underwear I've worn since Tuesday. It's too cold to take "sponge baths" with baby wipes. Who wants to be naked in sub-zero weather? The baby wipes are frozen anyway.

Everything has to go into our sleeping bags at night otherwise, it will freeze – including all water. Even our pee bottles have to go in our bags. If it freezes, it will never thaw out up here.

Not sleeping well – could be the altitude, but more likely, it's nervous anxiety about our upcoming summit attempt. I wile away the night reading from Scott's log in full daylight. One of his passages reminds me why I'm up here:

> *Every day, some new fact comes to light – some new obstacle*
> *which threatens the gravest obstruction. I suppose this is the reason*
> *which makes the game so well worth playing.*

Robert Falcon Scott Journals, *Scott's Last Expedition, page* 114

January 18 – High Camp

Today is a rest day in advance of our summit attempt tomorrow. Good day to rest since weather outside tent is ugly. Windy and white-out conditions.

But Vern gets a report that the weather will clear tomorrow. So it looks like a go for our summit attempt.

At dinner, Vern recommends I take one of his compressor sacks in place of my backpack to save on weight tomorrow. Since we're only taking up food, water and storm gear in our packs, we don't need the volume of a backpack.

Even though Vern isn't happy with my decision, I stay with my pack. While it's four pounds heavier than the compressor sack, I believe my backpack gives me greater support for carrying at my hips rather than just my shoulders. Plus, my down parka is easier to get to from the top of my backpack when we need to bundle up quickly at rest breaks.

Most important, I've learned from marathoning not to change gear at the last minute. Once, I bought new shoes at an expo the day before a marathon. Not only did the shoes prevent me from racing at my goal pace, my feet were "ruined" for a month.

So I think it's just too late to change equipment now.

January 19 – High Camp
SUMMIT DAY!
Suzanna, Herbert and I volunteer to go up with Garrett on a slower-roped team
that will start out at 8 a.m. before the faster group leaves at 9. Vern believes this
pacing strategy will allow both teams to merge higher up the mountain, where
we can drop our packs for a final assault up the ridge line.

Only 10 minutes out of High Camp, my right foot falls into a crevasse and
I sink in up to my knee. My initial reaction is to try to step out. Mistake. I only
slide deeper in. I get my wits about me and extend my body on the surface as
much as possible, like I'm making a snow angel. I then kind of worm my way
out of the crevasse. Of course, I'm roped to my teammates, so there's no real
danger of falling into a bottomless pit. Still, it's pretty scary.

My crevasse

Doing a lot of pressure breathing now – breathing in as deeply as possible
and then exhaling as if I'm blowing out birthday candles. In camp, Vern
demonstrated how that kind of breathing increases the oxygen level of your
blood. On a measurement device he had, my oxygen reading went up almost 10
percent. That makes a big difference climbing at altitude.

At first, I find myself taking one pressure breath for each step forward. Then
it's two breaths, then three and then four or more.

Our two teams meet up at around 15,000 feet – just as Vern predicted. We
drop our packs and move up a steep gradient before reaching the summit ridge.
Really lucky with the weather. It's cold at minus 40 to minus 50 degrees but
sunny and clear with little wind. At the rocky summit ridge, the climbing gets
dicey. As we negotiate steep turns and narrow ledges, I grasp the overhanging
boulders for dear life.

4 pressure breadths = 1 step forward

Approaching the summit ridge

Moving up the ridgeline

After scrambling through all of this, we reach a safer, more level portion of the ridgeline. Now we can begin to enjoy the absolutely magnificent views. We can even make out the curvature of the earth at the edge of a vast expanse of white.

We reach the summit at 2:30 p.m. I grope in my inside pocket for the Chapman pennant and pull it out. I look at it with tear-filled eyes, thinking about all the summits it's been on. Then, the requisite photo-ops with me holding the pennant while my teammates join me in triumphant poses.

Suzanna and me holding the Chapman pennant on the summit

Me and John Rudolf on the summit

In his cybercast, Vern captures the moment:

> "Friends, family and loved ones and everybody else that
> is watching, this is Vern Tejas' group calling in from the top of
> Antarctica. We are looking north right now at the third, the
> fourth, the fifth and second highest mountains in Antarctica.
> It is a beautiful day above the clouds, a sea of white spreading
> out underneath this range in all directions. Everybody made it.
> Holy smokes they have been working hard for this one. I wish
> you could be here, this has got to be one of the best moments of
> my life up here. So please stay tuned and we will tell you when
> we get back down safely in one piece but right now we are
> celebrating and having a joyful moment. Everybody is taking
> pictures, clapping hands together, hugging, we would be kissing
> but we have too much ice on our face so it is quite dramatic.
> Ciao for now from the top of Mt. Vinson."

From the summit, we make it back down to High Camp in good time. I'm
one of the first to get in at around 6 p.m. So it was a ten-hour day. Pretty fast…
the normal time is around 12 hours.

Just woke up to a 9 p.m. dinner call. For the life of me, though, I just don't
remember getting into my sleeping bag.

Moving down

January 20 – High Camp

We left High Camp with heavy packs (maybe 70 to 75 pounds) for a one-day trek back to High Camp.

As we move down, we gather stuff we cached along the way at Camp 1 and Camp 2. So the weight increases, but thankfully we can offload some of it onto our sleds that are waiting for us at Camp 2. Need to also collect our cached wag bags to bring them back to Base Camp, where they will be flown to Patriot Hills and then on to Punta Arenas. Collecting these several-day-old bags makes me extremely grateful for the first time that everything freezes instantly in Antarctica.

Suzanna makes it back to High Camp

It's almost a whiteout. Kind of eerie to look around and see nothing but white. While it seems to be snowing, I know it's only ancient snow being blown around by the wind. Antarctica is actually a desert, so it snows only a few inches a year. The reason there's so much of it is that it never has a chance to melt.

Despite the worsening weather, we move pretty fast. If we make it to Base Camp before an Icelandic climbing team, we will be ahead of them in the queue for the Twin Otter flights back to Patriot Hills. Happily, our team, which actually starts running as we near Base Camp, beats the Icelanders by 15 minutes. So we'll get the first flight the next day to Patriot Hills.

This competition reminds me again of the Scott-Amundsen race to the South Pole. Sadly, after Scott found that Amundsen beat them by a month, he and his team tragically never make it back to their base camp.

Carrying heavy packs with sleds

In the final entry in his log, Scott manages after five days of silence to weakly scrawl the following words:

Thursday, March 29 – Since the 21st we have had a continuous gale from W.S.W. and S.W. We had fuel to make two cups of tea apiece and bare food for two days on the 20th. Every day we have been ready to start for our depot 11 miles away, but outside the door of the tent, it remains a scene of whirling drift. I do not think we can hope for any better things now. We shall stick it out to the end, but we are getting weaker, of course, and the end cannot be far.

It seems a pity, but I do not think I can write more.

R. Scott

For God's sake look after our people.

Robert Falcon Scott Journals, *Scott's Last Expedition*, page 412

Eight months later, a search party found the bodies of Scott and four of his teammates frozen in their tent.

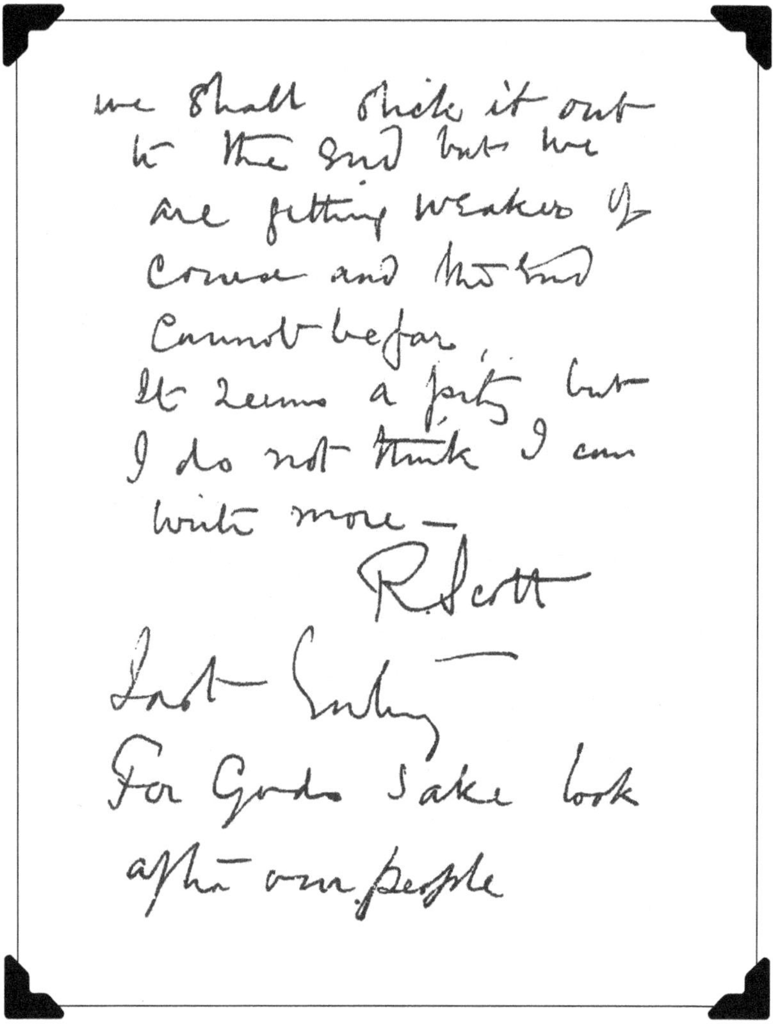

we shall stick it out
to the end but we
are getting weaker of
course and the end
cannot be far.
It seems a pity but
I do not think I can
write more —
R Scott
Last Entry —
For Gods Sake look
after our people

Scott's final entry

January 21 – Patriot Hills

Upon arriving in the Twin Otter to a celebration in Patriot Hills, we get the glorious news that the Russian Illuyshin is scheduled to fly us that evening back to civilization… and to hot baths.

But now, it's time to celebrate. We whoop it up with the best quesadillas and pizza I've ever had. I have my first Diet Coke in many a day.

Vern entertains us by playing a pretty mean harmonica accompanied by our bad singing but good cheer.

At 8 p.m., we take our long walk back to the Illuyshin ice runway, and we're off by 9 p.m.

January 22 – Punta Arenas

We arrive at our hotel at 2 a.m.

As soon as I walk into my room, I strip off base layers of underwear I've been wearing non-stop the last two weeks. I don't take them off as much as peel them off. The smell that exuded from my body was more akin to decay than typical BO.

The feeling of slowly sliding into a steaming bathtub was exquisite. Ahhhh… how luxurious it felt. It was truly a moment to savor.

I woke up still in the tub four hours later. The now cold water made me feel like I'm back in Antarctica.

Me and my Diet Coke

Back on the Illuyshin

Later that evening we all celebrate at Brocolino's Restaurant in Puntas Arenas. We have a great time reminiscing about our odyssey, reminding each other about all the highs and lows. In listening to my teammates recount all the little episodes that make climbing such an exuberant experience, I'm reminded that climbing isn't about reaching the summit. Rather, it's the coming together of a group of people all focused on a common goal. In pursuing that goal, our coming together inevitably is really about all the help and support we gave each other as well as the fun we had along the way.

It's about John keeping us laughing… Herbert helping me pull my sled out of a ravine… Dave helping everybody, including our guides, with such good cheer it was infectious… Alex doing the yeoman's work in chopping our snow blocks… and Suzanna inspiring all of us with her steely focus and drive.

It's kind of like Robert Scott's experience. Despite all of the bitter disappointments on his horrific expedition, he wrote on the back cover of his log a final "Message to the Public":

… for my own sake, I do not regret this journey, which has shown that Englishmen can endure hardships, help one another and meet death with as great a fortitude as ever in the past… Had we lived I should have had a tale to tell of the hardihood, endurance and courage of my companions which would have stirred the heart of every Englishman. These rough notes and our dead bodies must tell the tale.

Robert Falcon Scott Journals, *Scott's Last Expedition*, page 422

Anatomy of A Denali Summit Bid

Jim Doti

BEFORE heading to Alaska for a summit attempt on Mt. McKinley in 2010, I sent out a farewell message to friends. In that message, I tried to explain why my son, Adam, and I were leaving our loved ones to be cold, tired, and run ragged during a climb of North America's highest peak. My explanation called to mind Mark Twain's words:

> *Twenty years from now you will be more disappointed by the things that you didn't do than by the ones you did do. So throw off the bowlines. Sail away from the safe harbor. Catch the trade winds in your sails. Explore. Dream. Discover.*
>
> —Mark Twain

I'm now back home after exploring, dreaming, and discovering, but without another Seven Summit notch. Mt. McKinley, often called by its original Athabaskan name, "Denali" (The Great One), was simply too much for me. Yes, business demands were pressing. (Unfortunately, I brought a satellite phone to stay in touch with my office). In the end, though, I was sick of living in a tent, constantly longing for a shower. Even more significant, the allure of standing on Denali's summit was beginning to wane. If that were to lead to a lack of focus, it would be dangerous, particularly on Denali's infamous knife-edge ridgeline.

Last year, I wrote in my Log from Mt. Vinson that mountain climbing isn't all about reaching the summit. Rather, it's the journey. In any case, experiencing Denali turned out to be a great adventure. I hope that in reading the following log entries written during my Denali journey, you will begin to see why every now and then, one should "sail away from the safe harbor" to explore, dream about, and discover one of the most spectacular places on earth.

From my log, June 2010:

- Training for Denali is tough. Six months of bodywork buildup and running
  back-to-back marathons during the final month. On this final week before
  leaving, I do two running stress sessions and climb on local hills for eight
  hours carrying a 50-pound pack attached to the infamous David Whiting tire
  (named in honor of the eponymous inventor who used it for his successful
  Denali summit bid). I also weight train and do 100 push-ups,100 sit-ups,
  and 20 pull-ups or chin-ups per day. Finally, I climb the Alumni Tower of
  Chapman's Beckman Hall (120 steps or 70 feet) 25 times for a total elevation
  gain of 1750 feet. That's more than the Empire State Building, which stands
  1454 feet to the tip of its antenna. I do this stair climb while carrying a
  50-pound backpack, but thankfully, no Whiting tire is attached to it.

- Adam and I have a two-and-a-half-hour drive from Anchorage to Talkeetna.
  The lady van driver tells us her favorite part about living in Talkeetna is
  during the winter when there is almost 24 hours of darkness: "You can go
  out almost anytime and look up at the stars," she says wistfully.

Our van ride to Talkeetna

- Arrive at the almost 100-year-old Talkeetna Roadhouse at about 9:00 p.m.
  After taking showers down the hall from our rustic and creaky-floored room,
  we can't find towels. So we air dry while running back to our room
  "au naturalle."

- Have breakfast at the Talkeetna Roadhouse. It's everything my climbing buddy, John Dahlem, promised. The mega-sized cinnamon rolls dripping with glaze are scrumptious.

- Our scheduled flight from Talkeetna to Kahiltna Glacier Base Camp is delayed because of cloud cover. We drown our sorrows by sharing slices of blackberry and apple pie at the roadhouse. They ought to franchise this place.

Blackberry pie a the Talkeetna Roadhouse

- Flying out today is still impossible. Adam and I along with our head guide Todd Passey, assistant guide Joey McBrayer, and fellow climber Lillian Cuthbert, take a hike around a shimmering mountain lake surrounded by lodge pole pines and a prodigious display of wildflowers. It looks like a scene out of the children's book Heidi.

- Barbeque buffalo steak, caribou sis-ka-bobs, and salmon burgers over at Joey and his wife, Melis', home. Their "compound," as Melis calls it, consists of an 8x10-foot (80 sq. ft.) home and a separate 8x10-foot tool shed. Their new, two-story, 1000-sq.-ft. home is almost completed – a really cute house that just the two of them have built from scratch. Melis shows me the books she read to learn how to wire and plumb the house. Melis then builds a raging bonfire to keep the mosquitoes at bay as we enjoy our caribou sis-ka-bob appetizers washed down with a really good local beer.

- I help Melis get weeds out of dirt she's shoveled into a wheel barrel for a vegetable garden she's planting. Sifting through the wet, cool dirt feels good. Melis tells me that at Colorado College she majored in Russian and international economics to become a Russian economic analyst. But during a trip to Alaska, she realized that her real passion in life was to become an outdoor mountain guide. Then she met Joey, also a guide, got married and moved into their 8x10-foot nest.

Our picnic at Joey's

- We sleep in a former church that is now the equipment store for our guide service – AMS (Alaska Mountaineering School). We call it the "Church of AMS." Tonight, I play Beethoven's "Moonlight Sonata" accompanied by Adam, who rhythmically taps a punching bag that is inexplicably located near the piano. Our audience is a caged pet chinchilla. Standing on hind legs while grasping the cage with front claws, the chinchilla attentively watches and listens to our concert.

- At AMS headquarters, we pack lunches for three weeks of climbing. We select our favorite snacks and stuff them in three bags (one per week). We're told to limit each bag to no more than seven pounds and no less than five. The AMS shelves are laden with just about every candy/nut/dried fruit mix ever created. I load up on all my favorites: Almond Joys, Pringles, Snickers, salmon jerky, cashews, Rice Crispy treats and Fig Newtons. I also stash away bags of Tang that I can throw into my water bottles.

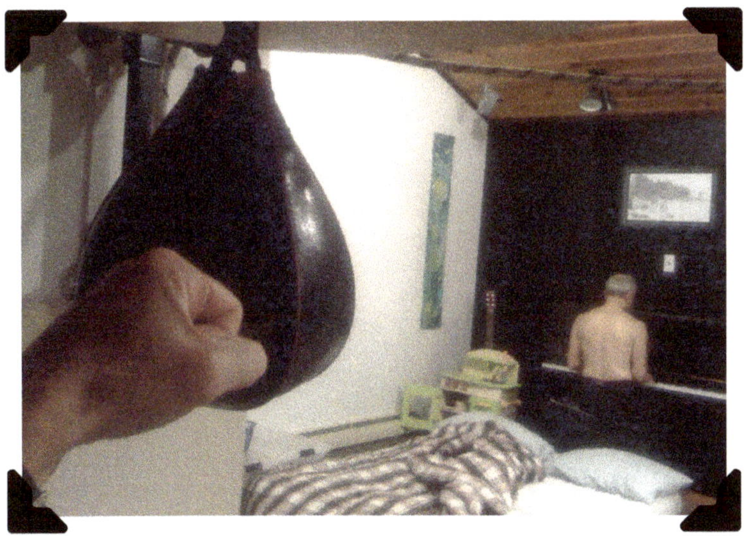

Adam punches a bag while I play the Moonlight Sonata

- Receive word this morning that flights are going out. We pack up fast at the "Church of AMS." On the way to the air strip, we see a "baby" moose munching grass on the roadside. We hear that after its mother was hit by a truck, the Talkeetna community helped feed the little guy through the winter. Now he looks strong and healthy.

- Glorious flight to the Kahiltna Base Camp (7200 feet). Absolutely amazing how we fly through mountain passes that seem only slightly wider than the DeHavilland DHC3 Otter plane's wingspan. It almost seems like we'd be able to stick our hands out and touch rock. This flight alone is worth the price of admission. We land at 10:30 a.m. on the Kahiltna Glacier, bumping along snow on the plane's ski legs.

- Too warm to climb safely to Ski Hill Camp (7800 feet), so we hang out during the day at base camp, practicing crevasse rescue techniques. In the heat of the day, snow bridges covering the bottomless crevasses are more likely to give way. That's why we wait until 8:00 p.m. to start our climb.

- The start of the route to Ski Hill Camp descends Heartbreak Hill. It's called that because on the way back it's an uphill.

- We arrive at 2:00 a.m. Remember, it's Alaska, so it's still daylight. Have a quick dinner, set up our tents and get in our sleeping bags. For some strange reason, all night my feet are freezing but my head is hot.

- Get up around noon for breakfast. Todd scrambles eggs with big hunks of butter, cheese, salami and potatoes. He revives stale cinnamon rolls by frying them in butter. After six hours of hiking last night, all these calories refuel our weary bodies.

Kahiltna Base Camp

Heartbreak Hill

- Outside, a raging snowstorm creates near whiteout conditions. Thankfully, it's not too cold, so we decided to climb just above Upper Talkeetna Camp (10,000 feet) to cache (store by burying in snow) our gear and supplies we won't need over night at Ski Hill Camp. Very tiring with a stiff, steady wind against us the whole way. After climbing for seven hours, we cache our provisions and place our now empty sleds in our backpacks for the return to Ski Hill Camp. The wind is with us and the sleds sticking out of the tops of our packs serve as a kind of sail. We make it back in a little more than an hour.

Ski Hill Camp

Caching our gear at Upper Talkeetna Camp

- A Denali climb is all about caching high, going back to a lower camp to sleep and then returning the next day to set up a higher camp. This process helps in acclimatizing to the lower air pressure at higher altitudes. It's also a way to limit the weight on any single carry. On these lower stretches, where we're packing food and fuel (used for cooking and melting snow for our water), we carry around 50 pounds in our packs and pull 75 pounds on a sled "hitched" to our backpacks.

- Over the last couple of days, Daniele Struppa, the provost at Chapman University and a fellow mountain climber who also happens to be a mathematician, shares an interesting e-mail exchange with me;

> **To:**   Jim
> **From:** Daniele
> To pass the time, I have a nice problem for you and your fellow climbers. There is a sphere whose diameter is six inches. We drill a cylindrical hole through the sphere, symmetric with respect to the sphere center. What is the volume of the part of the sphere that remains after the drilling?
> Talk to you soon.

> **To:**   Daniele
> **From:** Jim
> Don't you need the diameter of the hole to solve this?

> **To:**   Jim
> **From:** Daniele
> No… but, of course, that's the right question to ask. That explains why this problem is so beautiful and elegant.

> **To:**   Daniele
> **From:** Jim
> We can't figure it out. But it's killing us. What's the answer?

> **To:**   Jim
> **From:** Daniele
> Nice to hear that I'm keeping the team entertained. But as I was writing the answer I realized I stated the problem to you incorrectly. We don't know the size of the sphere, but the cylindrical hole is six inches. There are two spherical caps which are cut off as well. There

are two ways to solve the problem. One is analytical and the other relies on the question you asked me at the beginning, namely the fact that the radius of the sphere is irrelevant.

To: Daniele
From: Jim
Now at altitude where I'm not thinking straight, so forget about your "beautiful and elegant" problem.

- For dinner, Joey cooks up some broccoli cheese soup followed by bean burritos. Since we're burning around 5,000 calories a day, we need to eat mass quantities to keep our engines going. We're still low enough in altitude for the food to taste really good. But higher up, it won't be so easy. Closer to the summit, we'll have to start force-feeding – kind of like a French goose being primed for foie gras.

Our team waiting for Joey's special burritos

- Over dinner, we discuss the European financial crisis. Joey will soon be visited by his international banker father-in-law, so he's particularly interested in getting some basic economics to regurgitate to him. I don't recall ever having a more attentive student. Joey seemed particularly pleased when I said he would impress his father-in-law by telling him: "I'm afraid the U.S. will be in the same boat as the "PIGS" of the European Community if we don't solve our deficit problem."

- Climb the Kahiltna Glacier in the morning to just below Motorcycle Hill Camp at 11,000 feet. We make our way over the top of the glacier between beautiful, albeit dangerous, crevasses with magnificent Denali looming in the background. Even the crevasses, as dangerous as they are, are incredibly stunning. As I peer down these deep V-shaped chasms, I often see masses of ice in the form of stalactites and stalagmites. They give off different shades of blue, sometimes brilliantly so, depending on the depth of the glacier.

Denali looming in the background

- Observing how our guides Todd and Joey, instruct us, cook for us, watch out for us, nurse us, motivate us and, in general, lead us is nothing less than inspiring. I never cease to be amazed at how much I learn about leadership from mountain guides, particularly the really good ones, like Todd and Joey. They are remarkable individuals, and I am in awe of the depth and breadth of their abilities.

- Reading *Little Big Man* – a great novel written by Thomas Berger in 1964. The blurb on the cover says it's "…one of the best novels written in the 20th Century." Laudatory statements like that are pretty common. In this case, I believe it. There are few joys in life greater than discovering a new book that takes you into another world in which you want to be a part. *Little Big Man* will definitely be on my list of summer reading recommendations for our Chapman students. People often ask how I find time to read 500-page novels.

Try climbing up an Alaskan mountain with 24 hours of light and a lot of time spent cocooned in a sleeping bag waiting out storms.

Todd checking for crevasses before setting up our tents

- Strangely, tonight my feet are hot, but my head is freezing.

- Below Motorcycle Hill, I'm huffing and puffing. I rest my head on my ice ax as we stop for a break. Adam clomps over to me in his snowshoes and asks if I'm alright. I reply that I'm just tired. He helps me unbuckle myself from my backpack. That's no small feat given the number of rope lines dangling around a climber. One rope ties you to the teammate ahead of you and the one behind you. This rope also ties through your sled. If you fall in a crevasse, at least you won't lose your beloved pig (slang for sled). Another line attaches to your backpack and your body harness. Several other lines keep all these lines from tangling. With all these lines and carabineers (climbing clasps) tied around you, taking off a backpack can easily trip you up. That likelihood is increased by the fact that it's not easy walking around while wearing snowshoes.

- Adam helps untangle and unwind me. He sits me down and pulls out my water (tough to get with all the ropes, etc.) and snacks. As he dribbles cashews onto my bulky, exploration-style mittens, I work hard to get them into my mouth, which is partially covered by my balaclava (face mask). As Adam helps me, it brings back memories of when I helped him set up his first tent in the backyard; how I comforted him when he got attacked by bees as a little boy on our first backpacking trip up Bishop Pass; how I taught him to bait a line and build a fire. Now the tables are turned. Adam is comforting me; he's protecting me. Isn't there a line that says something like: "The greatest satisfaction of a teacher is when a student becomes an even better teacher"? In a way, our camping, backpacking and mountain climbing serves as a metaphor for life itself. A baby is born. That baby is nurtured and supported by parents and becomes a child, then a teenager, then an adult. Small changes imperceptivity occur, but over time the changes are relentless and become ever more perceptible. Borrowing from Alan Lerner's lyrics in Gigi, when Gaston (Louis Jourdan) realizes that Gigi (Leslie Caron), is no longer a child, he asks, "Have I been standin' up too close or back too far? Oh, what miracle has made you the way you are?"

Dangling rope lines

- On the way back down to Upper Kahiltna Base Camp after a second carry, I ask myself why I'm going through all this effort just to get to the top of a mountain. In the past, the word "just" would have had no place in my vernacular. Getting to the top was an integral part of the journey. But now, it just doesn't seem all that important anymore.

- Back at our tent, I receive satellite phone messages about Chapman issues as well as my corporate board responsibilities. While these matters seem to lure me back home like the sweet, seductive call of a siren, in the end, it's not the siren that lures me. Rather, it's the more prosaic call of a body yearning to be free of Denali's grip. So after summiting together with Adam on Mt. Whitney (twice), Mt. Rainier, Mt. Kilimanjaro, Mt. Aconcagua and Mt. Elbrus, it's now his turn to do it without me. I'll have to be content with basking in the reflected glow of Adam's joy in facing a challenge and overcoming it.

- When I tell Adam and my teammates I'm abandoning the climb, they try to talk me out of it. They bring up the fact that I'm throwing away six months of training. To my delight, this gives me an opening for an impromptu economics lecture on "sunk costs." Namely, that costs already expended have no bearing on future decisions. One must only consider future costs and benefits in order to make an optimal decision. My teammates stare blankly at me.

- Tonight, in our tent, I ceremoniously and reverentially present the Chapman pennant to Adam. It feels like I'm in the final stage of my leg in a relay race, and I pass the baton to the racer ahead of me.

- Another father and son climbing team, John and Ryan Dahlem, brought the Chapman pennant that I just passed on to Adam to the summit of Mt. Everest last month. So it's now been to the top of five of the Seven Summits – the highest mountain on each of the seven continents. If Adam gets it to the top of Denali, that will make it six with only the piddling little 7310-foot Mt. Kosciuszko in Australia to go. While I haven't done an exhaustive search, I believe that would make it the only university pennant to reach the top of all Seven Summits. And if USC ever gets around to trying to copy our feat, Chapman's pennant will always be able to lay claim to being the first to do it. Eat that – USC!

- Our guide, Joey, and I head down and then up Heartbreak Hill and arrive at Talkeetna Base Camp around 2:00 p.m. On Denali there needs to be a minimum of two climbers roped together. That's why Joey's with me. He'll head back with another guide as soon as I can get a plane ride back to Talkeetna. Unfortunately, there's cloud cover at base camp, so no planes are flying. We set up a tent, resigned to sleeping one more night on the mountain. As the day wears on, we hope for better weather tomorrow.

- But we luck out. At 8:00 p.m., the clouds begin to clear and all of a sudden we hear the unmistakable rumble of a DeHavilland engine roaring in the air. The plane makes it through and gets me back to Talkeetna, where Caitlin Palmer, director of AMS, is waiting for me. For anyone who's seen the video "Deadly Denali," Caitlin is the woman with the long braids.

- Caitlin reserved a place for me at the Chinook Wind Cabins, where I'm given the "Denali Lodge." The proprietress, Jane Steele, is weeding her garden at 10:00 p.m. (Do all Alaskans do their gardening at night?) We chit-chat about the various vegetables to which she's giving such loving care. I hear a strange whirring sound and realize it's a fan clipped to her belt that's dispersing an anti-mosquito repellant. She tells me, "It's better than rubbing that poison on your skin." I'm certainly not going to argue with her on that one.

- As I take off the underwear I've been wearing for the last few days, I realize I don't have any clean ones. They're all in a cache somewhere up on the mountain. No way I'm going to put these dirty, smelling drawers on tomorrow, so I decide to wash them in the kitchen sink. But since it's now around midnight and I have to get up at 5:00 a.m. to catch my van to Anchorage, I realize there won't be enough time for my underwear to dry. So I come up with the bright idea of drying them by warming them in the oven. (For those Seinfeld fans out there, I feel a little like Kramer, who decided to warm his winter coat in a pizza oven.) Unfortunately, as I'm luxuriating in a splendid, hot bath, I smell smoke and then catch sight of it drifting into the bathroom. I run out and open the oven to see my underwear in flames.

- I won't get into the details of how I dressed this morning for the flight back home.

- On the van ride to Anchorage, we come about as close as I've ever been to a head-on collision as a car on the opposite side of the road crosses the median and heads straight at us. My driver quickly veers off the road to avoid it. When we come to a safe stop, my driver, Bill Cutt, who may have saved our lives, takes a few moments to regain his composure. He confirms that it's also the closest he's ever been to a head-on. Ironic, huh? The most dangerous part of the trip turns out to be on a highway to Anchorage – not on Denali.

- At the Anchorage Airport, I check my e-mails and read a missive from my buddy Rick Reiff, who asks if I received word that our Chapman PR student team just won the coveted national championship. When we won in the regionals, beating USC, UCLA and UCI, I thought that was good enough. But to win the nationals – how sweet it is! My fellow travelers in the airport look and smile at me while I whoop and holler with joy.

End of Denali Expedition Log

Back home that night, sipping wine next to the fire pit in our backyard, Lynne asks me if I would do it all again if I had the chance.

In recounting all the laughs, the cold winds, the relentless climb up the mountain, the lessons I learned, the beautiful sights I saw, the new friends I met, and especially the passing of the guard between Adam and me, I conclude, yes, it was one of the most memorable adventures of my life. Mark Twain was right: "Explore. Dream. Discover."

Lynne then asks, "What's next?" In thinking about that one, I'm reminded of Adlai Stevenson's response to reporters when he was asked what he'd do after losing the presidency to Dwight Eisenhower for the second time in a row. Adlai said, "I think I'll sip wine and watch the dancers." Right now, that sounds pretty good to me.

Note: As related in the next log entry, Adam Doti summited Denali on June 23, 2010.

Summiting Denali

Adam Doti

OUR staging ground was Talkeetna, Alaska – a vibrant outpost where bush planes roar, and climbers gather like pilgrims. Talkeetna, a quirky Alaskan town bustling with climbers and bush pilots, felt like the last outpost of civilization before plunging into the wild. My Dad and I along with our climbing team spent a few days, extended by weather delays, prepping gear and feeling the nervous energy build. The days were filled with hikes along rushing rivers, visits to a tiny museum with a mesmerizing 3D Denali model, and endless debates over trail snacks.

Dad checking out the 3D Denali model

We even turned a pulse oximeter into a bizarre game, seeing who could push their blood oxygen levels to extremes. Then came the gear check – our lives spread out on a tarp. Our lead guide, Todd Passey, scrutinized every item with the eye of a seasoned veteran. Talkeetna was a comfortable 60°F by day,

Ready for takeoff

dipping to a crisp 40°F at night. We practiced rope work on local walls and shared stories around a campfire at the home of our assistant guide, Joe Stock. Anticipation crackled in the air as we enjoyed a super BBQ.

Finally, the moment arrived. We boarded a small plane, wings stretching overhead, and soared into the vast Alaskan wilderness.

Then, the surreal moment: landing directly on the Kahiltna Glacier. The plane touched down on an icy runway, surrounded by a village of tents and a few permanent structures acting as remote airport control. The air was thin and biting. Our gear was immense, sleds laden with maybe 75 lbs and backpacks bulging with another 50-65 lbs – a testament to the long haul ahead. These sleds,

Our constant companion

attached to our harnesses, became our constant companions, dragging behind us as we navigated the endless white.

The Kahiltna Glacier stretched before us, a maze of ice. Zigzagging around gaping crevasses became the norm. At camp, Todd drilled us on avalanche and crevasse rescue, the stakes feeling incredibly real. We made good progress until we turned towards Denali's shoulder, where my father, despite his strength, made the heartbreaking decision to turn back and end his climb. The emotional weight of that moment hung heavy. We've always climbed together as a team. Without him at my side left me with an empty feeling. But at least, I'll have Dad's beloved Chapman pennant with me. That pennant will serve as extra motivation to reach Denali's summit.

On the Kahiltna Glacier

The following days blurred into a rhythm of tent life, mess hall meals, and the strange games we invented to pass the time. The pulse oximeter reappeared, even clipped to our toes for laughs. A rogue raisin became "Wilson," our own Cast Away companion, perched on a ledge and the source of endless banter. We joked about "organic pop tarts" and the constant struggle to keep sleeping pads from overlapping.

Reaching Advanced Base Camp at 14,200 feet brought a new level of intensity. We stood at the foot of a massive headwall, above which lay the "football field," a deceptively flat area that offered a brief respite. Looking up, we spotted a harrowing sight: a cable system with a sled used to lower injured or deceased climbers. Reality hit hard.

Advanced Base Camp with Mt. Foraker in the background at 17,400 feet,
the second-highest peak in the Alaska Range, 14 miles southwest of Denali

Our team with Vern Tejas second from left

Here, we crossed paths with the legendary Vern Tejas, a silent reminder of Denali's formidable reputation.

The high camp latrine was a terrifying crevasse, our waste destined for its icy depths in a 5-gallon bucket, periodically emptied by Todd or Joe.

Summit day began at 2:00 AM, in the pitch black. Roped together, we climbed the steep headwall for hours. A guide pointed out a grim reminder: the location of climbers who had never returned. The mountain held its secrets and its tragedies. We navigated the West Buttress, a rocky spine that was treacherous with crampons.

We finally reached the football field, named for its flat and open expanse.

The West Buttress

On the "football field"

On the Denali summit ridge

Then, the ridge – a wind-scoured edge with cornices that looked ready to crumble.

We traversed, step by agonizing step until finally, we stood on the summit of Denali, 20,310 feet above sea level. I felt incredible, no altitude sickness, just pure exhilaration. The final touch was taking the Chapman pennant for photo I knew that Dad would prize.

The descent was a blur, the sled now leading the way, almost like walking a stubborn dog. Back at the airport camp, shots of Scotch whiskey were passed around – a celebratory ritual. We waited for the plane, our eyes fixed on the horizon, ready to leave the white wilderness behind.

The Chapman pennant on the summit

Shots of scotch – a celebratory ritual

Climbing Carstensz and Kosciuszko

Jim Doti

From my log, August 27 – September 11, 2015:

August 27

Picked up by limo at 10 pm at home in Villa Park. On the way to LAX, the limo driver told me, using a combination of English and Armenian words, what sounded like the entire history (a very sad one) of the Armenian people.

August 28 – 29

Leave LAX on Eva Airlines and arrive in Taipei on Saturday at 6:00 am. It took about 13 hours or so. When I get off the plane (very groggy), I realize that I lost my passport. I go back to the plane, and a flight attendant goes back to the plane and finds it on my seat where it evidently fell out of my back pocket. How stupid of me? Maybe this is a metaphor for the rest of the trip – doing stupid things and then, luckily, recovering.

Next flight is to Bali at 10:00 am, where I will meet up with my son, Adam. I have around 4 hours to kill. I do that by walking up a flight of 40 steps multiple times for training. Free samples of Chinese candies are given out by various shops. I love the bean paste candy and buy a box as a snack for the rest of the trip. I also get a free auto chair massage by entering a token an airport attendant gave me. Not bad!

The airport restrooms are the best I've ever encountered. They had plants growing on a shelf in front of the urinals. The paper towels were scented and had happy or sad faces to allow people to rate their toilet experience. My rating was happy face all the way.

While sitting in the waiting area, I met a Chapman grad '99 who was also flying to Bali. She was a peace studies graduate now working for an environmental firm. In the rush to get on the plane, we were separated and I never got a chance to get her name.

The flight to Bali from Taipei was about 6 hours. This leg of the trip was "coach" instead of "elite." My eyes were so tired it was difficult to read. I longed to be in a prone position. I saw a ridiculous but entertaining film, "San Andreas," about a massive earthquake in California.

Upon arrival, I was picked up by a Balinese woman named "Carol" and drove to "Kapu Barong Villas and Spa." The two-hour drive was through rush hour traffic. I dozed off most of the way. The few times I would awaken, I found it bizarre that there were hundreds of places to buy lawn ornaments like elephant Gods, temples, Buddhas, etc.

Soon after arriving, I met up with Adam and his wife, Brenda, and went for dinner together at a restaurant called "Bridges," where I had a great barracuda dish. When I finally got to bed that night at 10:00 pm after 20 hours of flight and a two-hour cab ride, it was the first time I was able to lie down in a prone position. That was one of the more luxurious feelings I've experienced in a long time.

August 30

Walked down to Adam and Brenda's fancy room (their own pool!) and went for breakfast. I ordered "Belgium waffles" but in Bali that is closer to French crepes. Whatever they were, they were GOOD.

I swam in a beautiful hotel pool and did 10 laps for training purposes. Afterward, it was restful and relaxing to lounge and read "Pirate Hunters" on Kindle.

At 12 noon, we dropped Brenda off at Bali Airport. Then Adam and I went to the "Ramada Resort Brittany Bali" hotel. On the way back from the airport, Adam told a funny story about Brenda and his trip to the largest temple in Bali. Adam explained that a monkey took a woman's glasses but was bribed to give them back. The monkey kept the glasses and turned down the water that was offered, but the monkey gave the glasses back in return for a wrapped Kit Kat bar.

Lounged all afternoon on the beach with Adam, munching on satay and drinking local beer. During the two hours we were on the beach, we were pestered by four Balinese women trying to persuade us for them to give us manicures. It didn't seem like we'd be needing manicures for our climb, so we turned them down. I found it fascinating watching them weave corn rows on gleeful little girls.

At night, we met up with our climbing guide and leader, Todd Passey, and went to an Irish bar. We had a bad fish dinner – my first bad meal on the trip.

August 31

After breakfast at the hotel, we met up with Scott Chapman and then had a gear check in our hotel room. I stupidly left my GoPro camera back home. I brought all the camera attachments but not the camera. Hope I didn't throw out the

Adam and me, with guide Todd Pasey, at Irish bar

Gear check with Chapman pennant safely in tow

camera with all the packing material. (Alas, I later found out that I did.)

Our plan was to relax and have dinner before flying out to Timika, New Guinea, at around 12 midnight. Before leaving for the airport, we had a beachside dinner and saw a glorious sunset. Adam, Scott, and I met additional climbing partners, Mila from Indonesia and Ralf Laier from London, England.

We are now at the Bali airport waiting for our flight to New Guinea. I'm feeling refreshed after taking a two-hour nap after dinner. It's now 1:00 am, so I guess it's Tuesday.

September 1

We arrive in New Guinea at 6:00 am. Adam and my seats were in the emergency exit, so we couldn't slide the seats back at all. That forced us to sit in a vertical position for the four-hour flight. For our breakfast arrival, we were given candy bars called "Deka Crepes" followed up by chocolate-flavored biscuits. Excellent!

We were driven in vans to the "Komaro Tame Hotel and Resort." The room didn't have towels and looked like a flop house. I then spent the morning doing emails with my associate, Dorothy Farol, working on various Chapman matters. I found it pretty amazing to be conducting Chapman business in New Guinea, 7,100 miles from campus.

At our "resort" breakfast, I had some sort of rice with bits of chicken in it. I also had a noodle vegetable buffet entrée that was like Lo-Mein. For the rest of the day, we just hung out, but at 4 pm, the helicopter pilot gave us a briefing on procedures. Most worrisome is that we can't take off if the weather at base camp is cloudy ("Cloudy – no fly"). Sounds like there's a strong possibility of waiting around like we did in Punta Arenas on my Vinson climb in Antarctica.

Played one of my teammates, Ginge Fullen, in backgammon in the afternoon. He is an expert player, but I still beat him 11-8. He's a very interesting guy who is a deepwater diver who repairs underwater oil rigs in the North Sea. He hails from Fort William, Scotland. Ginge has a goal to climb the highest point in every country except Nepal. When he tried summiting Mt. Everest, he had a heart attack and had to go back. So Nepal is OUT. In bed by 9 pm. Just finished reading "Pirate Hunters". Absolutely great book. Now it's sleep time.

September 2

Our flight is delayed until 10:30 am. Scott just got bitten by a mosquito. He's paranoid about this because he had contracted malaria on a previous trip to the Southeast. Just received the following message: "Cloudy – no fly."

Ginge just beat me 11-3 in backgammon. I have a vague feeling he's hustling me.

Update report: "Cloudy – no fly."

We are watching "Fight TV in our "mess hall." Here's an interesting sumo wrestling factoid: The oldest sumo wrestling champ in modern history was 37 years old. For lunch, we are eating some sort of mystery meat on rice. It seems like I've consumed more rice in the last four days than I have in a lifetime. I haven't been doing any outside running or other exercising since I'm afraid of being bitten by a malaria-ridden mosquito. But I am going a little stir-crazy, feeling a little bit like the Tin Man before Dorothy came to the rescue. So, I improvised a quarter-mile loop around our hotel grounds and walked/ran for 45 minutes. In spite of this short workout, it felt good to get moving again.

I reversed yesterday's loss to Ginge of 11-4 with a win of 12-4 today. We had dinner at another Indonesian restaurant serving up the usual Asian (Chinese) rice, mystery meat and fish plate.

Still waiting around in what Adam characterized as our "minimum security prison," an apt description given the fact that it's unsafe to leave the hotel perimeter and not really safe to walk inside the perimeter, given our fear of contracting malaria.

During our waiting, I finally figured out something that I've wondered about for years. It involves how to unloosen a double show lace knot. If you pull the wrong lace, it tightens the knot; if you pull the right one, it loosens it. But

Our hotel is surrounded by a barbed wire wall

That's me demonstrating the Doti Knot Rule

how do you select the correct lace to pull???

Given the luxury of all our free time, I figured out that if the second knot is tied left over right, then the correct lace to pull for loosening is the left lace. This Doti Knot Rule applies to both shoes. Voila! It seems to me that this rule is more useful than solving Fermat's famous theorem about prime numbers.

Had the usual dinner outside the hotel (safer travelling in a group). We are increasingly talking about our favorite hamburgers (mine is In-N-Out). We even argued about whether a truly great hamburger should be accompanied by a hearty red chianti or a good German beer.

September 4

At breakfast, Ralf saw me eating my improvised rice pudding that I concoted by combining steamed rice, sugar, water, Cremora and some sort of coconut jelly. Ralf was impressed.

Just can't take any more noodles. Ralf asked how much I'd pay for a bowl of freshly made muesli with a little cream, honey, and yogurt (my go-to breakfast). When I said $50 bucks, he responded, "Is that all?"

Scott came down to our mess hall wearing his lucky Hawaiian shirt. He was confident that wearing that shirt would give us the luck to clear our flight. Just got word that the flights were cleared for takeoff and to get our butts moving. So Scott's shirt worked.

Before we cleared out of the hotel, I asked the hotel manager if I could buy one of the pillows in my room. It's just my pillow type: flat and firm. It's strange that I hate the soft and squishy pillows usually found at posh hotels. I've found my kind of pillows are at the motels at the bottom of the rung scale. Since our current hotel is at the lowest, I don't find it surprising that it has the best pillow. Call it the "Doti Pillow Rule" if you like. The hotel manager is even nice enough to offer the pillow as a gift. I thanked him profusely and gave him a 100 thousand rupee tip (around $7).

There will be three flights, and Todd, Adam, and I are scheduled to leave on Flight #2.

Just got word: "Cloudy – no fly." Scott evidently took his lucky shirt off too soon.

Lose two sets of Backgammon to Ginge today: 11-4 and 11-7. Walk 7 miles, last three with Scott, who was not wearing his lucky shirt.

Nothing to do now but wait for more noodles at dinner. I finished reading "Publishing" by Gail Godwin. Meh.

We've just been notified that because of the recent shooting in Tamika, we are ordered to stay in the hotel and eat at the hotel "restaurant."

September 5

Got word at breakfast that we're flying out today. I am on flight #2, and Adam is on flight #3.

Very interesting flight. It reminded me of illustrator Carl Bark's illustrations in an Uncle Scrooge comic book story, "Flight over Shangri La." We flew over a gold mine that is supposedly the largest open pit mine in the world. Pretty ugly blot on the landscape.

We landed at base camp and set up our tents. Everyone has their own individual tent. The weather is relatively warm at 50 degrees. Carstensz Pyramid looms over us and looks very intimidating. The face looks like a vertical climb.

Base camp

We took a practice hike and climbed 800 feet to the pass that leads to a lower campsite.

There was a discussion of the possibility of making a summit attempt today since our teammate, Mila, decided to do that. After some back and forth, we decided that it would be safer to acclimate overnight and make a summit attempt starting at 2 am tomorrow morning.

I play backgammon with Gringe and lose another match. I owe him $17 for my losses.

Mila arrives back in camp after successfully summiting. It took her and her guide only 8 hours. She told us it was very cold with rain/snow on the summit ridge. She fell four times trying to jump over the infamous two chasms after the Tyrolian pass. Of course, she was tied to a safety rope. On Mila's way down there was severe water runoff from the rain and melting snow that created very slippery conditions rappelling down the face. The whole experience sounded pretty intimidating.

So far no altitude sickness for Adam and me, although a few teammates are sick. We eat a light dinner of mostly rice to carbo load for tomorrow's planned ascent. Whether it's because of the altitude or nervousness over the pending climb, I toss and turn in my sleeping bag and feel cold all night.

September 6

We start our summit attempt at 2:20 am. Early going is tough – almost all scrambling and climbing 70 degree walls using our ascenders.

Getting up the steep face

On the ridgeline

Scott, Adam, Todd and me on the summit

But I get in the groove and make good progress. (Thank goodness for all the pull-ups I did while training for the climb.) It takes about three hours to make it to the ridgeline.

On the ridge, there's a lot of scrambling while tied to a fixed line as a tether. We are lucky that the Tyrolean Gap was changed about a month ago so one can now walk over it like on a tightrope with steel cables on both sides for balance. After the Gap, we are confronted with the two "notches" or gaps (4-5 feet wide). I don't know how I was able to manage jumping over them, but I did. We make it to the summit at around 6:30 am.

But now the weather is turning with rain, snow, and sleet pelting us. After quick photo-ops at the summit, we start our descent at around 7 am. Making it over the two gaps is even harder and scarier than on the way up. One of the gaps involved placing two feet on one side of the gap and then letting the body fall forward, catching the other side with two hands. With Todd yelling, "You can do it, Jim," I leaped off and raised my right arm to an ascender above me. Catching it, I pulled myself over. Whew! Scariest thing on the climb.

On the way down, I wrapped the fixed line around my arm to simulate rappelling. Once we were off the ridge, we rappelled (maybe 15 times) to go down the steep face. Several problems developed. One was that the rappel line was unusually thick and difficult to thread through my rappel device. Another problem was that the rappel lines got tangled up with the fixed lines. Yet another problem was that some of the rappel lines ended up short of a level spot to stand. That made it critically important to rappel down slowly, untangling the line as we descended and watching carefully for the length of the line we still had.

On one rappel where the line was too short, I had to find a foot hold, and then scramble rather than rappel down a 90-degree wall. When I did, I inadvertently removed my tether, placing me in instant danger. I was lucky that Todd saw me and scrambled up to tether me up again. Ironically, Ralf made the same dangerous mistake I did at almost the same spot. In his case, though, Todd was able to catch him as he almost killed himself falling backward. I can only guess that our mistakes resulted from our being super tired, wet from all the waterfalls around us, and being frazzled by the short rappel lines.

We finally made it back to our camp at noon with Adam, Scatt, Todd and me leading the way with Rolf and other guides behind us. That made the climb from start to finish about 10 hours, with most of those hours being pretty grueling.

I had a hot chocolate (best ever) and hobbled over to the tent, where I slept like a baby.

Rapelling down

Almost down

September 7

When we got up at around 8 am, Gringe was leaving alone for his climb. There was a downpour of rain all night.

Now, it's time to start worrying about our helicopter pickup. We got word pretty early that there would be no pickup today. "Cloudy – no fly." Ginge got back after his successful summiting in 7 hours. The guy's a Superman! After dinner, I paid Gringe the $17 I owed him. It was well worth it given all the backgammon strategy I learned watching Gringe in action.

September 8

Scott wore his lucky Hawaiian shirt not long after we got word that the helicopter was on its way. Thank goodness for Scott's shirt. We had heard rumors that the pilot was soon going on vacation. Our flight schedule was #1 for Rolf, Mila and Scott. #2 for Adam, Todd, and me. #3 for Gringe and a Swedish guy who got altitude sickness and didn't make the climb.

Adam's happy to be on board

Adam was so worried about making it out that he demanded that Scott not take off his shirt until we were on the helicopter and in the air. Unfortunately, while flights #1 and #2 made it out, the helicopter was grounded before it could go back to pick up Gringe and Per. Since Per was still sick, we were relieved to find out that they were flown out of camp the next day.

After arriving back in Tahita, we were driven to a sad-looking hovel of a hotel where we showered before being driven to Tahita Airport for our flight back to Bali.

We arrived in Bali and went back to the same hotel. Todd, Adam, and I went to the Hard Rock Café for hamburgers and fries before bed. They seemed even better than my favorite In-N-Out burgers and fries.

September 9

Adam arranged a flight to Sydney for tomorrow. Since today is a free day, Scott and I go snorkeling and go on a tour of Turtle Island, where we have photo-ops with turtles, fruit bats, and a huge eagle of some kind. Some guy ferries us around in a motor boat to see the various sights. Thankfully, we opted not to go scuba diving since it turned out that the dive site was only 15 feet deep. So we just snorkeled and saw some reef fish, but it was super crowded.

This evening we had a celebratory dinner where we received our climbing certificate and gift of Indonesian shirts. Carol, our tour guide in Bali, brought us to a really neat beachside BBQ where there was an incredible sunset. The fish (grouper, clams, shrimp, and some mystery fish were fantastic. It was a spectacular evening on a remote Bali beach. It was a perfect way to end the Carstensz Pyramid part of our trip.

Our fish dinner on a remote Bali beach

September 10

Adam and I arrived in Sydney, Australia, at 10 am and rented an SUV to drive to the Thredbo Ski area – the site of Mt Kosciusko, the tallest peak in Australia.

On the drive down south to the ski area, we see an incredible number of kangaroos and wombats on the side of the road killed by cars. Sad. Except for all the roadkill, the scenery was beautiful. There were no billboards and many vineyards and sheep and cattle ranches along the way. Looks kind of like Route 101 in Northern California.

We use Yelp to find the "best" meat pie place on our route. We find it in a picturesque little town in the middle of nowhere. Reminds me of Old Towne in Orange, California. Not only were the meat pies terrific, but even better were the apple danishes.

We arrive in Thredbo at 4 pm, where we settle in a nice B&B ski lodge and rent our equipment for tomorrow's climb. Weather reports call for clear 20-degree weather. Perfect!

Had a nice Australian steak dinner in town.

"Best" meat pie in Australia

September 11

Got up around 7 am. Adam asks me to fake having breakfast at the B&B so we don't offend the owners of the B&B, who are evidently very proud of the breakfasts they serve their guests. Actually, I find some really good stewed prunes on the rather sparse breakfast buffet table. After telling the owners of the B&B how much we enjoyed their wonderful breakfast, we went to another place that Yelp rated as the best in town.

I have a stack of four delicious pancakes floating in maple syrup covered with berries and bacon slices. After all the strange rice-infused breakfasts we had in Bali and New Guinea, this breakfast was like heaven.

Our B&B in Thredbo

We start our climb and the weather is perfect. Adam goes ahead of me, but I follow his bootprints in the snow. On the way to the summit, we see other climbers carrying skis so they can ski back down after summiting. Drats! We both regretted that we didn't rent skis so that we could do that. Too late now. We're already halfway up the mountain. After a three-hour trek up Kozi, we summit around noon. We meet a group of young people celebrating on top. After getting our photo with the Chapman pennant we head back down.

On top of Australia

On the way down, I use snowshoes. Adam goes ahead of me, so I am mostly alone in the quiet of the mountain. Maybe it's the satisfaction of climbing both Carstensz and Kozi, but whatever it is, I really enjoy the peace and solitude of the two-hour trek down the mountain (Hill?).

On the way down

We make it back around 2 p.m. and drive back to Sydney. We counted 89 dead kangaroos and 30 dead wombats. We didn't see any live "roos" until we stopped for a rest and saw a small group of them hanging out near the side of the road. As we continued our drive to Sydney, I read to Adam who was driving from Scott Chapman's e-mail log of our Carstensz trip. Not only was it hysterical, but all true. (That log follows this one.)

Upon arrival in Sydney, we dine on hamburgers and a beer sampler at King's Warf, followed by a snifter of Elijah Wood bourbon. We cap off a really neat day touring the Sydney Opera House while watching fireworks explode over the harbor.

Beer sampler at King's Warf

The Challenge of Climbing Carstensz Pyramid

Scott Chapman

THE board meeting had just ended. Chapman University president Jim Doti turned to me: "Adam and I are planning to climb Carstensz Pyramid this summer. Would you like to join us?" Pyramid? I pictured a Mayan ruin deep in the Yucatan. "It's the eighth summit of the Seven Summits". I knew the Seven Summits – the tallest mountains on each continent. "Some people think Australia's 8,000-foot summit is not in the same league as the other six, so they include an eighth summit -- the tallest mountain on the island of Papua in Indonesia, just north of Australia. Carstensz Pyramid is over 16,000 feet."

Of course, I said yes immediately. I had read about Jim's previous adventures on Kilimanjaro, Elbrus, Aconcagua, Vincent, and Denali. Now I had the chance to join the latest adventure myself!

From my log, August 2015:

Day 1
August 31. Dinner on the beach in Bali, a few hours before our red-eye to Papua. The team was assembled: Jim Doti (several marathons every year), Adam Doti (multi-day adventure races without sleep), Ralf Laier (10 first ascents of unclimbed peaks in Antarctica), and Todd Passey (guide: just back from a summer above 13,000 feet in the Alps). "So Scott, how did you train?" I was trying to figure out whether our wine and running club had done more wine drinking-or more running this summer. It was hard to say.

Adam: Can you believe that up until 50 years ago, cannibalism was rampant in Papua? True, they do still practice some cannibalism now, but it's not so much for food – more for intimidation.
Ralf: You know the town we are flying to in Papua? Two people were shot and killed there last week.

Todd: The gold mine right below the summit is strictly off-limits Recently, a climbing team went to the mine for refuge after one of their porters died and the porter's tribe wanted to kill a climber for revenge. The mine security people locked the climbers inside a container for days until they finally let them use a sat phone to call someone, who called a US senator who eventually got them out.

Day 2

After our red-eye flight to Papua, the team gathered in the lobby of our crumbling, walled hotel compound together with three more climbers (Ginge, Per, Mila) and our Indonesian guides (Josh, Matt, Poxy).

Ginge, an Englishman living in Scotland, has a unique mountaineering background. In the 1990's he began a quest to climb the highest peak (or get to the highest point) of all 195 countries in the world. After a heart attack and airlift from camp 1 on Everest, he will not go above 6000 meters again, but he can still get to the high point of 182 countries. Carstensz Pyramid will be his 166th.

Our Indonesian guides were very experienced in climbing Carstensz. Poxy had climbed it 56 times. They told us to be ready for a helicopter briefing at 4 o'clock for our flight to base camp the next day. So for the rest of the day, we had nothing to do but relax. It was actually nice to completely unplug everything and laze around without a care in the world.

"Don't leave hotel. Dangerous."

"Hey, what do you think? How many of these mosquitos are carrying malaria? I hear that more and more are resistant to the drugs we're taking."

OK. Back to my room to read and watch the only English language channel I could find, Fight TV: non-stop boxing, sumo wrestling, and martial arts.

Finally that afternoon, it was time for the greatly anticipated helicopter briefing. We all sat down and waited for the official from the helicopter company (Jacob) to launch into his briefing.

"If cloudy, we no fly."

Silence. Was that it? Was that the whole briefing?

"Is it supposed to be cloudy tomorrow?" "When you say cloudy, do you mean here or on the mountain?" "If it's cloudy on the mountain after our climb, do we just have to wait until it clears? Or could we hike to a different pickup location?" "When it gets cloudy here, how many days does that typically last, worst case."

"Papua very cloudy."

OK then.

Day 3

Rain.

I made a bet Todd as to whether it would clear up later and we would fly –a packet of Gu for a Power bar. In the meantime, there was nothing to do but sit and tell stories.

Jim: Hey, Adam, tell them about the monkey in that temple in Bali.

Adam: This monkey ran over and grabbed a lady's sunglasses, then ran into the bushes. One of the locals knew how to get the glasses back. He threw the monkey a KitKat bar. The monkey dropped the glasses and ran away to eat the KitKat.

Jim: What I like about this story as an economist is that it shows that even monkeys understand the basics of business. Although the monkey could have kept both the KitKat and the glasses, he knew that if he did so, he wouldn't get more KitKats in the future. His best strategy to keep getting KitKats was to drop the glasses, setting the precedent for a trusted exchange.

While pondering that, I felt something on my elbow. I slapped it and got blood all over my fingers. Oh, that's just great, back to the safety of my room and more Fight TV.

Lunchtime.

"Which of the sumo wrestling schools do you suppose is the most successful?" "I don't know, but my question is this: How successful does a sumo wrestler have to be in order to get paid more than an NFL lineman?"

The guides come over.

"Not flying today. Try again tomorrow."

Silence. I handed over a packet of Gu.

"Hey, have you guys ever seen snail racing? It's a well-known fact that the best-trained snails come from northern England."

Day 4

The guides told us at breakfast that we were going to fly. They came around to each of our rooms with a big scale and weighed us with our bags and gear. Then everyone sat in the stairwell with our bags, happy to be heading up the mountain soon, just waiting for the guides to come back and take us to the airport.

Waiting … slapping mosquitos … waiting …

"Did you guys see the Ricky Hatton – Floyd Mayweather fight?" "Mayweather's right jab is so fast! And he had a 7-inch reach advantage on Hatton. Only one way it could end." "Yeah, but he's boring to watch. Did you see his fight against Pacquiao?"

Lunchtime.

Jacob, the helicopter guy, came to our table. "Windy on the mountain. No fly today."

Silence.

Jim: Do you ever wonder which end you should pull when you double-tie your laces? One end tightens the knot, and the other end loosens it. I finally realized this: If your second knot is right over left, then you should pull the left single end, but if it is left over right, you should pull the right one. See, watch this.

Ralf: Hey guys, you want to see a magic trick? I'll reach into Todd's mind and cause him to freely choose an object that I've already texted to his phone.

Day 5

Rain.

I decided to wear a Hawaiian shirt to breakfast. I figured that if I wasn't wearing my mountain gear, so I wasn't actually ready to fly, we would definitely get the green light.

Nice shirt. I explained why I was wearing it.

"Elbows must be legal in kickboxing."

"They are in a lot of leagues, but some leagues have banned them – along with head-butting – too many deaths."

"Wow! Nice take-down!"

No news.

Me: That's it. I'm going to the helicopter company to get an update.

"Weather on the mountain is good. First group fly soon."

After I reported the news, everyone immediately got excited and told me to be sure to take my lucky shirt up the mountain. We wouldn't want to get stuck there after our climb. Bags were loaded into the van. We were ready to go.

Ready to go …

Ready to go …

We eventually got the bad news.

No fly today. Bad weather.

Silence.

Back to Fight TV – AND … (drum roll) … a newly discovered movie channel! All the classic movies you always wanted to see. For example, who could forget the masterpiece, "Robinson Caruso on Mars"?

Dinner.

Weather should be good tomorrow morning. Group one be ready at 5:30, group two at 7, … A lot of happy faces.

Day 6

The first and second groups flew. I was in the third group. How can I describe the flight? For the first part, we flew low over dense jungle (Vietnam war movie – Platoon?). Next, we quickly ascended steep jungly slopes (King Kong, especially the remake). Then we flew over the world's largest gold mine, cut out of the jungle and into the slope of a mountain (Avatar). Finally, we landed on the treeless rock and scree at 14,000 feet (Seven Years in Tibet).

The weather was good at 11 a.m. when we had all made it up to base camp. The next day was also supposed to be good in the morning, but deteriorating in the afternoon and bad for at least a day or two after that. So if we didn't catch a helicopter back the morning of the next day, we would likely be stuck at base camp for a few days (or several days).

Todd, Jim, Adam, Ralf, and I debated plans.

"OK guys. We could gear up and make our summit bid right now, or we could give ourselves a day to acclimatize and go early tomorrow. If we go now, we have the highest chance of getting a helicopter down tomorrow if they are flying. But we would be climbing down in the dark."

"It is supposed to be an 8-hour round trip, right? If we start early enough tomorrow, say 2 a.m., then we could be back by 10 to still take a helicopter out. The downside is that we would be climbing up in the dark."

"As a rule of thumb, weather is typically best on a summit first thing in the morning."

"OK. Let's do the 2 a.m. start."

Mila, on the other hand, decided to gear up and go for the summit immediately, taking Poxy as her guide, and Ginge decided to give himself 2 nights to acclimatize before climbing. We heard Mila come back that night – she had successfully made it to the summit and back in 8 hours.

Day 7 - Summit Day

Poxy, Matt, Todd, Ralf, Jim, Adam, and I got our start at 2:25 a.m. The skies were overcast, but it was not raining. Most of the early part of the route was rock climbing at about a 70 degree angle, with good hand and footholds. The entire route has fixed ropes that are anchored at various places by bolts, pitons, etc. We protected ourselves from falling by clipping our ascenders to the ropes. Since ascenders will move up a rope but not down, when there were tough spots with no good handholds, we just pulled on our ascenders to get past that section. We did all of this in the dark with our headlamps and with an occasional light spritzing of rain.

Dawn came, but it was still cloudy. To reach the summit ridge, we climbed a last pitch that was steeper but with good holds when you needed them. Traversing the summit ridge took close to 2 hours, with the most challenging and exposed climbing of the entire route. First came the Tyrolean traverse: holding two cables with your hands (and clipping into them for protection), then walking 25 feet on a lower cable, looking down at the 2,000-foot drop below you. Next, a ten foot gap had to be crossed by climbing down a bit, doing a big step, then climbing back out. Another gap a little later had to be crossed in a similar fashion.

Eventually, we reached the summit. It was still cloudy, so we couldn't see in the distance, but we could see our base camp 2,000 feet straight down. We took every imaginable picture combination with different people and different banners provided by our Indonesian guides, but most importantly, we took a picture of the Chapman University pennant. That same pennant had been to the top of all Seven Summits, and now here it was on the Eighth.

As we started heading back along the summit ridge, snow started to fall. Crossing the gaps was even more exciting in this direction. In fact, the second gap required a trust fall: "Stand on the rock and just fall forward until your hands hit the wall in front of you. Don't pay any attention to the 2,000-foot drop below you."

When we made it across the summit ridge, it was time to start rappelling down. It was tricky since the multiple fixed lines were always getting tangled with each other and time-consuming since we rappelled one at a time. A lot of the descent, though, was not rappelling; it was down-climbing. The basic technique was to wrap a fixed line around your arm and use that for friction as you climbed down, sometimes forward, sometimes backward. In addition, you clipped to the rope so that if you started to fall and couldn't stop yourself you would at least be stopped at the bottom of that fixed rope, where it attached to an anchor in the rock. But a fall like that would not be a good thing, so despite the fatigue from altitude and all the climbing, you had to be alert and at the top of your game with every step.

As we descended, rain began to fall. Mostly just a steady rain, once a little bit of hail, but then the heavens opened with a downpour. Our descent route became a series of waterfalls. At one point, I had water pouring down the back of my neck. But I was rappelling and definitely not going to take my hands off the rope, so what can you do?

Eventually, we made it back to base camp. A 10-hour roundtrip. We all congratulated Mila on what a stud she was for making it in 8 hours! Due to the rain, there was no chance of us getting a helicopter down the mountain, so it was just hot drinks, cookies, and recovering in our rain-pelted tents.

Day 8

We woke to a steady rain. At breakfast, the conversation was mostly predictions for when the weather would be good enough for us to fly out, and various alternative proposed plans if that couldn't happen for a few days. Also Ginge was making preparations for his summit attempt if the weather cleared (Per was having problems breathing and would not make a summit bid). As the morning wore on and Poxy had some radio calls with the helicopter pilot, it looked increasingly unlikely that we would fly that day.

Then after talking with Poxy in Indonesian, Mila let us know that the pilot was only available for two more days. The helicopter company couldn't get any other pilot since all of the other qualified pilots were fighting a forest fire in Sumatra. So if we didn't fly out in the next two days, we wouldn't be flying out at all. Mila said that the backup plan was to make the 2 hour hike to the mine at night and get smuggled out by people that the guide company knows there. Oh that sounds like a great idea.

As soon as I heard that, I went back to my tent and put on my Hawaiian shirt (over all of my cold-weather gear). A little later, the skies cleared up a bit, Ginge set off on his summit bid, and Poxy got a call from the pilot telling him that he was on his way. I was scheduled to go on the first flight down (with Ralf and Mila).

Adam: "Be sure to keep the shirt on until we're all down. If you want to take off some layers at the airport, that's fine – just figure out a way to do it without taking off the shirt."

Ralf, Mila, and I made it to the airport just in time for a direct flight to Bali. As our plane was taking off, Ralf saw our helicopter back on its pad with Jim, Adam, and Todd outside of it.

The trip was a success. I could take off my Hawaiian shirt.

Here I am wearing my lucky Hawaiian shirt

The Turquoise Goddess ... Mt. Cho Oyu

Daniele Struppa

THE year 2002 was probably the most important year in my recent life. After serving for five years as Dean of the College of Arts and Sciences at George Mason University, I was tired of the pettiness of academia and of the interminable silly battles that we had to engage for a few crumbs (as H.Kissinger seems to have said "the reason that university politics is so vicious is because stakes are so small") and I had decided to quit my job as a dean and professor and begin a new career as a mountain porter in South America. I loved climbing mountains, I had discovered that I could acclimatize easily, and I felt that moving to the Andean region could give me great opportunities to indulge in my passions for mountains, women, and freedom. I would not be making much money, but I had personal experience of the fact that living in places such as Bolivia, Ecuador, Peru, Argentina, Chile was not an expensive endeavor, and I was sure I could gobble up enough to make a decent living.

So, I went to visit Alan Merten, at the time the President of George Mason University, and I told him I wanted to quit the university. His surprise was palpable, and he asked me to wait a few days while he was trying to make sense of what seemed an unreasonable decision. During those days he consulted with the chairs of the many departments in my college, with my associate deans, and came back to me with a proposal that, as Don Vito Corleone would have said, I could not refuse. George Mason would grant me a paid leave for one year so that I could climb whatever I wanted, as long as I agreed to return as Dean at the end of the leave. Sensing the strong desire to keep me at George Mason, I negotiated another component of the deal: after four years as Dean, George Mason would grant me another fully paid leave to climb some more.

The generosity of this offer was such that it was truly impossible to refuse the deal, and my dream of becoming a porter in the mountains of the Andes seemed to be on hold for at least four more years.

As I was preparing for the leave, I decided to climb several peaks. I was going to climb as much as I could, and I signed up for a bunch of trips with

Mountain Madness, the outfit that I had used in the past to climb Aconcagua, Kilimanjaro, the Cascades, and the Cordillera Real in Bolivia. Mountain Madness had been founded by Scott Fischer, a strong climber who pioneered many routes and played a crucial role in opening the way to amateurs towards the summit of Everest, where he perished in the 1996 tragedy that is recounted in Jon Krakauer's *Into Thin Air*. I had (and still have) great confidence in that company, and I was excited about traveling again with them. At the time, their president was another very strong climber, Christine Boskoff, and I will never forget her kindness in sending me a beautiful fleece with the Mountain Madness logo. Christine, sadly, would die a few years later, in 2006, while climbing Genyen Peak in China.

My plans were to start with the French/Italian/Swiss/ Italian Alps, followed by Mt. Elbrus in the Caucasus (the highest summit in Europe), followed by Cho Oyu (a splendid peak in the Himalayan region that, at 26,864 ft, is the sixth highest mountain in the world), and finally Mt. Vinson in Antarctica (the highest mountain in that continent).

But, as many have said before me, if you want God to laugh, make plans. So, most of what I had planned was not going to happen.

What derailed the plan was love…There was a colleague of mine, a junior faculty in the Department of Communication at George Mason University, that I really liked. She was a runner (we ran together a half-marathon) and a beautiful and funny woman. Unfortunately (for me) Lisa was married, with a beautiful daughter (Elena), and I did not harbor many hopes for a future with her (I was married as well, but my marriage was not going too well, so that was not really a consideration in my mind). However, just a few days before the beginning of my leave, June 1st, 2002, I learned (by pure chance) that Lisa was getting divorced, and that she would be in Moscow (on a research trip) on July 19. My plans changed instantly, and I arranged my climb on Elbrus to coincide with Lisa's trip, so that I could be in Moscow on the 19th of July, just before leaving for Tibet and Cho Oyu.

I spent June on the Alps, climbing many beautiful mountains, though the climb that I remember more vividly was the Arête du Cosmiques, on Mont Blanc, a splendid rock-ice mixed climb that really pushed me to my limits.

It is not a very long climb (I think it took me five hours) but I found it quite terrifying for the exposure and the fact that I was climbing with ice crampons, something that is very uncomfortable whenever the rock is dry, as it was in many points on the route. Be that as it may, I was able to complete the climb, whose ending is truly surprising and probably deserves a quick description. After several hours of rock climbing, rappelling, ice climbing, and some dry pointing, the Mountain Madness guide encouraged me to reach the end of

The route to the arête in clear view

the route, where I was surprised to see a throng of Japanese tourists who had taken a gondola ride up the mountain on a terrace, ready to take pictures of the 'hero' reaching the top of the climb. I could not resist snapping a picture of that precious moment.

As I found out later, the Japanese tourist books apparently suggest to the travelers to position themselves on this specific terrace in the hope of capturing a glimpse of the brave climbers reaching the top of the arête. One of the ladies even asked me to take a picture with me, both of us holding an origami crane in our hands!

Waiting for the "hero"

After my moment of fame, and after a few more climbs in the Alps, I stopped by Milano (my hometown), I washed my clothes, had dinner with my Italian math friends Irene and Fabrizio, and moved to Russia. The climb of Elbrus was uneventful and not too interesting, and I summited on July 17. We returned to the base of the mountain on the 18, and I was ready to be in Moscow on the 19.

There I met Lisa, feigning interest in her research trip, but before the day was over, I could kiss her, and our love story began. It was hard for me to leave the next day, especially because she was a very beautiful woman, recently divorced, and I was going to be away for several months…a dangerous situation for a newly begun romantic relationship.

On the way to Tibet I stopped by Doha, in Qatar, where I gave a bunch of money to a florist, with the request that he would regularly send a bouquet of roses to Lisa, my desperate attempt to make sure she would not forget me…The florist kept his word, and Lisa (whom I married in 2003) still has some of those roses.

Cho Oyu, also known as the Turquoise Goddess, was first climbed on October 19, 1954 by Herbert Tichy, Joseph Jöchler and Sherpa Pasang Dawa Lama. Their feat is described in Tichy's 1957 book, *Cho Oyu: by favour of the Gods*. There is a beautiful legend that tells us how Cho Oyu was in love with Chomolungma (Everest) but was rejected by Chomolungma. Her sadness was such that she turned her back to Chomolungma and now faces away from it.

The trip to Cho Oyu began in Kathmandu, the capital of Nepal, in my opinion one of the most beautiful and haunting cities in the world. It was there that we made sure to have the equipment necessary for Cho Oyu, including special gloves that would protect us once we reached 26,000 feet. In Kathmandu I met our guide, a very experienced and extremely strong climber, Damian Benegas, and my two climbing partners, a merchant marine captain and a Duke University oncologist. Great people who would become friends and whose company I greatly enjoyed in the months ahead.

From Kathmandu we flew to Lhasa, the capital of Tibet, where, after a quick acclimatization, we boarded a truck that, over several days, took us to Tingri, where we caught our first sight of Cho Oyu.

Cho Oyu from the Advanced Base Camp

Tingri is just a very small hamlet, with a few homes where people use yak's dung to heat their homes and parabolic mirrors to boil their water. After a couple of days to get our things together, we proceeded to base camp, at 16,000 feet. The camp was beautifully located in an ample valley, with a river, the Ra Chhu, running through it and a constant strong katabatic wind flowing down from the mighty Turquoise Goddess. Two more days of acclimatization and we moved to Advanced Base Camp (ABC) at 19,000 feet.

That transfer, that we did in a single day, was long and presented some challenges such as the forging of the Ra Chhu, where one of our companions fell. He was not hurt, but he had to continue the climb in freezing cold clothes…something I would not wish on my worst enemy. During this trek we were accompanied by our yaks, who were carrying our supplies, and it was a sad moment when one of them fell to his death while navigating a narrow ridge. We finally made it to ABC, somewhat exhausted, and happy to retreat in our tents, located on a fairly wide area on the moraine. The plan was now to take a few days to rest and continue the acclimatization with a series of carries to Camp One.

Before we could leave ABC, the porters who were staying with us required our participation in the puja ceremony, with which the climbers make offerings to the mountains and ask for permission to climb and help in returning safely. A very touching ceremony that remains one of my strongest memories.

Our team after the puja ceremony.
That's me, second from left in the front row.

At that point I had imagined the next portion of the climb to be easy, with Camp One being 'only' at 21,000 ft, but the route between ABC and C1 was more tiring than one might expect. The first three hours were spent navigating the moraine, up and down, up and down, so that at the end of those hours, one was at what was called Lake Camp, still at 19,000 feet. It was there that one could look at a rather unimposing scree slope, known as 'pain hill'. The reason for the name became clear to me when I first had to go up that hill. Despite its unassuming aspect, the scree on the hill makes the climb an exercise in frustration. As I was going up, I was remembering the Canaleta on Aconcagua, which, in comparison, seemed a simple training ground. Once, after at least two hours, I finally reached the top of the hill, a new panorama opened up to my eyes. I was now on the other side of the mountain, and snow and ice were everywhere. The camp itself was nested on a wide ridge, and the tents were surrounded by deep snow. What a spectacle!

Camp 1 at 21,000 feet

That night was really hard for both me and my tentmate, the oncologist. We shared the tent, and we found it very hard to breathe in the thin air at 21,000 feet. The next day we trekked back to ABC to rest and prepare for another trip to Camp One. I confess I hated the idea of having to go back once again through the moraine and then again on pain hill. In fact, I thought that a better idea would have been to make a permanent move to Lake Camp, at the basis of the hill, in order to avoid the tiring and frustrating hike through the moraine.

It was at ABC that we were reached by very sad news. Another experienced Mountain Madness guide, Gabriel, had fallen to his death during a climb in the Condoriri region. He and I had climbed together in that region just a year earlier, and I remembered him with great affection. That cast a sad pall on the entire expedition.

We returned once more to Camp One. I could feel my health begin deteriorating, though the route to the top was now visible.

My ability to move upwards was rapidly diminishing and my breathing was getting increasingly labored. It was not a good sign. And so, after a brief attempt to reach Camp Two, I had to stop before the next big obstacle (an ice cliff that had to be climbed on fixed ropes) and turn back. I was very upset but my body was giving me very precise instructions, and I had to start planning my departure.

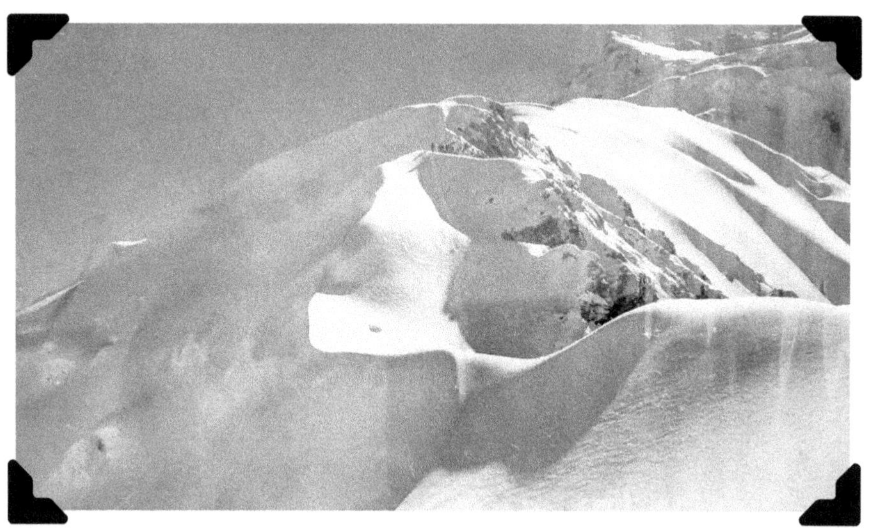

The route to the summit

I went back to ABC, hoping to feel better, but I was completely exhausted by the time I reached the camp, and it was clear I needed to go down, fast, if I did not want to risk worse consequences.

After a sleepless night, I said goodbye to my teammates, and I began my descent in the company of a Sherpa. We did not have a common language, but we managed to enjoy each other's company, and I am indebted to him for his support through what was a very long day. By the time we reached Base Camp, however, my breathing had significantly improved, and I was able to take care of myself without any more help.

The question, now that I had abandoned my team, was how to get back to Kathmandu. It was a more delicate question than one might think because I was on a Chinese climbing visa that included the members of the expedition, and I did not have an individual Chinese visa on my passport. Thus, it was not possible for me to cross into Nepal legally, something that worried me quite a bit. I was told that, at Base Camp, there was a Chinese officer who would be willing to transport me to Nepal at the price of $500, and since I did not have any other alternative, I decided to visit a very large tent, where I was told he had his quarters.

After some negotiation, we agreed he would transport me the next morning. I paid him in advance and went to sleep in my tent with some anxiety as to whether he would actually follow through and take me to Nepal in the morning.

We were supposed to meet at 6.00 am, and I was up already at 5.00, worried that he might leave without me. But my fears were misplaced: he came to my tent at 6.00, brought me some boiled eggs to eat and some Coca-Cola to drink, and off we were towards Nepal, along the so-called Friendship Highway that China had constructed years earlier.

It was a fairly uneventful ride, and after several hours we reached the border. The border itself was just before a long bridge (the Sino-Nepal Friendship Bridge) that was joining two sides of a deep canyon excavated by the Sun Kosi River.

There we had a very nice Chinese lunch, kindly offered by the officer who was driving me. What I did not expect, however, was the fact that, after lunch, he explained to me that this was as far as he could take me. Since I did not have a visa, I could not pass the border legally, and I had to try to reach the Nepali side by climbing down to the river, follow the river for a few hundred meters, and then climb back on the Nepali side. No…I really did not like that plan at all, and I could just envision the articles in the Washington Post where their news would be reported as 'American climbers detained in China under suspicion of espionage.' This was definitely not how I wanted my travel to continue. But the officer that had accompanied me seemed pretty comfortable in saying that the border was very porous and I did not need to worry about this last step.

And so…I did what he had suggested to me, and a couple of hours later, I was finally on the Nepali side, where a Mountain Madness van was waiting for me. The return to Kathmandu was quick and I was happy to be back to civilization after spending so many days in altitude. There was only one more thing to check…was Lisa still waiting for me? I remember sending her a tentative email explaining that I was back in Kathmandu, and it is hard to describe the happiness that filled me when I got her enthusiastic response.

Our love story still had some challenges to address, in particular the jealousy and envy of many of our colleagues (back to the pettiness of academia), but the ending was as happy as one can hope for; we got married a year later, we made two beautiful children, and eventually moved to Chapman University, where a fellow mountain climber, President Jim Doti hired me as Provost and Lisa as his first Presidential Fellow and Full Professor in the Department of Communication.

High Altitudes, Deep Bonds:
A Father-Son Journey to Everest and Back Home

Ryan Dahlem

CLIMB safe. Climb confident. These were the simple words of advice my mother offered every time my Dad and I headed off on another climbing adventure. This time, as we prepared to board a flight to Nepal for a two-month Mt. Everest expedition, they carried even more significance. We had completed years of training, numerous climbs around the world, and months of meticulous planning. But this was Mt. Everest. Sensing the magnitude of our departure, my Mom added a well-timed boost of confidence: "And I just know you are going to make it."

That boost helped, though there were still times when I wondered how we ever got to the point of attempting to climb the highest mountain on Earth. The answer traces back to my childhood, when my parents, both educators, planned vacations that entailed piling my older brother and me into our VW bus and heading out on camping adventures throughout California. Yosemite, Death Valley, Idyllwild, we saw them all from the windows of that bus and the vestibule of a tent.

The pinnacle of these trips was a 72-mile backpacking trip across the Sierras when I was 12 years old that culminated with a summit of Mt. Whitney, the highest mountain in the lower 48 states at 14,497 feet. Adding to the challenge, a bear raided our camp one night and took most of our food, making the final leg of the trip even more grueling. But it created a family bond and sense of adventure that continues to this day.

Years later, my Dad and I set out to climb Mt. Rainier. At 14,410 feet and a fully glaciated peak, Rainier was the most technical climbing we had encountered, requiring ice axes, crampons, and roping up as a climbing team to navigate crevasses. We signed on with International Mountain Guides, where we met American climbing legend Phil Ershler. Phil had climbed Mt. Rainier over 500 times and was the first American to summit Mt. Everest from the

North side, a feat he accomplished solo during the final push to the summit. He also completed the storied Seven Summits, the highest mountain on each of the seven continents, then climbed all seven again with his wife Susan, becoming the first husband-wife team to accomplish this feat.

Dahlem family vacation: 72-mile backpacking trip across the Sierras

Our climb on Rainier with Phil was an inflection point in our shared pursuit of adventure. Summit day was extremely hard. We reached the top in bad weather, tagging the summit and turning around without a photo or a view. But the elation we felt after descending and the connection we formed with Phil, was compelling. We returned home and dove further into the sport of mountaineering, immersing ourselves in climbing books and magazines. We attended talks of other climbers and spent hours at REI, building up our gear closets for the next adventure. Most importantly, we called Phil and shared how much we enjoyed the climb, including the challenges, and asked a question that would inform the direction of our lives for the next decade: What's next?

Phil encouraged us to consider an attempt on Mt. Kilimanjaro. At 19,340 feet above sea level, the "roof of Africa" promised a significant high altitude challenge and unique geographical experience of hiking from a tropical rainforest to the glaciated peak, analogous in climatic zones to traveling from the equator to the North Pole. We trained hard for the climb, spending weekends on Southern California's "Big Three" mountains: Mt. Baldy, Mt. San Jacinto, and Mt. San Gorgonio, all over 10,000 feet. We also returned to Mt. Whitney, once the culmination of our family's backpacking trip, and now just a training peak for a summit nearly a mile higher.

We were successful on Kilimanjaro, thoroughly enjoying all aspects of the expedition, from the cultural exchange to the safari that followed. We also discovered a synergy to our relationship that made for very good climbing partners: we traveled well together, embraced training and preparation as an important and enjoyable part of the experience, cherished learning about new places and cultures, and supported one another through the inevitable hardships inherent in climbing big mountains. There was also a perfect intersection of our life trajectories that provided a window for pursuing these climbs together. My Mom and Dad were settling into their status as empty nesters and eyeing retirement. I was a recent college graduate working and climbing in my spare time before settling down to start my own family. I often joked that my Dad and I were living the same life journey, just in reverse.

Subsequent climbs included a return to Mt. Rainier for a weeklong seminar and another summit; a successful expedition to Denali in Alaska, by far the greatest challenge we faced and our steepest growth as climbers; a trip to

Dad and me on the summit of Vinson Massif in Antarctica

Russia to scale Mt. Elbrus, the highest peak on the European continent; an expedition to Argentina to climb Cerro Aconcagua, the highest mountain outside the Himalayas at 22,841 feet, a new altitude record for us; and the most unique travel experience of all, a trip to Antarctica to climb Vinson Massif and learn how to survive in temperatures that average -20° F through the summer climbing season.

During this time, my Dad and I were training and climbing together every chance we had, seizing the opportunity of this very special window to pursue our dreams together in the mountains. We trained hard by carrying large water jugs up the Big Three, topping off water bottles of grateful hikers on the summit before pouring out the rest to descend with lighter packs. We dragged tires chained to our backpacks to simulate the load of pulling a sled on Denali and Vinson and continued this training practice for other mountains, not because they required sleds but because the workout was so physically and mentally grueling. We would "yo-yo" a mountain by hiking up and down, then turning around to hike up and down again to create days with 16,000 feet of total elevation change. We tackled the grueling "Cactus to the Clouds" hike up Mt. San Jacinto for a vertical ascent of 10,700 feet, followed by a 2,300 foot descent and a merciful tram ride down to the desert floor.

Pulling tires to simulate sleds for a grueling workout

We were in the best shape of our lives, waking up each morning to train hard–whether together or apart–and always with the next goal in sight. And while we never set out to climb the seven summits, especially after barely surviving that first Rainier climb with Phil Ershler, we took stock and realized we'd now climbed five of the peaks – call them the "middle five." The remaining two were the shortest, Mount Kosciusko in Australia, essentially a moderate, 10-mile day hike at 7,310 feet, and the tallest, Mount Everest at 29,035 feet, the highest mountain on Earth.

Might the seven summits actually be a goal for us? Would our training in Southern California translate to climbing in the Himalayas? We were confident about the day hike in Australia, thinking it would be a satisfying culmination to the journey, so we began imagining traveling to the Himalayas. We were eager to trek through the Khumbu Valley to experience this special mountain range and part of the world for ourselves and set our own eyes on what the Sherpas and Tibetans respectfully call "Chomolungma, Goddess Mother of the World." But could we actually climb it? Feeling the weight of this challenge, we decided to venture into Himalayan climbing on a much lesser-known yet formidable peak, Cho Oyu, the sixth highest mountain in the world.

At 26,906 feet, Cho Oyu was serious business. We continued to train hard for the physical challenges of the climb, carrying water jugs and pulling tires, yet quickly realized the mental preparation was even more challenging. The expedition would take six weeks, a long time to be away from family, friends, and work. We planned to climb the mountain from the North side, yet the Chinese government would not issue our visas in advance, so we would travel to Nepal with no guarantee of even entering Tibet to attempt Cho Oyu. We would be spending a considerable amount of time living at Advanced Base Camp at 18,500 feet, an elevation close to the summits of our previous climbs yet nearly 8,500 feet below Cho Oyu's peak. If we did reach the summit, we would be crossing into the "death zone," elevations above 8,000 meters where the human body cannot sustain life. To this end, we had to fill out a "Body Disposition Form," a sobering document that reflected the nearly impossible task of recovering a body from extreme altitudes.

My Dad and I had some very real conversations as climbing partners, and of course as father and son. What if we got into trouble as so many climbers do? Would we have the mental clarity and humility to turn around if needed? We certainly thought so, but we'd read too many stories where good judgment was compromised with catastrophic consequences. How would we navigate Himalayan climbing, where climbers are roped not to one another, but to fixed lines on the mountain, meaning climbers often climb apart, not together? I also had some worries that were harder to voice. Is this climb worth our lives? How would either of us face my Mom if something went wrong?

Our Cho Oyu expedition turned out to be more than we expected, both for better and for worse. It was a magnificent introduction to the stunning beauty and enormity of the Himalayas. Called the "Turquoise Goddess" for its icy hue, the relentless nature of Cho Oyu led us to nickname the mountain "Chew on You." Brutal storms shredded tents and delayed summit plans. Vertical ice and rock pitches at extreme altitudes tested the limits of our endurance. And the tragic deaths of two climbers during our summit bid, one a renowned climber we befriended for weeks at Advanced Base Camp and the other a climber aided by our IMG guides when we witnessed him in distress during his descent, cast a sense of sadness over Advanced Base Camp as we said goodbye. In the end, we were very fortunate to reach the summit of Cho Oyu on a spectacularly clear morning and, most importantly, return home safely.

The purpose of climbing Cho Oyu was to test ourselves in the Himalayas. In many ways, we didn't "pass" as much as we survived. We could expect similar conditions and risk calculations on Mt. Everest, though the expedition would be two weeks longer and the summit more than 2,000 feet higher. We debriefed our Cho Oyu expedition, including our growth as climbers and the inherent challenges of 8,000-meter peaks, and decided if there ever was a time to attempt Everest, this was it. We were also both moved by the awe-inspiring view of Everest when we stood on the summit of Cho Oyu, just 12 miles away. Our next goal appeared before us, literally and figuratively, in vivid, alluring detail.

Summit of Cho Oyu with Mt. Everest in the background

That is how we ended up making an attempt on Mt. Everest, representing an incredible journey rooted in those early adventures in the VW bus. We hugged my Mom goodbye and boarded our flight from LAX to Kathmandu, feeling positive, optimistic, and as ready as we could be for the adventure ahead. "Climb safe. Climb confident. And I just know you are going to make it." With my Mom's signature advice in our hearts, we set off for Nepal and the highest mountain on Earth.

This was our second visit to Kathmandu as the gateway to the Himalayas. The city is a fascinating destination unto itself. The streets are a kaleidoscope of color, sounds and energy. Ornate temples and ancient shrines dot the city. Busy roadways buzz with a mix of cars, motorcycles, rickshaws, and vendor carts moving in frenetic patterns. There are Buddhist prayer flags adorning buildings and hanging from rooftops, and crowds gather at the sacred pilgrimage site, Swayambhu, or familiarly known as the "Monkey Temple."

Bustling streets of Kathmandu, Nepal

Everest Base Camp is a distant 175 miles from Kathmandu. In the early days of mountaineering expeditions, climbers would trek to the mountain on foot. Today, you fly on a small fixed-wing plane to the tiny village of Lukla, home of the Tenzing-Hillary Airport, built by Sir Edmund Hillary and named to honor his partner on the first summit of Everest, Tenzing Norgay. It is considered by aviation experts to be one of the most dangerous airports in the world, with a single runway only 527 meters long (typical airport runways are over 2,500 meters), perched on a steep cliff with no margin for error. Only highly experienced pilots are permitted to land in Lukla, but for anyone attempting to climb Mt. Everest, this is the entry point to the Khumbu Valley and the more modest 35-mile trek to Base Camp.

The Khumbu Valley, carved out by Everest's massive glacial runoff, is lined with villages and tea houses along the Dhudh Kosi River. The region is heavily influenced by the culture of the local Sherpas, an ethnic group indigenous to the high Himalayas, primarily in Nepal. The term "Sherpa," often misused as the description of a climbing guide or porter, literally translates to "people from the East" and represents a rich cultural history and religious tradition heavily influenced by Tibetan Buddhism. The Sherpas of the Khumbu Valley live and work at high altitudes and have adapted to this environment for generations. As a result, Sherpas, who work on the mountain, are physically very strong and capable of navigating the extreme conditions of Everest.

There is no motorized transportation in the Khumbu Valley, no trains, trucks, or motorcycles. Everything is moved on foot by porters or by yaks, large pack animals that carry the heaviest loads of goods up and down the valley. Most of the gear and food for expeditions is brought into Base Camp by yaks, though helicopters are increasingly used to shuttle goods, and even climbers, directly to the foot of the mountain.

We set off on the spectacular trek that took us through remote villages, always with the stunning backdrop of Himalayan peaks in sight. On day three, we arrived at the major trading hub in the valley, the town of Namche Bazaar. Perched at 11,000 feet, Namche is nestled in an amphitheater-type bowl in the mountainside that draws locals from nearby villages for its weekly market. There, everything you can imagine is available, from building materials to fresh produce and an open-air butcher shop. We spent my birthday in Namche Bazaar, a wonderfully unique location to celebrate. The climbing team presented me a makeshift cake from a slice of local pie and a straw as a candle. It was inspiring to turn a page of life in Nepal with my Dad. I wished for a successful summit and return for all our team members, then blew out the "candle."

Our next stop was a Buddhist monastery, Tengboche, the most important sacred place in the entire region. Trekkers are welcomed into Tengboche to learn about the religious traditions and experience the remote serenity of this temple at nearly 13,000 feet. We were fortunate to be granted an audience with a lama incarnate and receive a blessing for our well-being and a safe expedition. The lama tied red protection cords, or sungdis, around our necks and presented us with khata scarves as a ceremonial gift. The Sherpas hold deep spiritual reverence for the Himalayan mountains as sacred, holy spaces inhabited by the Gods. The lama gave us inspirational advice for our climb as well. He encouraged us to "maintain inner peace, especially when storms happen around you," and to "love and take care of your teammates." I carry these lessons with me today in so many aspects of my life. Our visit to Tengboche was an amazing cultural and spiritual experience that provided a sense of calm and a deeper connection to the region and its people.

Tengboche Monastery
at 13,000 feet

Tents at Everest Base
Camp: home for six weeks

Along the trek to Base Camp, we also had somber reminders of the magnitude of the challenge ahead. We encountered people with altitude sickness being carried down to lower elevations. We passed small monuments called chortens lining the trail to memorialize climbers who perished on the mountain. We saw the chortens for Rob Hall and Scott Fischer, famed mountain guides most associated with the 1996 tragedy chronicled in the cautionary tale *Into Thin Air*. We'd read that story and heard details of it many times, but to face their names in stone was a poignant lesson on the risks of climbing Everest.

We took eleven days to complete the 35-mile trek, slowly adjusting to the increasing altitude, and arrived at Base Camp feeling the effects of being back up at 17,500 feet. It is both exhilarating and intimidating to stand at the base of Mt. Everest with another 11,500 feet rising above you. Looking up, we swallowed hard and realized this was now the beginning of the climb.

Base Camp is a makeshift town of tents perched on a moraine of rock and ice continuously in motion as the Khumbu glacier grinds down the mountain. It is broken up into neighborhoods by climbing teams, each with its own hub of activity. The 24 climbers and crucial Sherpa support team on our IMG expedition were nestled together near the lower portion of Base Camp. Phil Ershler was there with us, guiding as always, providing welcome familiarity as we began this daunting challenge. My Dad and I had two individual tents, side by side. We settled in for the next six weeks of life in this dynamic environment that would become our home after each rotation up the mountain.

Before we started to climb above Base Camp, our Sherpa team held a religious ceremony called a Puja to pray for and bless the climb. It involves various forms of offerings, chants, rituals, dancing, and prayers, with specific intentions for safe passage up the mountain and, importantly, back down. It created a deeper connection with teammates, honored the cultural traditions of the Sherpas, and set a spiritual foundation for the journey ahead.

Preparing for the puja ceremony at Everest Base Camp

We then began a cycle of climbing rotations designed to acclimatize the body to the lack of oxygen at high altitude. We would climb to Camp 1 at over 19,000 feet, stay the night and then return to Base Camp to recuperate. A few days later we'd climb to Camp 2 at 22,000 feet, stay a couple nights, and then descend to recuperate. Each rotation pushes higher, challenging the body to become more efficient in oxygen consumption. Climbing to these altitudes, you are at your physical limits at the top of each rotation, getting little sleep, losing weight, and wearing down physically and mentally.

Throughout this process, we became closer to our guides, Danuru Sherpa and Dawa Sherpa, with whom we had climbed on Cho Oyu. They are among the strongest climbers we've ever encountered, and among the most generous, humble and peaceful people we've ever known. On our rotations up the mountain, they would carry twice as much gear as us, yet patiently wait for our much slower pace. They wanted to be as efficient as possible on the mountain to return home safely to their families, but they selflessly waited anyway. While we were immersed in navigating our first attempt at the summit of Everest, this would be Dawa's 8th and Danuru's 13th summit if we were successful. We would have never been able to attempt this climb if it were not for the climbing expertise of Danuru and Dawa. We also enjoyed getting to know them and hearing about their families. They shared how they used their earnings from lengthy expeditions to send their children to private schools in Nepal, hoping to create new pathways in life that did not involve the perils of high-altitude guiding.

Below Camp 2 with me, Dawa Sherpa, Danuru Sherpa, and my Dad – Mt. Everest is in the background

After a month on the mountain, we made our final rotation to Camp 3 at 24,000 feet, spending the night without supplemental oxygen inside a tent perched on the steep Lhotse Face. Worried about the ability to sleep at this altitude, I was pleasantly surprised at how quickly I dozed off after the exhausting climb up. I was disappointed, however, when I woke up a short time later and spent the bulk of the night navigating a piercing headache, gasping for air at times, and waiting for the sun to finally rise so we could descend.

After this last rotation, we returned to Base Camp to rest, savoring the relative warmth and ability to eat and sleep at 17,500 feet now that our bodies were acclimatizing. The wait then began for a weather window that would allow us to climb back up through the camps to make an attempt at the summit at 29,035 feet. This would require a window of five to seven days of good weather, which, if lucky, would occur in mid-May when the jet stream annually moves north off the summit.

We checked the weather forecasts constantly, and after 10 days of waiting at Base Camp, our window finally arrived. We retraced our steps back up the mountain, spending a night in each of the four camps, energized by our acclimatization and how much more quickly we were ascending than our earlier rotations. A day of high winds delayed our ascent to Camp 3, but we were back on course the following day and in position for a summit attempt from Camp 4 at 26,000 feet. For this final rotation, we began using supplemental oxygen at Camp 3, which further aided our progress by making us feel like we were about 2,000 feet lower. While I noticed the difference, I did wonder how we would perform near the summit, where even with this assistance, the body cannot function normally.

My Dad and I readied ourselves in the tent at Camp 4, not saying much as we recognized this would be our one shot at the summit after nearly two months away from home. We planned to begin our summit bid at 8:00 p.m., hoping to reach the top just after sunrise with plenty of daylight for the descent. As we put on our climbing gear, the tent began to rattle with the wind, and we were met with an unexpected snowstorm when we exited. Knowing that climbing Everest is hard enough in ideal conditions, and climbing in a storm could be deadly, we had the first of many decisions to make that night. We decided we'd come too far not to attempt the summit, and set out in poor conditions with the mindset that we'd climb for short stretches and reassess along the way.

This plan worked, allowing us to scale the triangular Southern face of the mountain, ascending to a perch known as the "balcony" at 27,500 feet on the Southeast ridge. There, we changed oxygen bottles, plugging into a fresh bottle and saving the partially used one for the descent. Unfortunately, my Dad's oxygen set was leaking, but Danuru was able to fix it, and we carried on. We were grateful to Danuru and Dawa for their help that night, including carrying our second bottle of oxygen up to the Balcony. They were again incredibly patient, climbing at our pace, which extended their exposure high on the mountain.

During this next stretch, I had several conversations with my Dad to see how he was doing and to discuss the weather, which was treacherous and made climbing up through fresh snow even more exhausting. At one point, he stopped and said he wasn't sure if he could navigate the descent if he made it to the summit. In a role reversal, he repeatedly asked me how much farther it was, just like I asked on so many of our long road trips as a child. We discussed what it would mean if we split up, if I were to continue on and attempt to summit for our family, knowing this wasn't the outcome either of us wanted. I encouraged him to go a little farther, and after a few more rest breaks, he seemed to catch a second wind. At one particularly steep section, I checked in with him again, and he said, with newfound energy, "You're up – go."

We continued through the iconic sections of the upper mountain, including the South Summit and the Hillary Step. Finally, after nearly 12 hours of climbing, we looked ahead and saw a small group of climbers stopped in a huddle. We soon realized this was the summit and took the last steps to the top together. We shared an emotional embrace, took some photos, which all have a white background as the weather obscured any view, and recorded video messages before turning to descend. Our time on top of the world was a brief yet profound

Me and Dad at the summit of
Mt. Everest at 29,035 feet

shared experience. As much as we wanted it to last, we also understood that we were only halfway, and the safety of our tent was 3,000 feet vertical feet below.

Most accidents on Everest happen on the descent, so we did our best to stay mentally aware, carefully rappelling several ice and rock pitches before arriving back at Camp 4 after another five hours. My Dad, in his hypoxic state, tried to convince me he descended a new route, bypassing the Hillary Step – something we would later laugh about while recognizing the impairing impact of extreme altitude, both physically and mentally.

We made it back to Base Camp after another two days, for a total round trip of eight days on our summit bid. Safely down at Base Camp, we spoke between our adjacent tents the next morning, trying to piece together the hazy details of our summit night before packing up and beginning the trek out, tears streaming down my face as we left what had been our home for over six weeks. Once back in Kathmandu, we could further relax, released from the mountain and able to embrace the vibrant city that welcomed us to Nepal and would soon bid us farewell.

The journey home from Everest began with a heartfelt reunion with my mother and the strange, often disorienting task of reconciling two vastly different worlds: the harsh conditions high in the Himalayas and the familiar comforts of life back home. As I pulled into the driveway, I gazed at my house with a sense of distance, as though I were a visitor returning to a place I once called home. Sixty-six days away had created an emotional gap that would take weeks to fill in.

That first night, my father and I indulged in a feast of our favorite foods,

Finally home after 66 days
My Mom's advice of "climb safe, climb confident" paid off

culminating in generous servings of Häagen-Dazs ice cream—an attempt to recover the 25 and 15 pounds we had lost, respectively. We watched video footage of our climb, marveling at how even a large-screen television could not begin to capture the sheer immensity of the Himalayas. For others, the images were striking; for us, they were small cues, evoking the full emotional and spiritual depth of the experience.

Just two days after our return, we were honored guests at the Chapman Economic Forecast, invited by our dear friend and University President, Jim Doti. During his introduction, Jim projected a photo of us on Everest's summit, proudly holding a Chapman pennant—a moment captured just ten days earlier. He seized this moment of institutional pride, and we were more than happy to provide him with bragging rights over rival schools whose banners had yet to reach the top of the world.

Soon, the comforts of daily life once again gave way to that familiar,

Flying the Chapman pennant on the summit of Everest
for our dear friend, Dr. Jim Doti

post-expedition question: What's next? This time, the answer was clear: Mt. Kosciuszko in Australia, the final peak in our Seven Summits quest. But this adventure came with a delightful twist: my mother would join us. Free from the rigors of high-altitude acclimatization Hand demanding training schedules, the trip was pure joy. We hiked the gentle five-mile trail to the 7,310-foot summit in the balmy summer of the southern hemisphere and toasted to the completion of a ten-year journey. We wore shirts emblazoned with a bold "7" on the front. Curious glances from fellow hikers questioned our celebration—until we turned around and revealed the back, listing the six previous summits. With that, the summit turned into a communal celebration, a wonderful shared moment as we successfully completed our journey.

In the years that followed, my father and I continued to explore trails

Summit of Mt. Kosciuszko with me
flanked by my Mom and Dad

together, often reminiscing about Everest as the miles passed beneath our boots. Our lives, once so deeply entwined by this shared goal, gradually began to diverge. I immersed myself in work, while my parents embraced the freedoms of retirement. I met and fell in love with someone who, among her many wonderful qualities, shared a love for hiking—and who happily joined my father and me on the summit of Mt. Whitney and a special climb of Mt. Rainier that included my brother. Eventually, we were married, complete with a puja ceremony at the rehearsal dinner to bless our new adventure, and turned our focus toward building a family while my father still had a few more big challenges to pursue.

There remains an ongoing debate about the true "seventh" summit. While we chose Mt. Kosciuszko—the high point of the Australian continent—others argue that Carstensz Pyramid in Indonesia, the tallest in the region of Oceania, is the rightful final peak. The controversy, as legend has it, stems from the second-place finisher in the original race to complete the Seven Summits. We didn't let the debate trouble us. But my father, ever the adventurer, set off for Indonesia to quiet any lingering doubt. I wasn't able to join him, caught in the pull of career and young family life, but he called from the summit, and we celebrated the moment just as we had so many times before. He went on to ski to both the North and

South Poles, completing the prestigious "Explorer's Grand Slam," a feat achieved by few people and, at the time, by no one his age. I was, and remain, deeply proud of my Dad– for his stamina, his spirit, and his unwavering pursuit of big dreams.

One part of our Everest climb that has never faded is our enduring bond with Danuru Sherpa, who guided us on both Himalayan expeditions. When my parents returned to Nepal years later to retrace our path to Everest Base Camp, they took a detour to visit Danuru and his family in the village of Phortse. Not long after, Danuru came to the United States to guide climbs on Denali and visited us in Southern California. It was an honor to host him, to share the Pacific coastline with the man who had led us across the highest mountain range in the world. Now living in Golden, Colorado with his family, Danuru realized his dream of providing his children with a life free from the dangers of high-altitude guiding. We visited him there, enjoying a meal together at the Sherpa House Restaurant, run by a fellow Sherpa who also chose a new path.

On the flight home from Everest, I scribbled a note in my journal: This

My day, Dr. John Dahlem at the South Pole,
completing the Explorer's Grand Slam

climb will be the lasting legacy of my relationship with my father. At the time, it felt both obvious and profound. Through the years, that sentiment only deepened—commemorated by our annual photo on May 24th, the anniversary of our summit, and shared in countless stories, talks, and long hikes. The summit had become a spiritual touchstone, something I could return to again and again, especially when we were apart.

That connection took on even more significance years later when my father was diagnosed with pancreatic cancer. In the face of such a stark reality, the memory of Everest became a wellspring of strength—a vivid reminder of his passion for life, love of family, and willingness to pursue audacious dreams. He rarely spoke of his illness in detail, but he relished recounting our adventures. Those conversations, more than anything, were what we both cherished most.

As his final days approached, we hung prayer flags above his bed and invited two Buddhist monks to offer blessings. I reminded him of our puja ceremonies in the Himalayas—those sacred moments when we asked the mountains for safe passage—and now, we wished him the same for his journey ahead. We also welcomed an Episcopal priest to bridge the chapters of his life, from his youth in Los Angeles to the summits he climbed around the globe. He passed peacefully at home, surrounded by our family, his eyes open and a smile on his face as he set off on his next adventure.

In accordance with my Dad's wishes, we held a Celebration of Life that drew several hundred people, including Phil Ershler and many climbing friends. Jim Doti delivered moving remarks and announced that Chapman's climbing wall would be renamed to honor my Dad. Danuru and his wife, Palhamu, traveled from Colorado to pay tribute, sharing stories of their youngest child, Tshering John Sherpa, whose middle name honored my Dad.

The legacy of our Everest climb lives on—in me, in our family, and in all those touched by my father's remarkable life. The summit was never just a place. It was a moment in time that represented a larger journey and an enduring bond between father and son.

Our last Everest Summit Anniversary, with the third generation of Dahlems, Colin John, peeking out between Dad's legs, May 24, 2024

My Hero, John Dahlem

Jim Doti

Eulogy presented at the *Celebration of Life of John Stephen Dahlem*

July 24, 1943 – November 8, 2024

JOHN Dahlem is one of the finest men I have ever known.

I met John on Mt. Aconcagua almost 20 years ago near the Polish Glacier where he and his team were going down the mountain while my team was headed up. We chatted a bit and left with the words, "Let's get together when we get back." I assumed that would be an empty promise. But I now know that John does not make empty promises. He called, and we did meet when I got back, and, as they say, "It was the beginning of a beautiful friendship."

John later was my coach, helping me prepare for my Mt. Vinson climb in Antarctica. His training involved me climbing up and down the highest hill in Peters Canyon, pulling a long, heavy chain wrapped around a huge tire – the kind of tire used by semi-trucks. The chain, I imagined, was like that connected to the anchor of the Titanic. He wanted me to pull the tire at a fast pace. I didn't think I could do that, but I needn't have worried: We'd have to stop every few minutes to meet and greet his many former students who were also hiking.

I asked myself, "Who is this guy?" Not only does he seem to know everyone, but everyone seems to love him. I recall thinking how I wish I had such a beloved coach when I was in high school. But better late than never. His coaching transformed me from a weak and timid climber to a tougher and more confident one—no wonder all of his former students flocked around him at Peters Canyon.

In the years that followed, John was able to find immigration records relating to the migration of my parents and grandparents from Italy. He presented me with a 50-page book that he prepared about the history of the historic Chapman-owned residence that was built in 1915 and became my Chapman office after I resigned as president and rejoined the faculty. He attended all of my annual forecast conference presentations. After each one, he'd send me the notes he took of my presentations. Those notes were better than my own!

I began to ask myself, "Where does John get all the time to do these things for me?" This puzzled me especially since I knew he was doing these kinds of things for his many other friends. What was John's secret sauce? I still don't have a definite answer to that question, but I suspect that it has something to do with his incredible wife, Sioux, who has been at his side through thick and thin.

John and I spent a good deal of our time together discussing leadership, but not directly. In spite of his many notable accomplishments, John was a very modest man. I didn't even know that he was a highly decorated company commander in the Vietnam War until I read an account of it in someone else's book.

As a result, I had to work hard picking John's brain in my goal of trying to discover why he was so incredibly successful in everything he tackled. But I finally figured it out. He did not come out and say it. But by watching John in action, listening to him talk about his former students, and seeing how he treated me as a friend, I learned that leadership isn't just about things like strategy or making tough decisions or taking calculated risks. What John taught me is that leadership is mainly about treating people with dignity and respect.

What more can one ask from a friend than to learn a lesson like that?

I recently completed a book about the 25 years I served as president of Chapman University. What I wrote about John is the following:

> *One of the neatest parts of mountain climbing is the people one meets along the way. A dear and special friend I met on the slopes of Mt. Aconcagua is John Dahlem, himself a climber who has made it to the top of all Seven Summits, the highest point on every continent. My good fortune in meeting John makes all those tough times trying to make it to the summit well worth the effort. When John passed away, President Daniele Struppa and I decided to add his name to what will now be known as the* Dahlem-Doti-Struppa Climbing Wall.

John and Sioux at Everest Base Camp

PART TWO

RUNNING and BIKING

*The obsession with running is really an obsession
with more and more life.*

—George Sheehan

The bicycle is a curious vehicle: its passenger is its engine.

—John Howard

A NOTE BY JIM DOTI

FOR me, becoming a distance runner was an afterthought. When my son, Adam, expressed an interest in climbing Mount Whitney with me, I was in my mid-fifties and happily faking cross-country skiing on my NordicTrack ski machine. Since those were the days before AI, but thankfully, after the advent of search engines, I Googled "What is the best training for mountain climbing?"

While I didn't get any recommendations relating to NordicTrack skiing, I did find that the most often cited suggested preparation for climbing involved distance running. That recommendation, along with the look of utter joy on the face of my friend, Ann Cameron, after she ran her first marathon, led me to conclude, "Anything that good must have something to it."

Indeed, it did. It wasn't long before running became an integral part of my life. In fact, if someone were to ask me, "Who are you, Jim Doti?" my response would be, "I'm a runner…oh, and an educator, too."

Actually, that's not quite accurate. To separate the term "runner" from my career or family life is impossible. They've all become so intertwined that being a runner is an integral part of who I am. As the great runner Joan Benoit Samuelson said, "As everyone knows, running is about more than just putting one foot in front of the other; it is about lifestyle and who we are."

The connection between climbing and running is made clear in "What… No Porta Pottie?" Running the Mount Meru International Marathon was an afterthought to that of climbing Mount Kilimanjaro. In the "Race Even Marathoners Fear," I show that one of the great joys of running is allowing one's thoughts to wander, like wondering about where Jimmy Stewart parked his car near the Golden Gate Bridge in the classic film, "Vertigo."

"From Arusha to Fort Sill Via Boston" explains how running a marathon in Africa led to adopting an 18-year-old Tanzanian son who went on to run the Boston Marathon with me. In light of that, how can I separate my running from my life?

"Beating the Heat in Boston" includes handy tactical information on how to run the Boston Marathon when the temperature hits 90 degrees. "Running a Marathon in the Black Forest" describes how one can be the fastest American marathoner even with a time of 4:54:39.

Being editor of this book gave me the authority to also include an article on biking across the state of Iowa from the Missouri to the Mississippi. And what an adventure it was! Lesson learned from that experience? Two words – Pickle Juice!

"Taking Back Boston" describes what it was like running Boston one year after the tragic bombing. This article also explains how the legendary runner Katherine Switzer inspired me by writing a note to me upside-down.

If there is one article in this log that shows the connection between running and life, I hope it's captured in "Boston Strong and the Story of the Pebble." This article also goes a long way in showing how the real reward of running is not found in the flashing time on the screen at the finish line. Rather, the true joy is found by the people you meet along the way, people like my seatmate on the bus ride to Hopkington, Liz Chute, or the couple who provided me with warmth and succor at the race's end – Liz and Phill Gross.

My polymath friend Dan Temianka's "My Road to the Vermont 100 Mile" is one wild and crazy ride. How wild and crazy, you ask? Well, it's not often that a person can possibly have saved another person's life by taking the wrong turn. Dan describes how that was done.

If there are readers of this adventure log who, like me, wonder how the human animal is physically capable of completing an Ironman, wonder no longer. Dan shows how it can be done while surviving the experience in "Destination Ironman Canada." If this story inspires you to shave a lightning bolt on the back of your head, welcome to the club.

Finally, for all those data analysts and statisticians joyfully living in the new world of AI, "The Impact of Age on a Senior's Running Pace" may strike your fancy. I wrote this piece to empirically examine how biological age has affected my running time. It ended by convincing me that continuing to run is more important than achieving new PBs (Personal Bests).

I began this note by reminding the reader that I started running in order to help me climb mountains. I'll end it with a quote by health and wellness coach Lea Genders that mirrors my thoughts to a tee.

I started running to lose a few pounds, but I ended up finding myself. I set out to change my body but instead changed my life.

What ... No Porta Potties?

Jim Doti

IT was August in 2003 and there I was, at the appointed time, under the clock tower in Arusha, Tanzania, to run in the Mount Meru International Marathon. Said to be at the midpoint of Africa between Cairo and Cape Town, the clock tower is where the marathon materials directed runners for the start of the race. But where were the porta-potties and thousands of people I had come to expect after running the likes of the Chicago and Los Angeles marathons?

At the start line by the clock tower

I saw only about 50 Kenyan and Tanzanian runners and a small band that inexplicably played music that sounded vaguely like Dixieland jazz. There was also a handful of runners that didn't look like the locals. Seeing my puzzlement, one of them approached me and introduced himself as Don Harris, a sponsor of the marathon. He then proceeded to introduce the other three members of his relay team. I was startled when the last runner he introduced said, "You know me, Jim. I'm from Orange County. You even tried to get a donation from me for Chapman University."

I did, indeed, know John Michler, a local engineer. Given that I'm president of Chapman University, it's not surprising that I had asked him to give to my favorite school. But to meet him like this in the middle of Africa was quite a shock. The poor guy must have thought my persistence as a fundraiser led me to tail after him all the way to Africa.

It turned out that John, Don Harris, and the rest of his relay team are members of World Runners. They explained that this group raises funds to further the mission of its parent organization, Global Partners for Development, which provides educational opportunities and supports projects to promote self-sufficiency in developing countries like Tanzania. The team members would run the race knowing that they would be helping to accomplish things like providing educational opportunities for young people and developing clean water systems and nutrition programs for the villages.

At this point, however, my attention was focused not so much on the valuable work of Global Partners and World Runners as it was on my competition. In addition to Don's relay team, there were the 50 or so lithesome African runners who all looked like they were easily capable of a sub-three-hour marathon. And then there was me, a relatively new marathoner, who at age 57, would be happy to complete the race in four to five hours.

Given my concern, I asked if the stadium where the marathon ended would stay open for late finishers. They assured me it would and not to worry about it. "Don't worry about the porta-potties either," John added. "There are plenty of places to pee in bushes along the road.… Just wait until you get out of town."

One minute into the race, and I'm already all alone

So with that last admonition, I lined up in the back of the Kenyans and Tanzanians and told myself it was too late to back out now. In front of us stood two "officials," one on each side of the street, with a string held high in the air and pulled taut between them. Suspended from the center of the string was a large piece of paper with the word "START" written on it. For any runners who might still be confused, as I had been, the start line was now clearly designated. A horn sounded, and we were off.

About one minute into the race, I was all alone, except for some early Sunday morning traffic. Evidently, there was no traffic control for the marathon. Carts pulled by people, donkeys, or cows assumed the right of way.

Thankfully, I had a secret weapon. I had contracted with a local guide named Martin to drive my wife, Lynne, and son, Adam, ahead of me through the race. They would provide me with water every few miles and also make sure I stayed on the marathon course. Since I'd been warned that the route was poorly marked, it was a comfort that Martin knew the way. As I left the city outskirts on the main road, it was a great relief to see the three of them waiting for me. Martin alerted me to a turn I needed to make onto a dirt path bordered on either side by coffee plantations.

A young boy picking coffee seeds

Running through coffee plantations may sound somewhat idyllic. Unfortunately, the path was about 10 miles long and filled with huge potholes. Avoiding them required all the attention I could muster. Once again, I was happy to see my "pit crew" waiting for me about halfway through the 10-mile stretch. As I ran toward them, Lynne exclaimed, "You were pretty brave back there, not quickening your pace with that huge bull charging you." Given that I'd been fixated on the potholes and oblivious to the close proximity of any agitated bovine creatures, I replied, "What bull?"

I quickly concluded that to make it to the finish safely, I'd have to widen my range of vision and be a little more aware of my surroundings. I noticed, for example, a small dog-like creature bound out in front of me. Martin, an incredibly knowledgeable expert on anything flora or fauna, later told me, "That wasn't a dog. It was a tdik-tdik, the smallest antelope in the world. You were lucky to see one – I didn't think there were any in these parts."

After negotiating my way through the potholes, bulls and tdik-tdiks, I found myself on the main road again, headed back toward Arusha's city center. People appeared along the side of the road and seemed to wave and smile at me. Lynne later explained that my "fans" were actually making hand signals that communicated their belief that I was "mjenga" (crazy in Swahili). But at the time, I was happy that I was no longer alone.

Loved seeing all the cats waiting for goat scraps

Not only did I think I had what I thought were enthusiastic supporters, but in Pied-Piper-like fashion, I had attracted a group of kids who joined me in the marathon. While I was running in the latest running gear, these kids ran barefoot or in flip-flops. Amazingly, they kept up with me and several even rotated their hands in the universal signal to speed up. Since I was nearing mile

20 at this point, I responded with the universal shrug that said, "Sorry, I'm doing the best I can." At least I didn't take the walk breaks I'd planned. These kids probably wouldn't fully appreciate the efficacy of the Galloway run/walk plan.

The "Pied-Piper leading the way

Nearing the outskirts of the city, I finally saw in the distance an actual marathon runner. Suddenly, I remembered a story Jeff Galloway shared during a running school he had held at Chapman University several months earlier. Jeff related the inspiring story of Dave Waddle, one of his teammates in the '72 Olympics. Although an injury had hindered his training for his 800-meter competition, Dave was just barely able to qualify for the final race. Well into that race, he was 40 meters behind the field. Still, he did not give up. Dave decided he wanted to finish next to last rather than in last place. He focused on the runner just ahead of him and overtook him. He followed that strategy, runner-by-runner, until he was just behind the wall of lead runners. Suddenly, right at the finish, there was a parting in the wall, and Dave dove through to break the tape and win the gold medal.

My goals were less ambitious, namely, coming in next-to-last place instead of dead last. Feeling pretty good now that I had fan support and my small running partners, I imagined I was in the final stages of the Olympic marathon. Gaining ground, I soon noticed that I was back in the city. But unbeknownst to the townspeople of a dramatic turn taking place in their city's marathon, they were going on about their daily business.

It was clearly apparent that Sunday is Arusha's big market day. The congestion was far worse than earlier in the morning when I started the race. I was now running in traffic congestion that rivaled anything I've experienced in Southern California. In spite of that, I ran on, still focused on the runner who was now just slightly ahead of me.

A burst of speed finally got me ahead of a Kenyan runner who looked to be about 100 years old. Nevertheless, I wouldn't be last… or would I?

Martin was no longer keeping up with me, and with a sudden dread, I realized there'd be no way for him to get through all the traffic. Cars, carts, and wagons were darting out here and there, and even on foot, it was a struggle. To make matters worse, I had no idea how to get to the stadium where the finish line was. I realized I could let the centenarian Kenyan overtake me and then follow him in, but my pride wouldn't allow for that.

Luckily, the stars were aligned in my favor. The World Runners relay team had completed the race a half hour earlier and figured I might need some help. John Michler kindly came out to meet me and ran the final mile a second time to escort me to the finish.

My finish time: 4 hours, 36 minutes. Placement: 43rd out of 44 runners.

The winner of the race was a Kenyan, David Kipligat Kwino, who finished in 2 hours, 15 minutes. His prize was a Samsung cell phone handset worth Tsh 300,000 and talking airtime valued at Tsh 100,000 (total is equal to about $400.) Unfortunately, the air time will be of little value to David since the local cellular phone services provider, CelTel Tanzania, doesn't have any coverage in Kenya.

The first-place finisher in the women's category, in 2 hours, 40 minutes, was Fabiola William, a Tanzanian from the Kilimanjaro Police.

After the race, Martin and the rest of my pit crew joined me. They were there to hug and congratulate me as I received a signed certificate of completion. There was no medal! Nor was there any food to restock my depleted glycogen stores. So when Martin suggested we go into town for lunch at his favorite Chinese restaurant, Shanghai Gardens, I readily agreed, not even thinking about whether Chinese food was on Jeff Galloway's list of acceptable post-race foods.

While we dined on what tasted to me like the best Chinese food I ever had, Martin and Adam argued over whether the background song being played was sung by Phil Collins or Elton John. Here I was in the heart of Africa in a Chinese restaurant, hearing a debate between an American and Tanzanian over the song stylings of two "Western" singers. We truly do live in a global society.

I learned a great lesson in competing in the 19th Annual Mount Meru International Marathon. Up to now, I have evaluated marathons not unlike those who critique marathons on the websites I always check before entering

a race. It's always about how many water stations there were, the variety
of performance drinks offered, the clarity of mileage markers, the post-
marathon smorgasbord of bananas, bagels, and energy bars, and perhaps most
importantly, the weight and attractiveness of the marathon medal. Now I know
that a marathon's real value is the sights, sounds, experiences and most of all,
the people that form memories that will last a lifetime.

The Race 'Even Marathoners Fear'

Jim Doti

JUST a few months after climbing Denali's glaciers, my son, Adam, and I were at it again. This time it wasn't climbing a mountain but rather "climbing" the hills of the San Francisco Marathon. Its course is infamous for including what seems like every hill in San Francisco. A recent Wall Street Journal article proclaimed it the race that "even marathoners fear."

I flew in from Berlin to LAX the day before the race and then hopped on a flight to San Francisco where I met up with Adam. He had arranged for us to stay at his buddy Brian's pad. But when we got there, the apartment building's key pad wouldn't work. We had to buy a 9-volt battery and install it to get in. I texted Brian: "Hey, your landlord owes me $7.50!"

Any guy would love Brian's apartment. It looked like a small version of an REI store. In addition to various bikes on racks and equipment galore, there was a 20-ft. kayak behind his couch. Adam told me all of his buddies refer to the kayak as Brian's girlfriend.

Weather on race day was near-perfect, nice and cool. I fueled up with a Venti coffee at Starbucks to offset the effects of jet lag.

At the start line, Adam and me, anxious to get going

The race was terrific. There's so much to see and experience in San Francisco. It all started in Embarcadero on mostly flat ground along the docks. It wasn't long, though, before we encountered a steep uphill rising to the Golden Gate Bridge. I noticed the parking lot where Jimmy Stewart parked his car in the movie, "Vertigo," before rescuing Kim Novak from drowning (at least, he thought he was rescuing her).

Jimmy Stewart parked here

Then it was on to the Golden Gate Bridge itself. I've run this marathon twice before in total fog. This running was the first time I could actually see the bridge. According to my GPS watch, each length from the beginning to end of the cable is 1.2 miles long.

Hey! No fog for a change

After the bridge, it was not long before we were running almost every path of Golden Gate Park. I've driven through the park countless times, but running it made me realize how beautiful it really is. Not only did the ponds, streams, flower beds and plazas catch my eye, but also grazing buffalos and a windmill that I'm sure rivals anything in Holland.

After being in the midst of this bucolic setting, it was a bit of a shock to leave it and soon experience the sound of screaming fans encouraging runners through Haight-Ashbury – the symbol of the counterculture movement of the 60s. Then we made our way through the Castro district and past more wharfs.

It was great to run with Adam and have the opportunity to observe the instincts he has honed through his adventure racing. I loved the way he was obsessed with cutting every turn into a straight line to minimize the distance run. As we approached each turn, I could see in his eyes a mental calculator rapidly determining the hypotenuse. His racing instincts also shown through by his forcing me to run through all the water stations. Adam isn't used to

Only in
Haight-Ashbury

Still smiling

pavement, though, and constantly complained that he'd much rather be running on dirt in one of his 100-mile adventure races.

We finally reached the home of the Giants, AT&T Park, which, like the sight of Fenway Park in the Boston Marathon, signals the end of the race. One more mile to go!

At the finish, instead of the usual dry bagels and bruised bananas, we found raisin scones and Jamba Juice. How's that for fine dining?

Adam and I finished together with a time of 4:27 – not bad considering all the hills and our stops for photo ops we just couldn't pass up. Moreover, this was Adam's first marathon ever, and I hadn't run longer than 10 miles since my last marathon three months earlier. The best part was our negative split – running the second half faster than the first half. Our pace times were 10:11 for the first quarter of the marathon; 10:14 for the 2nd, 10:13 for the third and a blazing 10:06 for the fourth. How's that for consistency?

Despite the gracious fare served to finishers, we were still famished. So Adam took me to his favorite breakfast/brunch place – "The Pork Store." My "Breakfast Tortilla Wrap" covered with a hot, spicy chipotle sauce and Adam's "Artichoke Greek Omelet" were fantastic, and the Bloody Mary bar offered 10 different kinds of hot sauces, including a "Habanera Stinger" that truly stung.

At the finish

Breakfast Tortilla Wrap and
Bloody Mary

From Arusha to Fort Sill Via Boston

Jim Doti

I knew we were in trouble when the fierce rumbling sound of the wind kept
us awake all night before the 2007 Boston Marathon. Whispering over to my
African son, Beatus, who lay awake in the bed next to mine, I said, "Can't sleep.
Can you?"

"No, Baba." (Swahili for father.)

"That wind out there doesn't sound too good," I added.

"No, Baba."

I first met Beatus Mushi nearly four years earlier in Arusha, Tanzania,
while there to climb Mt. Kilimanjaro and run the Mount Meru International
Marathon. I saw him standing by the sidelines at Arusha Stadium, where the
marathon ended. He approached me and asked in excellent English what I
thought of the race. Beatus explained that he was always interested in running
but didn't know very much about how to train for running long distances.
Basically, he wanted to learn more and do what it would take to complete
a marathon.

As our conversation continued, I learned that Beatus had dropped out of
high school to work and support his family after his father's death. But he always
remembered his father's words to him about the importance of education. So
he walked the countryside, looking hard and wide until he eventually found a
Roman Catholic high school that would let him enroll as a student in exchange
for cooking, washing dishes, scrubbing floors and cleaning the priests' robes.

I was intrigued by this very likable, soft-spoken young man. When I learned
that he did well enough not only to graduate but also to serve as class president,
I immediately thought that he was the kind of student I'd like to have at
Chapman University in Orange, California, where I serve as president. We said
our goodbyes, but not before exchanging email addresses.

Thirteen months, hundreds of emails and countless hours of bureaucratic
hassling later, I drove to Los Angeles International Airport to bring Beatus to
his new home and life as a freshman business and economics major at Chapman

University. As we drove from the airport to campus, Beatus filled me in on his trip. He recalled his first escalator ride at Nairobi's airport in a tone reminiscent of someone describing a scary horror flick, "I watched and studied it very carefully before I got on that machine."

He sat quietly for a time, studying the passing landscape. Suddenly, he broke the silence by slowly and thoughtfully stating, "Remarkable infrastructure." I'd never heard a California freeway referred to in such an unusual way. Even more surprising to me was when we passed a sign advertising Disneyland, and he asked, "Baba, what is Disneyland?"

No question, Beatus was in for quite a culture shock.

But Beatus quickly found a large circle of friends who helped him over many of the hurdles he faced. Still, they didn't always recognize that things they took for granted were unfamiliar to him. For example, it was several weeks into the semester when Beatus told me in a way that suggested he'd just solved a great mystery, "I now know why the water coming out of the shower is sometimes hot and sometimes cold."

All in all, Beatus adapted quite well. He worked hard and earned good grades, and he became a highly regarded and popular friend to his fellow students as well as a close and loving member of my family.

In addition to his coursework, Beatus held down a half-time job on campus. His first Christmas at Chapman he sent his mother $700 he had saved so that she could have running water piped to the two-room, cardboard-roofed home where she and his six siblings still lived. He continued to live modestly and save as much as he could to assure that his brothers and sisters would have a good education.

But despite all that had transpired since our first meeting in Tanzania, Beatus had never forgotten his dream of running a marathon. So it wasn't long before we started running together. We were only about a mile into our first run when Beatus asked with a cringe on his face, "Baba, what's this pain I have in my side?" I doubt my admonition to him that that side stitch was the first of many aches and pains he would endure as a runner was of much comfort.

Given my hectic schedule, Beatus had to run on his own most of the time. Since he was terribly fearful of getting lost, he identified a quarter-mile loop adjacent to the campus that he ran round and round and round… even for his 20 miler.

Beatus ran his first 26.2 miles in pounding rain at the inaugural OC Marathon on December 5, 2004 with a finishing time of 3:40:54. (Yes, it does rain in Southern California.) He remained determined to excel and push the envelope, so it wasn't long before he started asking me about Boston and qualifying times. For him, it was a time of 3:10.

Anxious to meet that goal as soon as possible, Beatus ran the Surf City Marathon in February 2005 and followed it up with the Long Beach Marathon in October. Frustrated that he still wasn't able to make his qualifying time, he came to me for advice. "Baba, what should I do to get to Boston?"

I knew the answer. "Beatus," I said, "You'll have to do what I did. Hal Higdon's novice plan gets you to the finish line. But to get to Boston, you have to move up to the advanced plan. If you're able to keep up with that kind of rigorous training, I know you'll qualify for Boston."

"Ah, I see," he responded, "It's the five P's."

"The five P's?" I asked.

"Yes, Baba, my father often told me, 'Preliminary preparation prevents poor performance.'"

"That's right, Beatus," I said, "It's all about the five P's."

So Beatus conscientiously followed Hal Higdon's advanced training program, and in December 2005, we headed to Sacramento's California International Marathon, both of us with our sites set on qualifying for Boston.

I'll never forget the moment I crossed the finish line at the steps to the State Capitol building and saw Beatus there cheering me on. After hugging me, he told me he hadn't qualified. Then, seeing the utter disappointment on my face, he smiled broadly and shouted, "I did make it, Baba! I ran it in 3 hours, 3 minutes." We jumped together, high-fiving each other ecstatically. We were going to Boston!

Now that we were here, our worries turned to the possibility that the Boston Marathon would be canceled. While that had never happened in the 110-year history of the race, this might be the year.

A Nor'easter was forecasted to hit Boston on Patriot's Day – the traditional day for the running of the Boston Marathon. The storm would start at night and pelt the entire northeastern seaboard with heavy rain and maybe even snow. As if that weren't enough, hurricane-force winds would blow from the northeast, directly against the runners that would start in Hopkinton, a town lying 26.2 miles southwest of Boston.

On Sunday, the day before the race, the weather was already miserable. We had box seat tickets for the Red Sox/Angels baseball game, where I would at last fulfill my lifelong dream of seeing the Green Monster, the fearsome 37-ft. left-field wall of venerable Fenway Park. However, given the rain, cold and wind, it was not a surprise when the game was canceled.

While our hearts were set on going to the game and we were disappointed, our greater concern was about the race. All reports called for a steady worsening of the storm, increasing the likelihood that the marathon would be canceled.

The sound of our alarm at 5:00 Monday morning wasn't needed to wake us. We had been awake pretty much all night. I tried to peer out through the rain that pelted our window and saw large trees downed during the night.

We turned on the Weather Channel and found severe weather alerts peppering the screen. The Nor'easter would hit hard until 12:00 noon. But, thankfully, there were no reports of the race being canceled.

I bundled up with multi-layers of clothing. A supposedly waterproof jacket and pants protected the two layers of thermals that covered my body. On top of it all, I wore a full-body vinyl poncho. I had even wrapped my feet with plastic bags to keep my shoes dry, at least until the race started.

We ran through the wind and downpour to our waiting cab, which would take us downtown to board one of the buses that would transport the 20,000 runners to Hopkinton. Along the way, our driver swerved around the sheets of aluminum siding and tree branches that clogged the streets. The wind was still steady at about 15 to 20 mph, but the 50 mph gusts had died down.

While still raining when we jumped off the bus in Hopkinton, it was not coming down in the buckets of water that had earlier lashed our faces. Maybe, just maybe, the Roman God of running, Mercury, was protecting us.

As we waited our turn for a porta-potty, I looked at the thousands of runners in line. It was reminiscent of photographs I've seen of German soldiers being led out of Stalingrad after their disastrous defeat.

Me and Beatus in the porta-potty line

But once the race started, we pulled the plastic bags from around our shoes and threw off the rain ponchos. We actually began to look like runners again as we took our first strides toward Boston. It was still windy, with big gusts, but the sky cleared a little, and the rain slowed to a drizzle. Even better, the temperature was near 50 – well above the predicted 35 degrees.

Funny thing about running. Once you get started, you begin to ignore the weather and listen to what your body is saying to you. Mine was telling me it was too hot and I should start taking off some clothes. So gradually, off came the various layers. Some I left on the wayside, some I tied around me. I tossed a pair of wind pants and later realized I had left my driver's license and credit card in a zippered back pocket. We had to run back about two miles to retrieve them. Thankfully, they were still there. But the trip added to our time since it made our marathon 30.2 instead of 26.2 miles.

By then, however, we weren't worried about our time. The weather had improved enough to actually begin enjoying the race. Now that I was running lighter, I no longer felt like Ralphie's little brother in the classic movie "A Christmas Story," when his mother bundled him up with so many winter clothes that he couldn't walk.

Compared to the Boston Marathon I ran two years ago, the crowds, though thinner, seemed more boisterous. Perhaps it was the imbibing they did to keep warm. One moment I'll never forget is arriving at an aid station just as a big gust of wind hit it. All at once, thousands of used paper cups filled the air. I've run through rain, sleet, snow, and even hail, but never a sea of cups. When we hit the 12-mile mark, we could hear the Wellesley women screaming a mile away. As we later approached the infamous Heart Break Hill at mile 20.5, Beatus and I were feeling so good that we gave it everything we had and ran all out to the top.

Reaching mile 23, we saw the distant CITGO sign beaconing the finish line. We knew we had nailed it. We had survived the Nor'easter.

Seeing that CITGO sign told us we nailed it

At mile 25, I looked to the right and saw it looming like a large green monster – Fenway Park. Gazing at it at that instant, at that point in the race, I realized that seeing it at mile 25 of the Boston Marathon was more special than being inside the stadium at a regular baseball game.

Beatus and I were together as we made our last turn to the finish line. It meant so much to me that, although he's a much faster runner, he wanted to run this race with his Baba. Knowing how far he'd come, from the tiny village of Arusha to a triumphant finish at the Boston Marathon, made me feel very proud. Given the extra four miles we ran, our time of 5:12 wasn't too bad.

I felt even more pride about one year later. It was the day that I presented Beatus Mushi with his Chapman University diploma.

But I don't think it's possible to feel greater pride in my African son than several years later when Beatus walked across a stage in Fort Sills, Oklahoma, to become a U.S. Army boot camp honors graduate. Imagine the glow on my face when Beatus received a special medal for being the second-fastest runner in his company of 250 soldiers.

Beatus and me at
the finish line

Beatus graduates with honors
at Fort Sill, Oklahoma

Beating the Heat in Boston

Jim Doti

WEATHER reports weren't looking good. Forecasts called for the temperature to hit almost 90 degrees in Boston on Patriots Day, just in time for the 116th running of the Boston Marathon on April 16, 2012. This was not a welcome forecast for the nearly 27,000 runners expected to race this year. It was particularly bad news for me. To say the least, I don't run well when it's hot.

In the 2005 Boston Marathon, when temperatures hit only 66 degrees, I struggled mightily. My slow time of 4:48 at that race put me in danger of missing my afternoon flight. As a result, I ran through the finish line, eating no food and drinking no water so I could get to my hotel ASAP to pick up my luggage, catch a cab, and make my flight. When I arrived at the security line at Logan Airport, I suddenly felt faint. Next thing I knew, I was in a wheelchair, and a stranger was holding a Gatorade bottle to my lips. It was all somewhat disconcerting, especially since I've never fainted before. On the positive side, I was whisked through the security line and caught my scheduled flight.

When I got back home and told my running friends about my experience in Boston's heat, I was severely chastised. "How could I not hydrate?" they would ask. "You skipped taking in some food at the end? You're such a numbskull." While my friends were obviously not very sympathetic to the demands of my flight schedule, their candor proved a point. So, I chalked up my experience at Boston as a lesson to be filed away along with all the other things I've learned on the myriad paths of multiple marathons.

That's what's interesting about the sport of marathoning. While the aging process and relentless breakdown of cells over time invariably mean slowing down and finally giving up on besting previous PRs, age begets experience, and experience begets wisdom. The wise runner knows that a marathon is more than just speed – it's also about endurance and knowing how to adjust to different conditions, including heat.

Running the 2012 Boston in 80-to-90-degree temperatures suggests all kinds of strategies. One strategy, of course, would have been to take the Boston

Athletic Association's kind, thoughtful, and unprecedented offer of a come-back-next-year deferral to runners who picked up their bibs but chose not to run. In making this offer, race organizers expected up to 2,000 deferrals. The actual number was far less. After all, this is Boston. Most of the runners here likely see the heat as an interesting test of their endurance skills.

In fact, the high temperatures turned out to be a sort of test for me as well. It was a test that pitted one theory of running against another. Those contrasting theories were debated over a magnifico carbo-loading dinner I had with a running friend at Mama Maria's in the North End of Boston, where we split orders of rabbit pasta and wild mushroom pasta. . . mmmm.

My dinner companion had qualified for Boston with a PR of just over three hours. In spite of the forecasted heat, he was hoping to break his three-hour mark and set a new PR for himself. Although I thought to myself, "This guy's bonkers," I more diplomatically reminded him that the heat should force him to plan a slower marathon – not a faster one. When I outlined my race plan, he gave me the sort of smirk Steve McQueen often used in "The Great Escape" – a smirk that registers loud and clear, "You run your race, and I'll run mine."

So what was my plan? I qualified for Boston at the California International Marathon in Sacramento in December 2010 with a time of 3:58:41 at a pace of 9:07. After my fainting experience at the 2005 Boston Marathon, I'd done some research on proper pacing when running in the heat. In his book Training Plans, Jeff Galloway recommends running 30 seconds per mile slower for each 5-degree temperature increase above 60 degrees.

Weather reports indicated a range of 83 to 88 degrees on race day in Boston. Assuming an average of 85 degrees (25 degrees greater than 60 degrees), that suggests slowing my pace down by 2 minutes and 30 seconds (5 x 30 seconds = 150 seconds) per mile. For me, it meant slowing from my qualifying pace of about 9:00 to 11:30, which would increase my finish time from about four to five hours. That's a big comedown, at least in terms of speed. But if endurance was my principal goal, slowing my pace was the only plan that would allow me to adapt to the likely conditions on race day.

There was one other strategy I used. It came from a tip I got at the race expo. While waiting in line to buy some Boston memorabilia, I sidled up to a fellow sexagenarian runner and started talking about various tricks to beat the heat.

This man of experience told me something he learned not on the race course but in the jungles of Vietnam. The trick he used was to wrap a cold, wet towel around his neck. Dredging up distant memories, he grew wistful as he described how he poured water from his canteen over the towel. As I listened, all I could think of was the fact that he used his limited supply of water to douse a towel rather than for drinking. Keeping cool, evidently, was more important to him than quenching his thirst.

That clinched it for me – I bought a blue terrycloth towel and cut it down to a manageable size. On race day, as we lined up in the corrals, I felt somewhat strange having a towel draped around my neck. One guy shouted as he walked past me, "Hey, I like the ascot!" Since I didn't have a comeback for that one (and still don't), all I could think of was how he'd be looking at me enviously after about an hour of running in the oppressive heat.

Another reason to be mindful of Boston's unusual April heat is that runners haven't had any summer training to help acclimate their bodies to hot-weather running. That means they will be particularly vulnerable to the heat unless, of course, one hails from the Southern Hemisphere.

A picture at this sign is a rite of passage for all
Boston Marathon runners

At the race's start in Hopkinton (10:30 a.m. for me), it was pretty obvious that the temperature was going to be as high or even higher than all the predictions. While I later learned it was about 80 degrees at start time, it felt even hotter in Boston's sweltering humidity. The heat wafting up from the asphalt pavement didn't help.

The gun sounded, and we were off. As almost everyone knows, the first half of the Boston Marathon is rolling but mostly downhill. From the start to mile 13, there is a net drop of about 300 feet. That's one of the tricks Boston plays on you. Not only is there all the release of pent-up excitement, but the downhill also seduces you to run faster in those early miles.

I've been seduced before, but not this time. I ran at a pace of around 11:00, figuring a quarter-mile walk through the aid stations at a pace of around 15:00 would keep me close to my 11:30 goal pace. The walk would also force me to take the time to hydrate by drinking enough water and energy drinks. Wearing my trusty and now vintage Garmin Forerunner 201 GPS, I carefully monitored my current as well as lap pace to keep close to my planned goals.

Even in the first few miles, my "Vietnam Jungle" towel seemed to be working, but only as long as it stayed wet and cool. Thankfully, the Boston Athletic Association had planned well. Because of the forecasted heat, the aid stations were supplied with extra water, allowing me to rewet my towel as well as my white hat every few miles. Even better, there were good Samaritans passing out ice along the route. Improvising, I placed a few cubes in the center of the towel and rolled it up like a sausage. The steady dripping of melting ice enhanced the towel's cooling effect.

When it's been hot in other marathons I've run (never as hot as this one), I would eventually reach the point where my head felt like it was ready to explode. Not this time. While I can't say I felt cool and comfy, my head didn't feel like it would detonate at any second.

I also ran in whatever limited shade I could find and even made a game of trying to run on the white median strips. The careful contingency planning of the Boston Athletic Association was made evident by the "shower tunnels" that were placed periodically along the course. Not unlike being in a carwash, runners jogged single file through these tunnels and received a cooling spray of water coming from all sides. More good Samaritans brought their garden hoses to the street side and seemed to enjoy spraying the passing runners.

By the time I neared the halfway point and started hearing the shrill sound of the screaming Wellesley coeds, I was feeling OK... not great, but I wasn't losing it. When going out too fast, a runner's body temperature eventually rises to the point where the muscles aren't getting the oxygen they need. Instead of the blood fueling the muscles, more and more of it is demanded by the body's cooling system. With so many parts of the body craving oxygenated blood, the heart has to go into overdrive by beating faster. And the problem is compounded as fluids are lost through sweat, and the blood thickens.

The fact that I was in good spirits while high-fiving the Wellesley women suggested that I wasn't putting undue pressure on my heart. But I still had a half marathon to go, so I wasn't quite out of the woods. Mile 16 also marks the start of a series of stepped hills, ending with the infamous Heartbreak Hill at mile 21. The net rise in elevation from mile 16 to the top of Heartbreak Hill is only about

The refreshing shower tunnels were a
welcome addition to the 2012 race

250 feet, but after running the first half of Boston, mostly downhill, one's quads start to rebel.

Uphills are particularly tough to take at elevated temperatures, so attacking the hills in the heat would not be the right strategy, at least not for me. My strategy involved shifting most of the quarter-mile walk breaks I was taking at aid stations to the hills.

No way, though, was I walking up Heartbreak. Heat or no heat, I attacked the venerable hill. The fact I could do so was yet one more indication that my pacing plan was still working. My Garmin also indicated my pace was holding steady and on track.

After Heartbreak, there is a sudden drop of about 150 feet through Boston College before the last four miles of flats that bring runners to Boylston Street. Figuring that I was nearing the marathon's end, I picked up my pace and stopped taking walk breaks. It seemed, though, that it was getting hotter, and, in fact, I later learned that the temperature was pushing 90 degrees. Maybe that's why I was feeling a little faint. The last thing I needed after getting this far was to blow it all in the final stretch. My faintness, though, didn't seem like the onset of hyperthermia. It was more akin to the feeling that follows skipping a meal or two.

Suddenly, I realized that I had forgotten to take any gels. Even though I alternate H20 and energy drinks at aid stations, my marathon regimen always includes a gel at mile 9 and another at mile 16. Maybe because of the effects of the heat, but more likely because my mind was focused on trying literally and figuratively to keep my cool, I didn't put down any gels.

Although, by this point, it was too late for it to have much of an effect, I frantically consumed a gel as quickly as I could. The funny thing was that my strength seemed to magically return. My sudden recovery was probably purely psychological since it seemed to coincide with my long-anticipated sighting of the huge Citgo sign near Fenway Park. That well-known beacon of hope for runners was my signal that I had nailed it.

As I turned the corner to enter Boylston Street, I felt chills, not from the onset of hypothermia but from the screaming crowds that made me feel like I was entering an Olympic stadium, not as an also-ran but as a gold medalist. I picked up my pace and gave it my all for that last half mile or so. Crossing the finish line, I hit the "end" button on my Garmin and saw my finish time of 5:03:23 and average pace of 11:35.

A Boston Marathon time over five hours does not immediately strike one as something to write home about. These seemingly sobering race results, however, did not get me down. Quite the contrary, I was elated. While I didn't beat the clock, I beat the heat. To me, that was something.

My post-race e-mail exchange with my carbo-loading pasta friend made it even better than "something:"

Carbo-loading Pasta Friend:
Wow. That was rough. I should have trained in the heat. First half at 1:30. Second half—I had nothing left. Ended up at 3:55. How are you?

Me:
I did the opposite. Started slow and finished strong with a negative split. That neck towel idea I told you about really helped. Total time was 5:03, which put me in the top 50% in the 65-69 bracket. Of my 40 marathons, this was easily the hottest.

Carbo-loading Pasta Friend:
You were right. I should have started slower from the gate.

Me with the smile of a happy survivor

Running a Marathon in the Black Forest

Jim Doti

A visit to the Porsche Museum in Stuttgart, Germany, was high on my
bucket list. Since I'd be in Europe to officiate at a Chapman University MBA
graduation ceremony at our Prague campus, I figured it would only be a short
trip from Prague to Stuttgart to finally get to see the new museum complex that
all my Porsche buddies have been raving about.

Looking at a map to confirm Stuttgart's location, I noticed the town of
Baden-Baden in close proximity. Bingo! Another bucket list entry. A number of
years ago, a friend told me that Baden-Baden is one of the prettiest places in the
world. He waxed eloquent as he described running along a footpath bordered
by a gurgling stream on one side and a dazzling display of towering trees and
wildflowers on the other. His description evoked images of the Garden of Eden
in my mind.

As I was finalizing plans to include all this in an expanded trip itinerary, my
associate, Ann Cameron, excitedly barged into my office to say, "Hey, there's a
marathon in the Black Forest right near Baden-Baden that's being run the day
before your flight home."

In the 26 years that Ann has been my associate at Chapman University,
where I serve as president, not only has she made it possible for me to do my
job, but she was the one who inspired me to run my first marathon 10 years
earlier. I'll never forget seeing her after she ran her first marathon. That look
of utter joy on her face led me to conclude, "Anything that good must have
something to it."

So here I am, 35 marathons later, with Ann giving me the lowdown on
the Schöck 39. Hornisgrinde Marathon 2011. I had never run a marathon in
Europe before, and to run one in the Black Forest of Germany was enticing, to
say the least.

The hard copy Ann gave me was a Google translation (German to English) of the Hornisgrinde Marathon website. It highlighted the boutique-like nature of the race, with only 300 or so entrants each year. The entry fee of €22.0 was roughly $30, so the price was right. That included a T-shirt and what the Google translation described as follows: "The first three in each category will receive a deed."

A charming addition to the usual race description and registration materials was the following Google-translated account of the marathon's early history:

1967, the gymnastics club began with the execution of people running events as part of a week of local advertising sports clubs from 24 June to 2 July 1967.

To avoid large differences in height in the marathon and to get more comfortable running temperatures, moved the people responsible for the running events in the height field. Start and finish were and still are the base station of the ski left on Hundseck Buhler Valleys. Nor could the leaders of the gymnastics club does not have guessed that the Hornisgrinde Marathon would develop into one of the most popular and most beautiful marathons in Germany and neighboring foreign countries.

In 1975, the event in "Hornisgrinde Marathon" has been renamed. In this event, the 8th Hornisgrinde Marathon, unmatched to this day they reached the record number of participants.

Klaus won the marathon places (Know-win) in 2:23:47 hours, as this time for the marathon Hornisgrinde almost was not possible, the route length was measured, and it turned out that the distance of 1.8 km to shortly.

Before 9 Hornisgrinde Marathon on 25/26. July 1976 was measured, the new marathon course and extended by the lack of miles.

Huh?......obviously, Google translations leave something to be desired. Nonetheless, I decided to register and received an e-mail in quick response:

Hello Mr. Doti,
I must know your correct year's issues for
proper registration.
Please tell us your correct year's issues by E-mail.
Thank you,
Best sportive wishes.
Martin Fritsch
Organisationsleitung Marathon

After thinking awhile about the pleasant German closing (Why don't we have something like "sportive wishes" in English?), I began to focus on the issue at hand, namely, "issues." Was Organislationsleitung Martin referring to a magazine subscription? Then it dawned on me. I went back to the registration form to confirm my suspicion that I missed entering my date of birth. I had, indeed, left blank the entry requesting my "vintage." I shouldn't have. After all, at 65, "vintage" is a pretty accurate description.

Thankfully, the two runner comments I found at MarathonGuide.com were written in English. One of them came from Joseph Sweenty in Glasgow, Scotland, who wrote:

"You will be running on cool, windy forest tracks and paths that resemble cross-country trails. The last kilometer is so steep it made last year's San Francisco Marathon look like Rotterdam the previous Easter."

Hmmm… I've run the San Francisco Marathon, so I get that, but what in the world does the metaphor "Rotterdam the previous Easter" mean? Ah… I think I get it. Rotterdam is in Holland. Right? Low country. Right? Flat. Right?

Anyway, this marathon was shaping up to be a real happening. My anticipation level was high.

After the Chapman MBA graduation ceremony, held in a beautiful Benedictine monastery in Prague, I rushed to board my flight to Stuttgart. Upon landing, I picked up my rental car, entered "Porsche Museum-Stuttgart" in the GPS and was on my way.

I found the building itself that houses the museum architecturally striking. It definitely produced a "wow" effect. Inside, though, I was expecting something more. Walking up a spiral display area, not unlike Frank Lloyd Wright's Guggenheim in New York, I passed just about every Porsche model ever produced. It reminded me of a very fancy automobile showroom.

Even though the museum was a bit of a letdown, I couldn't help but feel some satisfaction as I checked the entry off my bucket list and pointed the car toward Baden-Baden.

Arriving there only an hour or so later, Baden-Baden did not disappoint. It was all that was promised and more. Since its trailhead is at the town center, I immediately came onto the footpath my friend had described to me so long ago. Majestic trees and a magnificent array of flora, the likes of which I've never seen before, flourished along one side of the path. Beyond the silvery stream bordering the opposite side, I saw well-kept villas, castles and even a striking Richard Meir-designed modern art museum. All-in-all, it was, unquestionably, the most stunning, Shangri-La-like locale I've ever experienced.

Baden-Baden is famed for its thermal waters and exceptional spa facilities. In fact, the German word "baden" translates to the English "baths." So Baden-Baden is "Baths-Baths."

Baden-Baden

Among them is the historic Friedrichsbad, which opened in 1877 and hasn't changed much since. The English brochure in my hotel described it as follows:

"The relaxing and enjoyable experience that is unique to the Friedrichsbad is a result of the changing sequence of warm and hot dry air baths, a soap & brush massage, steam baths of varying intensity and a selection of thermal pools along with thermal water showers. Enjoy this fascinating journey to inner harmony and total relaxation!

Let yourself float off effortlessly and experience the wonderful feeling of finding your inner peace."

I was sold. A Friedrichsbad experience would be my gift to me after running the marathon. Not a bad incentive to keep my pace up, to say the least.

Marathon day arrived cold and drizzly. Although the ski area that was the location for the marathon start was only 20 minutes away, a dense fog made the drive stressful. I would have missed the mountain road turn-off if it weren't for a large blue "Schöck" sign advertising the race sponsor, a German construction company.

A large tent sheltered the marathoners from a drizzle that was quickly becoming a downpour. Posted near the entrance was a map and elevation chart for the marathon's point-to-point course.

Friedrichsbad Bathhouse

Map and elevation chart for the Hornisgrinde Marathon

As I studied the elevation chart and converted meters to feet, I realized that the course dropped 1000 feet in the first half and climbed 1000 feet in the second half. My anxiety level spiked. Having run Boston, I know from experience how long downhills followed by long uphills are tough on the hamstrings. But compared to the marathon I was about to run, Boston's 400-foot drop from the start to mile 16 and 200-foot gain from mile 16 to 21 is child's play. And unlike Boston, which mercifully drops 250 feet in the final five miles, Hornisgrinde challenges runners with its steepest ascent in the last few kilometers. All this somehow got lost in the Google translation.

I quickly paid my registration fee (there was no provision for payment on the website), pinned on the bib they gave me (there were no timing chips), and headed to the start line. There were no announcements, no national anthem and by then, thankfully, no rain. Someone shouted "Gehen," and the bunch of us were on our way.

At the ziel (start) line

I stayed near the rear, and it wasn't long before I was dead last, running all alone through the Black Forest. I wouldn't ordinarily mind this position, since I like finishing strong with a negative split. But given all I had seen so far, I didn't know what the race provided in the way of trail markers, and I was worried about losing my way.

So I quickened my pace, and it wasn't long before I caught up to a few stragglers. Good thing, too, since we soon hit a fork in the path. In the middle of the path was a branch about two feet long, which I would have guessed was part of nature's wonder. My fellow German marathoners, though, seemed to instinctively know this was a strategic marker that screamed out, "Verboten!"

Running along what appeared to be a logging road, we passed quaint and charming chapels, shrines, and ranger watch towers.

A chapel in the Black Forest

Every three or four miles, I came to an aid station providing water and two other beverages that tasted more like weak tea than any kind of energy drink. The volunteers were amazingly friendly and anxious to practice their English on me.

Friendly volunteers

The 1000-foot downhill during the marathon's first half didn't strike me as all that downhill. Perhaps, spread out over 13 miles or so, it doesn't amount to much of a grade change. By the halfway point, however, the achy feeling in my legs announced that my body knew something my mind didn't.

The funny thing and sad thing is that while I didn't seem to mentally notice the downhill, the uphill in the second half of the marathon revealed itself loud and clear. There would be no negative split for me.

Ordinarily, I don't like to walk up a steep grade or even walk through an aid station. The growing heaviness in my legs, though, led me to look for any excuses. How could I not stop for a great photo-op? Perhaps I should spend more time talking to the aid volunteers. And shouldn't I take a few breathers to soak up the sights, sounds, and wonders of the Black Forest? Isn't this a race that begs one to stop and smell the roses?

Yes, it is, and so I did.

The Black Forest is a glorious place. Parts of it are so thick with trees that the sky is invisible. And when there are clearings, incredible vistas reveal themselves.

I began to count the cut timbers along the side of the road and tried to mentally calculate how many of them it would take to build a house. I've discovered that mind games like this divert my thoughts from burning, screaming muscle groups.

As my fatigue grew and the number games started to seem too complex, I kept myself plodding along by chanting my new mantra: Friedrichsbad, Friedrichsbad, Friedrichsbad…

Near the halfway point

Counting the cut timbers

This must have worked because I began to notice that I was passing a few people, including an old guy who looked like he might be in my age division. Then, suddenly, out of the dark forest there was light. The trail came to an end at an asphalt road that appeared to head straight up. Maybe it was the bone-tiredness of making it to km 39 in a tough marathon, but this road looked like a stairway to the stars.

It could have been that I was hallucinating, for my brain was strangely telling me that a marathon is 44 km long. As a result, I mistakenly concluded that I still had 5k to go before it was all over. That may not seem like much, but with the "stairway to the stars" looming ahead, the thought of another 5k overwhelmed me. Slowly but surely, my run begat a jog that begat a fast walk that begat a slow walk. Even the old guy I'd passed earlier caught up and waved to me as he sprinted ahead.

Then, as I made it over a crest in the road, like out of a dream, a finish line appeared before me, "Is it a mirage?" I wondered. Then it dawned on me. Oh, joy of joys, a marathon is 42 km – not 44! My pace quickened. My aches and pains disappeared. And as my legs flew me toward the finish line, my delirium gave way to exhilaration.

Unlike Boston, it wasn't the crowd that fed my adrenalin. There was no crowd. There was only a guy with a stopwatch, standing beside an old folding table, matching bib numbers with finishing times. There was no customary draping of a medal around my neck. There were no medals. There was only a guy handing out an orange-colored cotton T-shirt with Schöck boldly blazoned on it. There were no bagels. There were no bananas. There were no free eats at all.

Then, a tent came into my sight. It appeared to have all the earmarks of an Oktoberfest celebration. Spilling out of the tent were my fellow marathoners, seemingly in the midst of one heck of a party. Beer varieties galore were being drunk not out of steins but directly out of super-sized bottles.

There was even an impressive table display of wines, brandies and liquors ready for sampling. I was so enthralled by it all that I didn't even think to check the race results.

Since the thick forest blocked the GPS satellites, my Garmin (the original, 4-inch- long model), was useless. I had no idea what my marathon time was. Not that I really cared much, but someone handed me a computer printout that was being passed up and down the party tables. In the number one position was Jacek Kurek, who finished in 2:54:14. I scanned down several sheets before my name popped up.

My time: 4:54:39! That's the slowest I've run since Boston '07. I placed 229 out of 244 runners but was third among four runners in my age group. That

An impressive display of wines, brandies and liquors

meant I'd be getting the "deed" promised to the top three finishers in each age category. If I hadn't eased up at the end and let my fellow sexagenarian pass me, I might have taken second place.

I noticed something else, though, as I scanned the list of finishers. There were lots of Germans, to be sure, but there were also Scots, French, Italians, Canadians, and even a runner from New Zealand. No one from the U.S.….. except for me! That made me the fastest American in the race. The fact that I was the only American in the Hornisgrinde 2011 didn't matter. I was number 1!

Is This Kilimanjaro? No, It's Iowa

Jim Doti

I was sucking in hair, and hot tea was sloshing around my feet. This wasn't some bad dream. I was flying to Omaha to bicycle 460 miles across Iowa – from Council Bluffs on the Missouri River to Fort Madison on the Mississippi – in what is known as RAGBRAI: The Des Moines Register's Annual Great Bicycle Ride Across Iowa.

Seated in C, I was tightly squeezed next to a woman in B whose voluminous hair spread like a weeping willow into the seats on both sides of her. I tried to push the hair away, but whenever the woman turned to talk with her husband in A, the hair would spring back to my face. My only relief came when she went to the restroom. Then, as she climbed over her husband to get back into B, she spilled the hot tea she was carrying, sending it cascading down my pants leg and into my running shoes. I was not off to an auspicious start.

When a Chapman grad and former student of mine, Mahmood Rezai, waxed eloquently about his four RAGBRAIs, he persuaded me to sign up.

Mahmood Rezai – the guy who got me in this "mess"

But now, as my first blast of Iowa's heat and humidity buckled my knees, I began to suspect that Mahmood's idyllic description of RAGBRAI didn't tell the whole story. I was even more certain of that when I arrived with my five teammates at our first campsite in Council Bluffs. The sight of endless rows of tents reminded me of Mathew Brady's photos of squalid Civil War army camps.

Our first campsite at Council Bluffs

Next morning, we were on our bikes at 6 a.m. After the ceremonial dipping of our back tires in the Missouri River, we were on our way. The first day's ride, designed as a warm-up, was a relatively short 54.8 miles.

The ceremonial dipping of the back tire in the Missouri River

Stopping for breakfast in the historic section of Council Bluffs, I enjoyed the most delicious oatmeal I've ever eaten with the biggest blueberries and raspberries I've ever seen.

Best oatmeal ever, bar none

At the day's halfway point, I indulged in deep-fried peanut butter and jelly sandwiches, ham balls on a stick, and for dessert – chocolate-covered bacon. Hey, this RAGBRAI adventure was looking up!

The second day's ride of 83 miles was the longest trek of the week. At mile 15, there was an "optional" loop that, if taken, extended the total distance for the day to 108 miles.

When I reached that point where "two roads diverged in a wood," I was feeling strong. Besides, there was the allure of a commemorative patch given to all who completed the "optional" loop. So I decided to take the road less traveled.

The morning air was cool, and with the wind at my back, I was breezing along. I closed the loop, picked up my patch and was soon back on the main route. But I still had 70 miles to go, and it was getting hot, really hot.

There was another problem. Everyone seems to think Iowa is flat. It isn't. RAGBRAI's total uphill elevation gain is about 19,000 feet. That's like climbing Mount Kilimanjaro from sea level.

By early afternoon, the temperature hit 100 degrees. I was experiencing leg cramps so severe that I had to start walking my bike up the seemingly endless series of hills. It was already dark when I finally dragged myself and my bike into camp. I hobbled along, tripping over tent wires, until I found my tent. Crashing on my sleeping bag, I luxuriated in the comfort of being in a prone position.

Picking up my Karras Loop patch

It wasn't even a minute, though, before excruciating leg cramps forced me back outside my tent. Standing upright seemed to ease the pain. Suddenly, out of nowhere, there was a loud clap of thunder and an unleashing of marble-sized hail that pelted my head. I escaped back into my tent, but as soon as I stretched out, the leg cramps returned. The only relief was to stand up, back bent, inside the tent.

Bending over in my tent in the middle of the night, dripping wet from rain and hail, I tried to figure out why I got myself into RAGBRAI.

As I hobbled out of the tent, my teammates berated me for not doing enough hill training prior to the trek. While that admonition was a bit late to do any good, they did offer some useful advice. What I needed, and needed fast, were pickles and pickle juice – supposedly the best remedy for cramps. So that explained all the makeshift pickle stands I saw along the route.

Lo and behold, a pickle stand was located just outside of camp. I joined a long line of weary, cramping bike riders who evidently also skimped on the hill training. Drinking pickle juice at 6 in the morning isn't the greatest. But once fortified with the potassium-rich mixture, the pain abated, and I was back to pedaling, stopping at every pickle stand along the way.

Pickle juice....my savior

My thoughts returned to the question I'd pondered in my tent: Why did I, along with 10,000 others, decide to battle the elements and torture our bodies to ride a bike across Iowa?

I posed that same question to other riders I met. Here are some of their answers:

- 72-year old man from Cedar Rapids, Iowa: *In January, in the dead of winter, the heat of summer sounds pretty good, so I sign up. Now that I'm in it, I can't wait for winter.*

- 67-year old man inside the men's room at Central College in Pella: *This is my first. I'm a virgin. Last winter, I was with a bunch of old fogies watching a TV show about RAGBRAI. They all said biking RAGBRAI was sheer madness. To me, it looked like an adventure, so I'm here.*

- 40 to 50-year-old woman from California: *I've been asking myself that same question ever since I started. I can't believe this humidity. Oh, this humidity.*

- 75-year old man from Hungary: *I came because I wanted to see the middle of America. I'm glad I did. I've never seen so much corn. Hitler was mad to think he could win a war against America. How can you win a war against a country that can grow all this corn?*

Corn as high as an Elephant's Eye

- 27-year old man from Salt Lake City: *I love its randomness. Every time you arrive in the next small town, you don't know what to expect. It's a total surprise. This is a far cry from everyday life where everything is so regimented and predictable.*

- 51-year old man from California: *Because it's the biggest and longest.*

- 18-year old girl from Portland, OR: *Because of the 'Walking Tacos,' I buy a bag of Doritos, crush it up, open the bag, and put in cheese, salsa, and ground beef. It's insane!*

- 58-year old man from Richmond: *Because it's like Woodstock on wheels.*

By the time I rode into Fort Madison at the end of the week and did the ceremonial dipping of my front tire in the Mississippi River, I'd given a lot of reflection to these insights. No doubt, there is truth in all of them. I guess every person has a reason for leaving behind the comfort of the old and opening themselves to the serendipitous discovery of the new.

For me, I concluded the reason for biking RAGBRAI was my watermelon experience. I was riding up a long, steep hill on another hot, sticky day. Every turn of the pedal was agonizing. As I crested the hill, feeling somewhat delirious, a farmer stood beside the road handing out free slices of watermelon. Now mind you, I've experienced all kinds of culinary delights in my lifetime, but nothing will ever surpass the luscious, luxurious and honeyed taste of that watermelon. To my dying day, the memory of that experience will always be with me.

Ceremonial dipping of the front tire in the Mississippi River at Fort Madison

Nothing like a free slice of watermelon

But now, as I write this, I rekindle other memories: Cooling off in an ol' swimming hole. Taking a nap on a hayloft. Riding a 1938 John Deere tractor. Being kissed by two of the sweetest kid goats you'll ever see, and enjoying the camaraderie of my biking team.

At the ol' swimming hole

Me and my goat friends

My RAGBRAI team

Taking Back Boston

Jim Doti

The Night Before

The night before the 118th Boston Marathon on April 21, 2014 was special for me since I carbo-loaded at the home of my cousin, Franco, and his wife, Anna. Running the race was really an excuse for me to visit with them.

Carbo-loading homemade pasta with my
Boston cousin Franco Siracusa

At The Start Line

As my son, Adam, and I wait for the starting gun to go off, I overhear a fellow runner telling her friend, "Whenever I run Boston, I feel like I'm Clark Kent turning into Superman." I know what she means. At this moment, I feel like I'm faster than a speeding bullet, more powerful than a locomotive, and able to leap tall buildings in a single bound.

Mile 6

Both sides of Waverly Street in Framingham are filled with screaming fans, 10 deep. Many are holding placards or wearing t-shirts emblazoned with a simple but powerful message: "Boston Strong." I see a young boy holding up a large photo of Martin Richard, the 8-year-old victim of last year's bombing.

Most of these fans have come out not only to cheer the runners on but also to honor those fallen in last year's race. As I run by the exuberant fans, I'm reminded of what the winner of the 68th Boston Marathon, Amby Burfoot, told us during the "Boston Marathon Legends" presentation at the previous day's race expo: "It wasn't the runners who were attacked last year, it was the spectators. So be sure to high-five as many as you can for 118 years of support and for giving fast and slow alike the thrills of a lifetime."

Me and Adam and at the start

Mile 12

As Adam and I near the Wellesley College campus, we hear the shrill screams of coeds who have lined Central Street. Most of the women have signs like "Kiss me, I'm Italian." One was so original I had to stop to take a photo. It was an equation that read:

$$f(x,y) = x \text{ kiss } y$$
$$f(you, me) = ?$$

Most pleasing to my ears were the shouts of "Go, Chapman!" when the coeds recognized the "Chapman University" name on my running shirt. One

Wellesley coed with that interesting equation

coed even stopped to tell me that she had wanted to attend Chapman, but Wellesley gave her a bigger scholarship. Oooh… that hurt!

Mile 16

Adam and I hit the first of the four Newton hills. These are not major uphills, but after running downhill for most of the previous 15 miles, my quads are starting to scream. It's also getting hotter. While 75 degrees may sound pleasant, runners generally start to heat up when the temperature exceeds 60 degrees. At this point in the race, I feel like my head's been zapped in a microwave oven for 40 seconds.

Mile 19

We hit the third Newton Hill. Pounding the pavement has become so painful that my pace has slowed to the point where even walkers are passing me. Now, more than ever, I need inspiration, and looking down at my race bib, I find it.

At the "Legends" talk, Kathrine Switzer spoke about how running makes us feel fearless in a fearful world. She told us that it was with that attitude in mind that she decided to be the first woman to register to run the Boston Marathon. That happened in 1967, five years before women were officially allowed to compete. The name she gave on her entry form was "K. V. Switzer." Race officials didn't realize that "K. V." was a woman. So, not suspecting anything amiss, they sent her bib # 261. But when a race director saw (Horror of Horrors!) a woman racing with an official bib, he tried to grab her off the course. An iconic photo of that scene with Kathrine evading "capture" has inspired male and female runners alike ever since.

Running legend Kathrine Switzer signing my bib

After her talk, Kathrine signed "Jim! Be 261 Fearless! K. Switzer" upside down on my bib. That is, I thought it was upside down until I looked down, huffing and puffing on that third Newton Hill, and saw Kathrine's message, reading from my perspective right-side up. It was as if she were beside me, whispering in my ear, "Jim, Be Fearless." I have no doubt that Kathrine Switzer helped me over that hill.

Mile 20.5

We hit the final Newton Hill, known to runners around the world as "Heartbreak Hill." For the first time in the eight Boston Marathons I've run, I'm forced to walk the last few steps to the top. I tell Adam to go ahead and finish without me, but he responds, "We started together, and we'll finish together." This brought to mind the words of another "Boston Legends" speaker, '83 champion Greg Meyer. He told us that everyone thinks his favorite Boston was the 1983 race that he won. "Actually," he said, "My favorite Boston was the one I ran with my son." Now I know what he meant.

Mile 25.8

When Adam and I turn onto Boylston Street to the cheers from throngs of devoted fans, I feel like we're entering Olympic Stadium. Just before crossing the finish line in five hours flat, Adam and I clasped our hands together outstretched, pumping the air above us.

The source of my inspiration

I was also thrilled to meet and talk about race strategy with my running guru Jeff Galloway

Me and Adam in lockstep

Past the Finish Line

As Adam and I join other finishers hobbling forward to have medals placed around their necks, I recalled Race Director Dave McGillivray's words at the "Legends" talk:

> *Remember, tomorrow is a special day.*
> *We're taking back Boylston Street.*
> *We're taking back our sport.*
> *We're taking back our marathon.*

That's exactly what my band of brothers and sisters in the race, the volunteers on the course and all the supporters in the stands did: We took back our marathon.

Me with Adam flashing 50 for completing my 50th marathon

Boston Strong and The Story of the Pebble

Jim Doti

COLD rainy, and headwinds the whole way. That's what we needed to be prepared for the 2015 running of the 119th Boston Marathon.

During the "Boston Legends" seminar at the marathon expo on Sunday, race director Dave McGillivray said he couldn't predict tomorrow's weather,

Boston Strong banner blowing in the wind

but we should expect it to be cold and uncomfortable. Jack Fultz described his experience winning the 1986 Boston Marathon in the rain. By the time he took the lead at mile 18, his bib number had washed off, and no one could figure out who he was. Amby Burfoot, the 1968 Boston winner, suggested we run with friends so we could curse about the weather together. Greg Meyer, the 1983 Boston champ, advised us to look at the bright side of the predicted rain and headwinds. "Just think, you can bitch about it the rest of your lives." He added, "No matter how bad it really is, people will say it was worse than it actually was."

Boston legends Amby Burfoot, Kathrine Switzer, Lisa Rainberger, David McGillivray, Jack Fultz, Lorraine Moller and Greg Meyer

So, rather than recount in this article why this year's Boston was worse than it actually was, I'd like to relate what made this year's Boston a very special one for me.

For starters, there was the bus ride to Hopkinton. Usually, that's a time when I engage in a few pleasantries with my seatmate before refocusing in quiet angst over the pending race. Not this time.

I learned that my seatmate, Liz Chute, hailed from Nova Scotia, where she and her husband operate a bed and breakfast called "The Pebble."

"How did it get that name?" I asked.

She then proceeded to tell me a remarkable story. When Liz was a young lass, a lad who was courting her took her for a picnic on the banks of the River Feale in Kerry, Ireland. Although Liz couldn't swim and was afraid of the water, her gentleman friend went for a swim. He returned about an hour later with something clenched in his hand. He opened it to reveal a beautiful little pebble he had found in the riverbed, which he gave to Liz.

Not long after, he proposed marriage and told Liz he wanted to take her to America with him. She declined, deciding that she was too young and not quite ready to leave her family.

Six years later, they met once again while Liz was vacationing in New York City. Over a candlelit dinner, Liz asked if he remembered the pebble he had given her. He said he had never forgotten the pebble and a day hadn't gone by when he hadn't thought about it and wondered if she had been thinking of it, too. At that point, Liz took the pebble out of her purse and gingerly revealed it to him.

They were married shortly thereafter and now own that bed and breakfast in Nova Scotia named "The Pebble." Whenever she's not running marathons, Liz wears the pebble mounted on a lovely necklace, so it's always close to her heart.

Liz related all this to the great Irish writer Brian McMahon, at a writers' conference held in her hometown. He was so touched by the tale that he used it in a short story titled "The Pebble," which he dedicated to Liz.

Liz Chute at home wearing the pebble and holding
a book of short stories that includes *The Pebble*

"Did he stay true to the story?" I asked.
"Well, except for some nudity he put in to jazz it up, it was pretty much the same," Liz replied.

As we got out of the bus and ran to the tent to take cover from the rain, I wondered if I'd ever see Liz again. Maybe not, but I knew the story of the pebble would never leave my mind.

In fact, as I ran through the start line for the race, the story was still with me. Instead of thinking of the rain, the cold and the wind, I was thinking of the pebble and wondering if my wife, Lynne, and I have something like it in our marriage of 38 years—something that is a symbol or memento of our love.

Try as I might, nothing came to me. I thought of paintings we both love. There is the jewelry, too. But I couldn't think of anything quite like Liz's pebble.

My thoughts were diverted from the "pebble" search when I hit mile 12 and first heard the screams of the Wellesley women, still a mile ahead of me. I always love their shouts and kisses. But, as a university president, I especially enjoy evaluating the originality of the signs they excitedly wave in front of us.

I have to give this year's co-eds a lot of credit just for showing up in the awful weather. Still, their signs deserved an "A." Here's a sample:

I came out of a warm, cozy library for this?

I'm Italian! Want some warm pasta and meatballs?

Kiss me. I'm a wet German scientist.

Hug me. I'm a Libertarian and love free markets!

Then, walking up the first of the Newton Hills, I found myself again pondering whether Lynne and I have a pebble in our lives. Nothing.

Approaching Heartbreak Hill, I committed myself to running the final crest of the "Newton 4" at a respectable pace. I huffed and puffed all the way to the top, where a young girl handed me a slice of orange. Wedging it between my teeth and lips, I imagined that I looked just like Mohammad Ali when he jumped in triumph, his mouth guard prominently on display, after beating George Forman in "The Rumble in the Jungle."

Then, all of a sudden, it came to me! I found the "pebble!" Maybe it was the image of Mohammad Ali that inspired me; maybe it was the sugar hit from the orange, or maybe it was running up to the top of Heartbreak Hill and knowing it was all downhill from here. Whatever it was, the "pebble" came to me.

Lynne and I have our books; not any one book but all the books we've shared together. When I first met Lynne at Chapman University, we were young assistant professors getting started in teaching and working like heck to get our articles published. We hardly saw each other. But when we bumped into each other, we'd trade book recommendations.

It all started when I enthusiastically recommended Wilkie Collins' *The Moonstone*, a rather obscure classic of 19th-century British literature. After reading it, Lynne told me she loved it so much that she had read Collins' *Woman in White*. So then I read that. This has continued on, as if it were a chain letter between us, to this day. That's it! All those books over the years are our pebbles.

By the time I hit Boylston Street to the still-cheering fans, I had shed my rain jacket and three layers of running shirts. Down to my remaining sleeveless Chapman University shirt, I crossed the finish line with the rain now coming down in a torrent and the winds kicking up like a Nor'easter.

That's me near the finish line

But I had one more delight awaiting me.

The previous night, I met with Liz (another Liz!) and Phill Gross, parents of an incoming Chapman freshman co-ed, Jessica. They invited me to stop in after the race to Phill's office suite on the 52nd floor of John Hancock Tower and even asked me to give them a change of clothes so I could take a hot shower in Phill's office suite fitness room after the marathon.

As I handed off my change of clothes, Liz asked, "What's your favorite beer I can have waiting for you?"

I told her, "Given the weather that's predicted, I think I'd rather have a shot of bourbon."

So just after the Boston medal was placed around my neck, I turned right at Clarendon Street and walked a half block to Hancock Tower, where it wasn't long before I was showering under a steaming spray of hot, soothing, and redemptive water.

Looking down the finish line from the
52nd floor of Hancock Tower

I joined Phill and Liz and their family and friends. After we raised our glasses and toasted "Boston Strong," I related the story about the pebble. Perhaps in passing on the story, others might take a moment to reflect on the pebbles in their lives. It's funny, though, that it was a Boston Marathon that helped me find mine.

Note: Brian MacMahon's short story, *The Pebble*, is included in *Baker's Dozen*, published by Poolbeg Press (1989).

Liz and Phill Gross

My Road to the Vermont 100-Mile Endurance Run

Dan Temianka

*Adventure is simply physical and emotional
discomfort recollected in tranquility*

—Tim Cahill

MY first discovery of true adventure was Jack London's *The Call of the Wild*, to which my mother introduced me when I was 12. She understood the vital impact of great literature. "I would rather be a superb meteor, every atom of me in magnificent glow, than a sleepy and permanent planet," said London. He awakened my spirit.

Some years later I read *Kon Tiki*, Thor Heyerdahl's thrilling account of his voyage from Peru to Polynesia in a makeshift raft of balsa and reeds. I wrote him a letter of admiration, to which he graciously replied.

In 2000, I planned a trip to Antarctica. To get there, I first had to travel to the colorful town of Ushuaia, at the extreme south end of Chile, Tierra del Fuego. We embarked *Clipper Adventurer* and traversed the Beagle Channel, named for Charles Darwin's ship. Then we dared the treacherous 600-mile Drake Passage, enduring 12-foot waves. (We heard that waves had reached 40 feet during the previous voyage, and one passenger had broken her arm in a fall from her bunk. Seatbelts, anyone?)

I will never forget the magical moment when we sailed into the Lemaire Channel in the Antarctic Peninsula. The air was pure crystal, the sky an aching blue, and the Una Peaks towered before us. A Weddell seal lounged on an iceberg nearby.

A physician by the name of Michael Rossove wrote a marvelous book titled *Let Heroes Speak* about the earliest expeditions to Antarctica, in which he quoted two sailors aboard *Erebus* in 1841.

Heyerdahl postcard

First, McCormick:

The wondrous scene nature has unfolded here, even beyond what might have been anticipated in this land of wonderment, has had the effect of riveting me to the deck for the last twenty-four hours... myself most anxious to trace this mighty wall of ice continuously... a night never to be effaced from memory's tablet to the latest hour of existence; and well was I rewarded for the temporary sacrifice of a night's rest and sleep by the grand and sublime panorama which... arrested my gaze... as the 'noonday' night of this high latitude wore on, and scene succeeded scene in nature's unrivalled display of her great Creator's works.

And Cornelius Sullivan:

All hands when they Came on Deck to view this the most rare and magnificent Sight that Ever the human eye witnessed Since the world was created actually Stood Motionless for Several Seconds before he Could Speak to the man next to him. Beholding with Silent Surprize the great and wonderful works of nature in this position, we had an opportunity to discern the barrier in its Splendid position. Then I wished. I was an artist or a draughtsman instead of a blacksmith and Armourer.

The eloquence of the common man.

In 1979, I ran my first marathon. I was ill-prepared, struggled to break five hours, and was half-lame for two weeks afterward. I resolved to learn good

Una Peaks

Lemaire Channel

training methods and gave serious analytic thought to the matter. Scheduling of training is the key; I set up a spreadsheet that I used for years. I considered the characteristics of athletic ability: speed, power, strength, flexibility, agility, coordination and balance, and stamina (endurance). Discipline, clothing, and equipment completed the list. Implicit in discipline is the idea of self-management, both in training and during races and tours – fluids, calories, electrolytes, pace, heart rate, temperature control.

Yours truly on the trail

I knew at the outset that I was no more than average in most of those athletic categories, but it intrigued me to know with certainty what my genetically determined limits were. That's all any athlete can do, no matter how gifted. I regularly did interval training to improve lactic acid metabolism despite knowing that speed was not my strong suit. Eventually I discovered that my endurance, augmented by strong discipline and my analytic approach, was well above average. Give me enough real estate, and I could pass some faster runners.

Pushing oneself to summit a mountain or run a hundred miles, or write a novel or complete a first 50-mile bike ride or triathlon, writing a symphony, building a pyramid or rocketing to the moon – why? It's about building and creating. "You have a very simple choice: to create or not to create," my father told me. Seeking one's limits is intrinsically, intensely, creative.

The 1990s were my multisport heyday. In 1992, having become a reasonably competent runner and cyclist, it dawned on me that I could become a triathlete if I learned to swim, so I did, engaging a swim coach and a trainer. Passion blossomed. Soon, I finished the Wildflower Half-ironman in very hot weather, narrowly avoiding the need for intravenous hydration afterward. I objected, in writing, to USA Triathlon's neurotic motto, "Never enough," and proposed "Finish healthy" as a much better alternative.

I completed more than 40 endurance events – marathons and ultras, duathlons, biathlons, three ironman triathlons, bike "centuries" and longer, including the Markleeville "Death Ride," 146 miles in the High Sierras – five mountain passes at about 8,000 feet elevation. I also did some one-off exploits. One year, I ran the Death Valley Marathon for the second time with two friends. It was a tough course, dirt roads and trails, with little logistical support – what we referred to as "fun." Not content with the race, however, I had brought along my Litespeed titanium racing bike, and at first light the next morning, I set out from Furnace Creek to Scotty's Castle, some 53 miles north, alone. Along the way, I stopped and experienced the quietest moment of my life, perfect stillness in the pristine desert, in beautiful mild weather (March).

Most of the road is at or below sea level, but it rises unexpectedly to some 3000 feet at the Castle, where I encountered a nasty cold fog. It was nearly dusk by the time I got back to Furnace Creek, and a California Highway Patrolman kindly escorted me the last few miles to our motel. I found my two pals curled up watching Steven Segal movies, washing down chocolates with cold beer, and heaping scorn on my exhaustion. Reliable buddies.

I was jogging along the boardwalk in Redondo Beach one morning in those years when I spied two older guys running the other way. One of them was wearing a red jacket emblazoned "American River 50." He had completed a 50-mile run! The glory of it seized me. I could not escape the commitment, and commitment is at the heart of adventure. I immediately registered for the race, a point-to-point run whose first half is mostly roads, paved and not, with sinuous, narrow trails after that and a four-mile climb at the end, when you least want it!

En route there were meadows, lilies, lupine, golden poppies, lavender irises, oak and pine in profusion, magpies, robins, finches, jackrabbits, squirrels, hawks, and those odd, shimmering, cola-black butterflies with blue spots on their tails, that fluttered up to your face to say hello (no, that was not just some endorphin-induced hallucination). And mucho poison oak – I was glad to be wearing full-length tights. If you needed further distraction – unlikely – there was always the magnificent American River rushing down below on your right.

I alternated running with walking, especially when I encountered mud. Fortunately, it was the slippery, rust-colored stuff, not the glom-on variety that turns one's shoes into 10-pound elephant turds. It was impossible to avoid, given the high berms of that very old trail, but after a while, it was fun – fingerpainting with your running shoes.

But my legs begin to whine and scold me, *yatta-yatta-blah-blah-nag*. Time for a serious talk. "Legs," said I, adopting the minatory tone of that pest-control mannequin with the dark spectacles and top hat, "do as you're told, or I'll clobber you with this wooden mallet!" They shut up temporarily.

I recalled the scene from Virgil's *Aeneid*, in which Aeneas lies wounded and exhausted on a rocky beach, viewing the remains of his storm-wrecked fleet. He turns to his lieutenant and utters one of the greatest lines in all literature: "Someday, perhaps it will be pleasant to remember even these things." What is my pain compared to that of Aeneas? I find solace, if not comfort.

At the 41-mile aid station I was energized by the theme from "Beverly Hills Cop." Doing some quick calculations, I was amazed to realize that a sub-10 hour time was a distinct possibility. But then my right knee conspired with legs, arguing, gnattering -- they were now the little exterminator man, and I the wayward mouse cowering in mute terror before the mallet. I flirted with a syllogism: pain is potentiated by fatigue; fatigue is amplified by hunger; I feel hungry. Therefore, eating will reduce my pain. This logic was undoubtedly specious, but it was also amusing, and the amusement and snack were distracting and reduced the pain. *Voilá!*

I reached the last four miles of gravelly uphill hell. My heart rate rose above 90%, but I held on. I thought of Tommy Lasorda and his dictum that the single most important quality in sports is *desire*. I wanted that sub-10 finish as much as he ever wanted a pennant.

The finish line! A carnival atmosphere, with tasty nibbles, ice-cold beverages, wonderful people, and the deep excitement of a race well bagged in a free country. And on top of that a way-cool black fleece finisher's vest, with zippered pockets.

Next, I took a step up: the first Catalina 100k Run – 62 miles. It began inauspiciously with a queasy 26-mile voyage from Long Beach on El Niño swells. The ship's steward ran out of barf bags. Most of the passengers were runners and their companions, wondering whether they would be able to hold down the traditional carbo-load dinner that evening, but by then, most of us had recovered.

The course route was shaped like a lollipop, doubling through the point where the narrow island is squinched into an isthmus at Two Harbors, but it was definitely not a piece of cake – mostly up-and-down dirt roads, some of them more like trails and a few miles of terminally fatigued asphalt roads. We had extraordinarily good luck with the elements, enjoying a clear post-squall window before the next storm.

We raced along verdant emerald-green slopes, with spectacular views of the glittering blue Pacific sprawling 40 miles in either direction. Where else can you see buffalo, billygoats, cactus, palm trees, and crashing surf all at once? At about 28 miles on the super-steep Kiss Your Knees Hill, the support crew had done a superb job of picking out a hiking detour around a treacherous landslide, planting little orange flags and yellow ribbons.

Aid stations every five miles or so were well stocked with a cornucopia of tasty stuff, from creme cookies to chicken soup and that Training Food of the Gods, salt. (Hyponatremia, eat death!) Plus some really lovely people.

"How you guys holding up?" I yelled when I arrived, startling them into spilling their beer.

"Cookies, pretzels, Vaseline, Gatorade?"

"No thanks, I don't like the taste of Vaseline."

"Aspirin, Tylenol, first aid – ?"

"Any cardiac catheters?"

A visit to my "drop bag" at 35 miles provided a change of shoes and a fresh pair of thick, snowy-white Thor-Lo socks with talcum powder in them – ah, heaven!

One runner complained that there "wasn't enough support." Every five miles isn't enough?? I noticed that this individual was not carrying his own water container. Two of the cardinal rules in endurance sports are (1) if you're thirsty, drink lots of fluids, and (2) if you're not thirsty, drink lots of fluids because by the time you get thirsty, it's probably too late... You dasn't run ultras without a water bottle or backpack. You wouldn't show up at a softball game without a mitt, would you? Go cycling without a helmet?

One delightful advantage of an out-and-back course is that you have an opportunity to see the front runners, sometimes top professionals, loping back toward you like happy mountain goats. It's a thrilling moment for mortals like me. They are almost invariably gracious, always quick with a smile and an encouraging word.

After that, the challenge became more mental than physical, or, to paraphrase Yogi Berra, "Ninety percent of ultra running is half mental." To keep myself going I recited that speech from the beginning of the movie "Patton" – "Now I want you to remember, that no bastard ever won a war by dying for his country..." (The great general also once remarked, "Accept the challenges, so that you may feel the exhilaration of victory.")

The most remarkable character in this race was Henri Girault, a sixty-ish French railroad engineer retired. He resembled Jacques Cousteau and had flown in from France, especially for the race -- his 369th 100k! His goal was to finish 400 of them, a distance equal to the earth's circumference. Having inflicted my broken French on Monsieur Girault at the starting line, I later atoned for it (or made matters worse) by bawling several stanzas of the "Marseillaise" into the stiff breeze at the summit on the west end of the island.

I had the privilege of running the last six miles with Henri – my father's name, by happy coincidence. "Oof! O la la," he puffed over and over. This patrician gentleman tried to insist that yours truly, a first-time 100k-er, cross the finish line before him! No way. I practically had to push him across the line ahead of me.

When I hobbled home the following day, my Spouse Unit inquired impatiently, with a puzzled frown, "Why do you do it if it's so painful?" My standard riposte: "Lots of worthwhile activities cause pain, honey, from pro football to childbirth."

Next, I set my sights on a 100-mile race. I had heard of a few events that involved running a zillion times around a city block. How boring! A dervish-like activity, reminiscent of spinning around to make yourself dizzy when you were a child. I chose the Rocky Racoon (yes, only one c) Trail 100 at Huntsville State Park in the Great Empire of Texas. "Pretty swamp" is not an oxymoron; it's a fair description of the steamy bayou where 104 ultra-souls convened.

The format was a 20-mile course repeated five times, each lap consisting of two out-and-backs around a raven-shaped lake, followed by a W-shaped squiggle that includes a final short out-and-back. Clear?

This criterium format is logistically simpler than a point-to-point, loop, or single out-and-back, allowing a single drop bag at the start-finish line. An added plus was becoming thoroughly familiar with the trails by the time night fell. This was attractive for the 100-mile first-timer (me), but the downside risk was that it's psychologically tempting to bail out at 60 or 80 miles, as you see your parked car beckoning to you repeatedly.

A delightful advantage of the multiple out-and-backs is that you get to greet your chums several times, whether they are behind you or ahead. You watch their psyched-up early-morning smiles degenerate via time-lapse photography into thin, embalmed grimaces; their high-fives become feeble flutterings; their high-spirited hoots fade into incoherent grunts. All while denying that you yourself have undergone such morbid changes. Fun!

My race bib number was zero, which faintly troubled me and perplexed the aid station volunteers. But then I was comforted by the realization that "zero" rhymes with "hero" and that I was zeroing in on my first 100 miler.

The course was excellently marked with yellow ribbons, pie plates with arrows, and glow sticks at night. Other than patches of muck and a riot of toe-stubbing roots, the trail was fairly smooth, punctuated occasionally by quaint boardwalk bridges over stagnant water. After dusk, we were serenaded by the chirring of crickets and cicadas as a humid breeze rushed through the trees overhead; fortunately, no biting insects were in evidence at that time of year. Choruses of whistling frogs drifted in the night air.

On the second lap I pulled alongside a runner who was ranging ahead, then speeding back down the line, shouting, hugging friends, singing. A gregarious, turbocharged deer. I was foolish enough to suggest that he might want to conserve his energy for later in the race. He responded by jumping in front of me and launching into a passionate rendition of "Guantanamera" at the top of his lungs. "How you Doin'??" he demanded and introduced himself as Gabriel Flores – winner of the previous July's 135-mile Badwater to Whitney race, probably the most ferociously difficult ultra in North America! This man had the energy of a nuclear reactor, palpable from 100 feet away. It transpired that another runner, an ordinary earthling like me, had paid Gabriel's expenses to act as his pacer in the race.

My split times ballooned. My cruising became paddling, then chugging, trudging, and finally hobbling. In the fourth loop, I entered the gates of Blister City. As Peter O'Toole remarked in "Lawrence of Arabia," after snuffing a match with his fingertips, "The trick is not to mind the pain." As darkness fell, the standard ultrarunner's lie, "Lookin' good!" seemed especially mendacious.

At about 85 miles I briefly took my only wrong turn of the race, which cost me about 10 minutes. At the 92-mile aid station, I noticed a young runner leaning back in a chair, snoring. But it was not snoring; it was a form of stertorous respiration that portends respiratory arrest, and a closer inspection revealed that he was clammy, diaphoretic, and unconscious. He was going into shock. With the help of a volunteer, I immediately laid him on the ground with his legs elevated, opened his airway, and shook him. Fortunately, he came-to promptly. He had no history of medical problems but had been drinking only water and half-strength Gatorade throughout the race and no salty food. Without a doubt, he was hyponatremic and hypotensive.

I fed him a teaspoon of salt, some crackers, and fluids, and he regained his strength remarkably fast. With no alternatives readily available, it seemed reasonable to attempt the rest of the race, so we took off and ultimately crossed the finish line together, breaking 24 hours. We were met by his wife, only eight weeks away from delivering a new little ultrarunner into the world. Had I not taken that wrong turn, I would not have arrived there at that critical moment...

Afterward, I spent a day "cocooning" in my motel room with cable TV, *New Yorker* magazines, and cooling footbaths. And I discovered that my finisher's pewter belt buckle had medicinal properties – whenever I rubbed it, the pain in my legs subsided.

The Vermont 100 Mile Endurance Run was known to be a couple of orders of magnitude more challenging, much hillier, and predicted to be very hot and humid that year. My plan was to keep my heart rate at or below 70% to the halfway point, walking the steepest uphills and staying well hydrated and well fed. I had logged some 2000 miles of running the previous year, with frequent runs of 25 to 40 miles, and had worked diligently with my trainer on lower-body strength, so I felt well prepared. I was used to running trails at night. I had learned to protect my feet by applying carefully shaped pieces of duct tape with benzoin to the soles of my feet. "The will to win means the will to prepare," said Juma Ikangaa, a Tanzanian marathon runner.

In the pre-dawn darkness, some 243 runners impatiently trampled the dirt in the huge barn at Smoke Rise Farm near Burlington, Vermont. At 3:45 a.m., fireworks burst above the green-black hills and we paraded past the owner's stone farmhouse, lit up for the occasion. He presided on the terrace in a tuxedo, serenading us with "Chariots of Fire" on an electric piano as we pulled up to the starting line. Magic was in the air.

An air horn sounded, and we herded off into the bucolic Vermont countryside: green forests and misty meadows; quaint old farmhouses nestling in rolling grassy hills; brick-red barns with black iron weathervanes perched on their spines; stone-walled garden plots bursting with black-eyed Susans, saffron daisies, creamy-orange daylilies, and Queen Anne's lace; marshes sprouting reeds and cattails like hot dogs on sticks; small seas of phlox and sprawling ferns; ponds and little crumbling cemeteries with tombstones dating back to the 17th Century.

Once the sun rose, the day heated up quickly. Riders on horses cantered past us in a simultaneous race. On a steep, hot-sunny hillside, two colorfully outfitted riders stopped to palpate their lathered horses' heaving chests, checking their heart rates.

Repeat after me: pace, fluids, calories, sodium and potassium, temperature control. Walk the uphills, gulp beverages, stoke the furnace, wolf down salt and oranges, slosh the scalp and chest with cold water, stuff ice in water bottles and hat. Do it all again and again til the queasiness eases and the energy level rises. Be relentless. Repeat to yourself: I want that silver buckle! (Finishing under 24 hours earned the buckle; longer than that, but under the 30-hour absolute cutoff, and you received only a tacky framed plaque.)

This was a tough race. The incessant hills totaled nearly 15,000 feet of climbing and descending each, and temperatures soared over 100 degrees – hottest in the 11-year history of the race – with more than 90% humidity. At 44 miles I encountered the gifted Ben Hian, already on his way back at 68 miles. He was smoking the course at an 8:30 pace but paid for it with excessive weight loss and was pulled by the race stewards. Rules are rules.

An orange crescent of harvest moon floated up from the horizon after dusk. I clicked my watch into Indiglo "night mode" (how quaint to think of that today!). Bullfrogs burped to each other in the darkness like the plucking

of thick rubber bands. Miniature shooting stars flitted in the trailside bushes --
fireflies. Glowsticks in trees marked the trail in the gloom ahead.

Ultras are usually social occasions, and this one was no exception. For
a while, I fell in with two French-speaking gentlemen. Another new friend,
Oscar, and I discussed everything from real estate to Freud. Later in the night,
I chatted with Don Allison, editor of *Ultrarunning* magazine, as we jogged over
the top of a hill into an exquisite view of a moonlit farmhouse, silo, and cows in
a field, a scene right out of Norman Rockwell.

"Have fun" was the oft-repeated First Rule of this race. The hardy souls who
stayed the course will claim to have done so, but there were definitely fewer
chuckles in the last 20 miles, notwithstanding the Rockwellian landscapes. The
hills seemed endless, the soft, broken singletrack trails interminable. Every aid
station was a welcome oasis, whether it was a rockin' barn party hosted by a
local fellow named Bill or a tilted, unmanned folding table hidden in the forest
with some bottled water and a few essentials.

Ultrarunners and endurance athletes dream that if they but train hard
enough, shrewdly enough, or just plain *enough*, they will enter a magical
stratosphere in which they can glide forever, effortlessly. The funny thing is, it
happens! The Germans would undoubtedly coin a long compound word for this
state of mind. I'll suggest *Wirkleistungfreude* – "power-joy."

Only 109 of 243 runners finished, the lowest finishing percentage ever in
that race. Of the 67 men in my 10-year age group, only 27 reached the finish
line; I placed fourth with a time of 23:38, earning the silver buckle, which I
still wear today. That was the pinnacle of my little amateur sports career.

Vermont belt buckle

The Vermont 100 was the main fund-raiser for VASS, the Vermont Adaptive Ski and Sports organization, which sponsored sportspeople with disabilities. How appropriate for an event that brings us face-to-face with our own limitations! And this is, after all, the deepest reason we keep coming back to these races: to reaffirm our belief in fairness, sportsmanship, camaraderie, and our indomitable spirit, despite the blisters and pain, the sometimes capricious elements and occasional disappointments.

George F. Will reminded us that "Greek philosophers considered sport a religious and civic – in a word, a moral – undertaking. Sport, they said, is morally serious because mankind's noblest aim is the loving contemplation of worthy things, such as beauty and courage. By witnessing physical grace, the soul comes to understand and love beauty. Seeing persons compete courageously and fairly helps emancipate the individual by educating his passions."

In these violent times, that's worth remembering.

Security is mostly a superstition.
It does not exist in nature...
Life is either a daring adventure or nothing.

—Helen Keller

I want to express my warm admiration for my wonderful friend and fine adventurer Jim Doti and his colleagues.

Destination Ironman Canada!

Dan Temianka

THE DECISION

I awoke at 1:15 a.m. on the night of February 15, 1992, with the realization that if I could learn to swim, I could become a triathlete. I was already a jogger and cyclist – both mountain and road –- how hard could it be?

"But why?" A Contrarian Voice demanded.

A reptilian lobe in my brain, now irrevocably engaged, replied with Ten Reasons for Doing a Triathlon:

1. "Because it's there," said I, arrogantly invoking the great George Mallory.
2. "It's the glory, stupid."
3. "You get to go swimming!"
4. "Then you get to go for a long bike ride!"
5. "And then you get to put on a fresh shirt and run around in the open air for a long time!" "That's only five," my inner voice countered. "And just what the hell are you trying to prove?"
6. "That's the wrong question!" I shouted. "If you insist, though, the answer is: I'm trying to prove that *I can do* it, you idiot!" "You're trying to be something you're not!" persisted the Voice.
7. "No shit!" I exclaimed. "And what happened to Browning's immortal advice, 'Ah, but a man's reach should exceed his grasp'?" Silence.
8. "I may be getting older, but I'm also getting faster, and I can prove it!" I added.
9. And: "To impress others." (I don't deny it.)
10. And finally, "Because it amuses me to define my limits. It's intellectually very interesting to know whether I can really alter and improve my physiology – VO2 max, lactate tolerance, cycling biomechanics, rotator cuff function…"

The substrate of tri training is your body and yourself - not wood or clay or words or *papier maché*. Make your body run like a sports car!

The Contrary Voice slunk away, and I embarked on a journey that involved intensive training, road trips with buddies, technical conundrums, international travel, injuries and "overuse syndromes," and a very flexible sports equipment budget. ("Honey, these pedals are even better than wallpaper, honest!")

The Training (and Tapering)

In *Jurassic Park*, Michael Crichton observed that "Most kinds of power require a substantial sacrifice by whoever wants the power. There is an apprenticeship, a discipline lasting many years. Whatever kind of power you want. President of the company. Black belt in karate. Spiritual guru. Whatever it is you seek, you have to put in the time, the practice, the effort. You must give up a lot to get it. It has to be very important to you. And once you have attained it, it is your power. It can't be given away: it resides in you..."

That's what I pursued for ten formative years. Happily, no dinosaurs were involved. I dove head-first into conditioning, in both the athletic and Pavlovian senses of that word. How I managed to do all that in the midst of a busy professional and family life remains a mystery to me.

Ironman! With a capital I, it refers to the trademarked event owned by World Triathlon Corporation and held at various venues around the world, most famously in Kailua-Kona, Hawaii. With a small i, in many other sites, the distances are the same: 2.4 miles of swimming, 112 miles on the bike, and a marathon run of 26.2 miles. (The swim is really longer than that for almost everyone because the fastest swimmers dominate the inner part of the course, so you position yourself more peripherally to avoid being thrashed by the big kids.)

I spent five days at a triathlete camp near San Diego. They determined our VO2 max, did a computerized analysis of pedaling technique, video'd our swimming underwater – the works. We were privileged to have several legends as mentors: Paula Newby-Fraser, the "Queen of Kona," champion swimmer Rob Mackle, and the great cyclist John Howard.

One morning, John rode with a dozen of us. He was wearing splashy tie-dyed shorts. I was laboring up a steep hill in my "granny gear," the lowest, when I suddenly felt a strong thrust on my back, as though by a giant's hand. It was John, his big right paw pushing my back powerfully as he casually scratched his ear with his left hand. Later that day we spent an hour practicing "hot stops" under his critical gaze. He showed us the video in which he had established the all-time world record of some 152 mph on his (modified and strengthened) bicycle behind a race car with a huge scoop at the Bonneville Salt Flats.

Heartrate monitoring came into vogue, and I had the privilege of spending time with Sally Edwards, who literally wrote the book on it, during a Caribbean cruise on which some 15 of us passengers were avid triathletes. There are several ways of determining one's maximum heart rate: the traditional formula, 220 minus age; a slightly more accurate formula that corrects for gender; and the best, empirical approach, if you are already fit enough to do it: just go balls-out in repeat intervals until you can't continue. Do that in each sport – swim, bike, run – because it can differ significantly for physiologic reasons that include weight-bearing, posture, and the effects of ambient water. Then, you can determine with confidence your percentages of the maximum that you want to stay within during your training and racing.

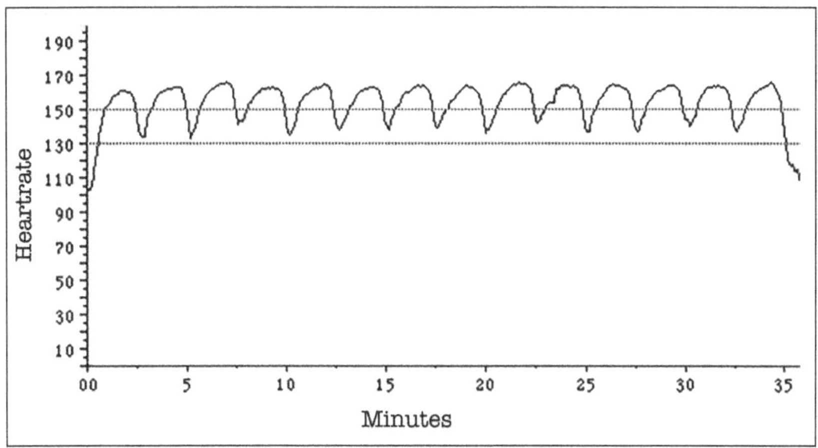

A sample heart rate tracing of an interval running session

After a while, you refer to the heart rate monitor less because you know from experience what your heart rate is at given levels of exertion when you start to breathe hard and know that you're approaching anaerobic metabolism. It's like a race car driver's familiarity with the sound of his engine – he relies less on the tachometer. But it's more uncertain under difficult conditions, especially very hot weather.

Scott Molina, one of the first great professional Hawaii ironmen, was also one of our mentors on that cruise. One morning, we all went out for an easy nine-mile run on Martinique. As we assembled on the dock, I said jokingly, "I'll race you!"

"I only race for money," he replied, dead serious. During one of our one-on-one sessions, he casually mentioned that he liked to do a 140-mile ride in the Mojave Desert in summer –- wearing a sweater for good measure. The inflection point of his lactate accumulation curve, even before his phenomenally intense training, was further to the right than Pluto.

Stravinsky had this to say on the topic of discipline: "Human activity must impose limits upon itself. The more art is controlled, limited, worked over, the more it is free." That's why schedules are of the essence in training.

To prepare for the ironman, the essential goal is base, which requires a lot of LSD workouts. (That's Long Slow Distance, not lysergic acid diethyldiamide.). You have to build it, no less than slaves (allegedly) carved stones for the Pyramids, and plumbers install the vasculature in a skyscraper. I decided that a weekly log of six to eight thousand yards in the water, 100 to 150 miles on the bike, and 40 miles on foot was the necessary minimum, including one long workout in each sport (i.e., at or close to race distance). In addition, I determined it was essential to do some multisport workouts ("bricks") of at least six to eight hours; otherwise, there was a risk of crash-and-burn on race day – the dreaded dnf, "Did Not Finish" – when my race was expected to last at least 12 hours. Plus, some interval workouts, i.e., high intensity, in all three sports, to prepare my body for the inevitable moments of unrestrained competitiveness.

Those "bricks" also served to develop transition mechanics. Greg Welch, another one of the early top pros, would place his wind trainer on a quarter-mile running track, go pedal-to-metal for 20 minutes, jump into his running shoes, sprint half a mile, and repeat…

Windtrainers and stationary bikes come in several forms and are useful in foul weather and at night. But there are also rollers, a simple rectangular chassis with two metal cylinders that support the rear wheel of your bike and only one cylinder in front, on which the front wheel perches precariously. You feel like a squirrel on roller skates. Their further advantage is that you quickly learn to maintain your center of gravity very tightly; elsewise you skitter off. No head-scratching or nose-picking! And coasting is impossible. You want to begin in a narrow hallway. I made a habit of riding them at least once every week or two as a supplement to my program. I'm the only guy I ever met who actually did a 100-mile ride on rollers.

That practice may have saved lives one morning. I was descending a steep, curving hill with a couple of pals. Suddenly, there were several pedestrians walking in an unexpected direction in front of me, one of them pushing a baby carriage. The only way past them was a gutter strewn with wet leaves. I unweighted my pedals and somehow steered through it.

Train to the circumstances and terrain of your planned race. It amazed me to see some triathletes do all their swimming in a warm, calm pool, wearing only a Speedo, and then on race day, they donned a bulky, full-length rubber wetsuit and jumped into cold, choppy seawater! Or trained on the bike entirely on the flats, then expected to hammer the hills effectively. Or put in all their running miles on asphalt but entered a half-iron race whose run included steep, single-track trails.

Outdoor workouts often present the "training opportunities" – rough ocean water, stiff currents, hot weather, gnarly trails, strong headwinds. They provide chances to improve your mental discipline as well. Tuck into them like a big meal!

Training is about recovery. When you're in good shape, even delaying your next workout until 30 hours later, rather than 24, can provide significant rest and recovery.

I tried every type of "power bar" and supplement on the market and took notes on how I reacted to them: Power Bar, Zone Bar, Thunder Bar, Clif Bar, Granola, Hammer Gel, GU, and so on. I'm an incorrigible label-reader and discovered that a few of them contained guarana, an herb with a form of ephedrine – a kind of "speed." Whoa, back off!

As to body weight, my advice is to ignore it because it's influenced by many factors, including muscle mass (a function of gym workouts), body fat percentage, and water, which makes up nearly two-thirds of our bodies. If you're really interested, body fat is measurable by a multiple skin-caliper method or, less commonly but more accurately, by an immersion tank.

Accordingly, what matters, in my opinion, in order of importance are:

- Exercise – am I keeping to my training schedule?
- Diet – is it right?
- Do I feel good?
- Am I performing well?
- Am I satisfied with how I look in the mirror?
- Do my clothes fit?
- (Body fat percentage)
- (Weight)

Train harder on your weaknesses, just as a tennis player works more on his backhand. That's the opposite of how kids practice the piano, preferring to play their best passages over and over.

Be prepared for pain and for being challenged as to why you're doing something that causes it. You're not being masochistic, and you've got lots of company – football players, boxers, and ballet dancers, for example (to say nothing of cosmetic surgery).

I had some interesting experiences. One morning in Scottsdale, Arizona, I went out for a solo ride, but by chance, fell in with a group of young Italians wearing colorful matching jerseys. They quickly picked up the pace, and I labored not to fall off the caboose. The lad in front of me looked back with a nod – they were giving me a chance to lead! I gave it all I had and managed to hold on in front for less than a minute. When I drifted back again, they dropped me like a red-hot rivet. It dawned on me that that was the *Giro Ciclistica Italia* – the Italian national youth team!

On Friday afternoons, I used to swim around Naples Island in Long Beach with one of my triathlete buddies. He was a faster swimmer than I was, but he had a thrashing, inefficient kick that was like the big scoop on the back of the car that led John Howard at Bonneville, so I could hang in behind him until the last 500 yards when he would always drop me just to keep me in my place. That roughly circular channel is just under three miles long, an excellent "over-distance" venue to train for the 2.4-mile Ironman swim. It goes through a marina with a substantial volume of boat traffic, from kayaks to sloops, and the water is none too clean. In perfect hindsight, it was too risky, but I got away with it.

I also liked to do the pier-to-pier swim, Redondo Beach to Hermosa Beach, on Saturday mornings, about two miles. One day, as I crawled north alone, a whiskered head, like something out of an old Katzenjammer cartoon, popped out of the ocean less than 50 feet away, peering at me intently. After a startled moment, I realized that it was a seal. I could swear he (she?) laughed at me before disappearing below the waves.

Another morning in that same area, there was a red tide. This phenomenon is caused by massive swarms of dinoflagellates, microorganisms that turn the water a dirty maroon color during the day but fluoresce brilliantly with turbulence at night.

Staring down through the murk as I stroked, I noticed a small sting ray. Moments later, I felt a violent shock on my right bicep, as though someone had zapped me with the cable from a car battery. I screamed and thrashed, but fortunately, the pain subsided quickly.

When I pulled ashore I found a tiny, trident-shaped barb in the rubber arm of my wetsuit. Serendipitously, at that time, there was a small marine laboratory at the end of the Hermosa Beach Pier, and they confirmed that it had come from a sting ray. I can only imagine what it would have been like if I hadn't been wearing a wetsuit!

The other side of training, and just as important, is tapering before a race. Tapering is an art form in itself, with the objective of preserving one's "training effect" (conditioning or base) while increasing rest and recharging. The duration of tapering is proportional to the duration of the race; for the ironman, 10 to 14 days is about right. While tapering, keep doing workouts in all three sports to maintain muscle memory and fitness, but go easier than usual. "Take your bike for a walk," someone told me.

Hardcore endurance athletes can get to a point where it's literally more difficult to refrain from training than to work out. A day off can be anxiety-producing, so I had one of those "logo watches" made to wear on such days.

The Recovery Time watch

Road Trips, Tours and Races

I am flooded with memories of road trips with my buddies, whose differences in personality would become vividly apparent. Jess quietly accepted any choice of music on the radio; the air conditioning practically set itself. Mark argued about everything, including the division of the check to the penny, at a lunch café. Steve was invariably enthusiastic about everything.

My favorite event was the half-ironman, which I did seven times at Wildflower, at Lake San Antonio, about 45 minutes via winding country roads northwest of Paso Robles, California. The first time, I barely finished in 7:25, in intense heat. Ultimately I got my time down to 6:36. It was a tough course, with a couple of killer climbs, an improperly banked descent that you had to be prepared for, and about two-thirds of the run was trails. It had a central transition area, and one year, as I descended into it on the bike, a huge cheer went up. "For me?" I thought foolishly. Then I realized that the great Scott Tinley was ahead of me – finishing the entire course. (That's one of the charms of triathlon, unlike other major sports: amateurs can rub shoulders with the top professionals!) And then it sank in that I still had to run 13.1 tough miles in the heat…

Mark was an experienced, fast triathlete; Jess was solid and taciturn. Steve had registered for the Olympic distance triathlon, his first, the following day. We always stayed at the best joint in town, the modest Black Oak Motel. Immediately after every race, we would reserve the motel for the following year.

Mark, Jess and I did well at the half-ironman on Saturday. That evening we sat around drinking beer in our suite as Steve nervously prepared for his first triathlon early the following morning, checking and re-checking his bike and equipment. Tires, gears, shoes, sun block, bike shorts, helmet, saddle bag, goggles, spare tire, sun block…

"You're gonna do great, Steve," I offered.

"Yeah, no problem," Mark chimed in.

A long silence. Jess had said nothing for some time. Finally, "Yeah, Steve, just don't embarrass us." Steve turned white as a sheet. In the event, he did well.

In sharp contrast, the Sourdough Triathlon was a homespun affair outside of Fairbanks, Alaska, approximately a half-ironman distance. It was run by a couple who reminded me of Ma and Pa Kettle. I threw my trusty Litespeed into my airplane travel box and got out of Dodge (aka L.A.) early on a Thursday morning.

"How many years have you been doing this tri?" I asked.

A pause, then Marcia said slowly, "Oh, about four."

"How many people did you have last year?"

"Oh, about 20."

"How much is the entry fee?"

"Well, Bob wants to do it again free this year, but I say we ought to charge a dollar, you know, to cover the potluck afterwards."

"Have you thought of getting some sponsors?"

"Oh, I think we had one of them once, but I don't remember what happened to him."

The finisher's prize was a handsome slice of varnished pine branch with "Sourdough Triathlon" inscribed on it. The day afterward, I nipped out for a 45-mile solo ride in the nearby mountains.

Most of the entrants were reasonably competent amateurs like me, but one was an air traffic controller who complained that he had just done "another bad ironman" – he hadn't quite broken 10 hours at Kona, the Hawaii Ironman! The demands we place on ourselves. Gustav Mahler wrote nine symphonies before his early death at 51; I've already outlived him by some 26 years and have yet to write a single symphony. What good am I? This is the negative side of excessive striving, what Carl Jung referred to as the "shadow."

I did the Phoenix National Trail 50 Mile Run, a hot, tough course. Afterward, by coincidence, I again met Gabriel Flores, the extraordinary ultra runner and the same Indian fellow I had met in Texas who had engaged him for support. Gabriel allowed how he was keen on growing his tire dealership; his material goals in life were clearly more important to him than his astounding athletic career.

There was a pause, and then the Indian man said, bobbing his head gracefully, "What matters is you are rich in heart." Without another word, Gabriel took off running. I have an indelible image of him gliding like a gazelle up the switchbacks on the mountain in the sunset. He needed to warm down…

Another road trip took the three of us to the desert east of L.A. for a ride. As usual, we spent a good hour lashing our bikes to the back of our SUV until, after a silence of at least two minutes, one of us would say, "These bikes aren't goin' anywhere."

At the Half-Vineman finish line

We set out early in the morning, but already the brisk winds were up, and Mark struggled in the lead. Steve and I huddled behind, making barely five knots in our lowest gears. Two hours went by. At last, we turned around. Almost immediately, our gears topped out at 45 mph. We sat up and spread our arms like sails without pedaling!

Another of my favorite half-ironmans was the Half-Vineman in Sonoma County, California. The swim took place in the Russian River, which at that time was so shallow that my hands scraped bottom.

Finally, I often recall the infamous Markleeville "Death Ride," which I did twice in the High Sierras. About 3000 riders showed up for the tour every year, bringing the best bikes made by independent artisans around the country. At one point, we descended the eastern slopes of the Sierras on smooth roads at 50 mph, gazing some 200 miles into the Mojave Desert to our left, with snow-capped peaks looming on our right. And then noticing the cattle grates ahead… Did I mention unweighting my pedals? Later, we heard that one rider had crashed into a cow.

The Bikes

I worked with a master bike-builder named Scott to assemble four state-of-the-art racing bikes with every available frame material – titanium, carbon fiber, chrome-molybdenum steel, and aluminum, respectively – and every brand of "group" (gears and brakes): Shimano Dura-Ace, Campagnolo Record, SRAM. One of the frames was a so-called "beam bike," an unorthodox configuration whose seat was separately mounted on a freestanding beam made of aluminum and carbon fiber. The Holland steel frame and Softride had exceedingly cool custom paint jobs.

Scott and I spent an afternoon experimenting with a hybrid handlebar, a combination of aero-bar and drops. A hacksaw and wrenches were involved. When it was finished, we gazed at it for a long moment, then looked at each other and said simultaneously, "That was stupid." I paid his fee.

One of my groups was the Mektronic, Mavic's first version of an electronic shifter. You had to install several button batteries to make it work, but ultimately, the co-processors all failed. Mavic retreated to their drawing boards; later on, Shimano and others perfected the system. Today, "e-bikes" are ubiquitous.

Ironman Canada

Penticton, Canada, is a pleasant small town on the southern edge of Okanagan Lake in British Columbia. Several city blocks downtown had an astonishing number of shops selling vacuum cleaners and sewing accoutrements –

My racing bikes, from left to right: Litespeed titanium with Dura-Ace;
Holland steel with Campagnolo group and aluminum wheels;
Kestrel carbon; Softride beam

Vac 'n' Sew, Vac & Sew, SewVac, and so on. Oddly, bike shops and athletic stores were harder to find. In preparation for the race, I went to a local barber and instructed her to shave a lightning bolt on the back of my head to induce greater speed.

We had a saying, "Nothing new on race day." The experience of Dave Scott, another legendary pro ironman, was one of the worst examples of breaking that rule. He had trained himself razor-sharp for Kona – the Hawaii Ironman –and tapered perfectly as well, but on the day before the race, someone persuaded him to change the height of his bike seat by half a centimeter. Big mistake! He pulled up lame before finishing his ride.

So that lightning bolt was my only new thing.

The key to speed

The day before the race, every competitor was required to bring his or her bike for a safety check by a "wrencher." Part of the physical examination consisted of putting his weight on the handlebars. When he did so for the guy before me, the handlebars broke on both sides! Years of sweat had rusted holes in them right through the tape. The entrant was enraged, but that repair guy may well have saved his life.

There is always a "valley of fatigue," as Newby-Fraser put it, when you slow or stop training, as I did during my 10-day taper. You realize how tired you are and how badly you have been abusing your body. But the worst is that, at the same time, your inner voice screams, "You cow-legged tub of lard! What are you doing sitting around on your arse? Your fitness is going down the tubes! Your VO2 max will be ZERO by tomorrow morning if you don't get out there and train!"

Some of the entrants succumbed to that urge, putting in serious workouts the day or two before the race to their detriment. Better to remind yourself that "The outcome is not in doubt," as Maggie Thatcher said during the Falklands War.

Your marathon time is going to be substantially longer in an Ironman than by itself. That should be obvious when you consider all the swimming and biking that precedes it, but you don't fully realize it until you're there.

By the way, there's a reason for the swim-bike-run sequence in longer triathlons: when an athlete is exhausted, the place you least want him is in the water. But it's also analogous to man's evolution to upright posture.

Man's evolution

A traditional "carbo-loading" banquet took place every year on the evening before the race. WARNING: The following anecdote is politically incorrect (but true)!

An Australian bloke named Stephen King (no relation to the author) emceed, presenting a slide show and video of previous races. He always wore a tuxedo. As he spoke, a young guy approached him from below the proscenium, walking in a labored, crablike fashion that suggested cerebral palsy. This impression was strengthened when he began speaking urgently in an apraxic manner with a pronounced (pun intended) lisp. "Mr. King, Mr. King…!" As he came closer to the podium, it was apparent that the speaker was being ambushed, and he became increasingly nervous, looking around desperately for help. "Mr. King, I have to athk you something!"

He began clambering spastically onto the stage, repeatedly slipping violently onto the floor, and we realized that it was a setup. Here we were, 1300 shaved-and-tapered triathletes who had trained intensely for months, cats on a hot roof before the race very early the next morning, and the stark contrast threw us into hysterics. I literally sobbed with laughter, and some of us writhed on the floor.

Happily, the fellow revealed himself to be quite healthy, to King's enormous relief, and they shared a hearty hug.

The weather on race morning was perfect, mild and sunny with a few little puffy clouds. Some easy-going swing music played from a speaker in the trees as all 1300 of us assembled on the grassy shore of the lake for the imminent mass start. I felt completely prepared and relaxed, with nothing to lose. At age 46, I had the additional small advantage of being at the front of my five-year age group. Let the pros and faster swimmers plunge ahead, I thought and steeled myself to wait a full two minutes by my Ironman watch until I started. A good strategy, well worth the small time loss!

The course in Lake Okanagan was a counter-clockwise triangle marked with orange buoys. Water temp was a perfect mid-60s, comfortable in my "Long John" wetsuit with a rashguard shirt under it. I soon found a swimmer who was a little faster and drafted him. After rounding the last turn, the sun was rising directly above the finish, so I didn't even have to look up from the water – just follow the light! Very cool. My time was 1:18, terrific for me. When I scrambled up onto the beach, an older race official grabbed my wetsuit and told me in a thick Dutch accent, "Now we peel you like a banahnah!"

Entering the big transition tent to jump into my bike clothes, I was pleasantly surprised to find many others there. "I'm damn well in this race!" I thought excitedly. I dashed out to the bike corral, surrounded by hundreds of cheering family and friends. What a thrill!

The first 30-some miles of the bike were a rather narrow winding road, so drafting, officially prohibited, was unavoidable, and it was slightly downhill. Dozens of us flew along together; the camaraderie was electric. Then we made a right turn and began the first of three long, moderately difficult climbs. The worst part was somewhere around 80 miles at Yellow Lake (very beautiful), which was followed by some screaming roller-coaster descents. Road conditions were generally good, other than some rough spots around 60 miles in a poor rural area.

The run was a fairly flat out-and-back, with a few short steep spots. A nippy headwind blew up in the last 10 miles.

Self-management is the key to success in endurance races: maintaining a good intake of fluids, calories, and electrolytes, controlling the pace and heart rate, and even little details such as not forgetting sunblock – you're gonna be out there all day, and sunburn hurts! Implicit in this is accepting the notion that setting limits will be more likely, not less, to lead to maximum performance. And unless you're one of the giants in the crowd, there will always be people ahead of you as well as behind you.

I remember a guy we often trained and raced with back in the day. He was an excellent cyclist and fast runner but hated swimming. He would always thrash his way through the swim and then go at warp speed on the bike, only to implode somewhere on the run and dnf. Then he would subject us to endless curses and "if-onlys" until the next race… I had no respect for him.

The volunteer crews at Ironman Canada were delightful, and the support was superb. At the end, they provided everything from hot chicken soup to jacuzzis and masseurs. A great experience all around!

The following year, I improved my time to 12:18 and change, which put me in the upper third of my age cohort.

At Ironman Canada on my Softride, 1994 and Litespeed, 1995

Over the years, I totaled some five million yards of swimming, 75,000 miles of cycling, and 32,000 miles of running. I toyed with the idea of tackling an even crazier goal: Ultraman Canada, more than twice as long as the Ironman. I honestly didn't know whether I could finish it, which made it almost irresistibly attractive, but wisdom prevailed. Discretion and valor.

At the finish line of Ironman Canada, 1994

My Finisher's Certificate and I got the way cool jacket
that only finishers were permitted to buy

The Impact of Age on A Senior's Running Pace

Jim Doti

I started long-distance running when I was 56 years old. Now that I'm approaching 80, I'm still in the game. I've now run 42 5Ks, 61 half marathons, and 60 full marathons.

My personal best (PB) 5K chip time in minutes was 21.70. (21 minutes and 42 seconds) at a pace (minutes per mile) of 7.0 when I was 57. I garnered my PB half marathon when I was 64 years old with a time of 1.92 hours (one hour and 55 minutes) at a pace of 8.79. My fastest full marathon took place when I was 62 years old at Sacramento's California International Marathon with a time of 3.67 hours (3 hours and 40 minutes) at a pace of 8.40. That race was my 4th Boston qualifier. Although I qualified for Boston six more times after that, I ran those marathons at successively slower paces.

Notice that all three PBs for the 5K, half marathon, and full marathon took place when I was 57, 64, and 62 years old, respectively. Since then, my race times have slowed with my pace for 5Ks, half, and full marathons on the rise. That result shouldn't be surprising given the impact of aging on muscle mass, telomere shortening, mitochondrial dysfunction, and decreased stem cell function.

As Haruki Murakami wrote in his wonderful memoir about distance running, *What I Talk About When I Talk About Running*:

> *I can try all I want, but I doubt I'll be able to run the way I used to. I'm ready to accept that. It's not one of our happier realities, but that's what happens when you get older. Just as I have my own role to play, so does time. And time does its job much more faithfully, much more accurately, than I ever do.*

How quickly the deterioration takes place, of course, differs from one person to another. No question, though, the breakdown of cells that accompanies the aging process will inevitably slow one's running times and increase pace times. My particular interest was how advancing age affected my pace times. I knew that they were on the rise, but I wondered if my rising pace times followed any discernible patterns. Since I kept a record of all the running times for my official races, I was able to analyze those patterns for my 5Ks, half marathons, and full marathons.

5Ks

Figure 1 is a scatter diagram that shows the relationship between my age and pace in the 42 5Ks I've run.

Figure 1, shows that there was no clear pattern between age and pace until I hit 65, when my pace began to steadily rise. Figure 2 shows that the increase after age 65 followed a linear trendline.

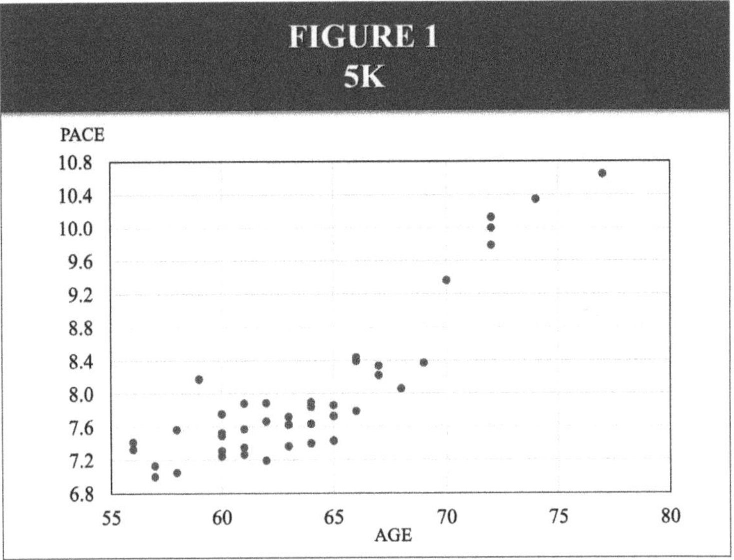

That trendline passed significance tests (not reported here) at the 99 percent level of confidence. Since it's a linear trendline, it suggests that every year, on average, my 5K pace increased by 0.28 of a minute (17 seconds). That is, at age 65, my average 5K pace on the trendline was 7.76. The following year, when I was 66, the trendline suggests that my 5K pace would increase by 0.28 of a minute from 7.76 to 8.04.

The regression results for this linear trendline are shown in Table 1.

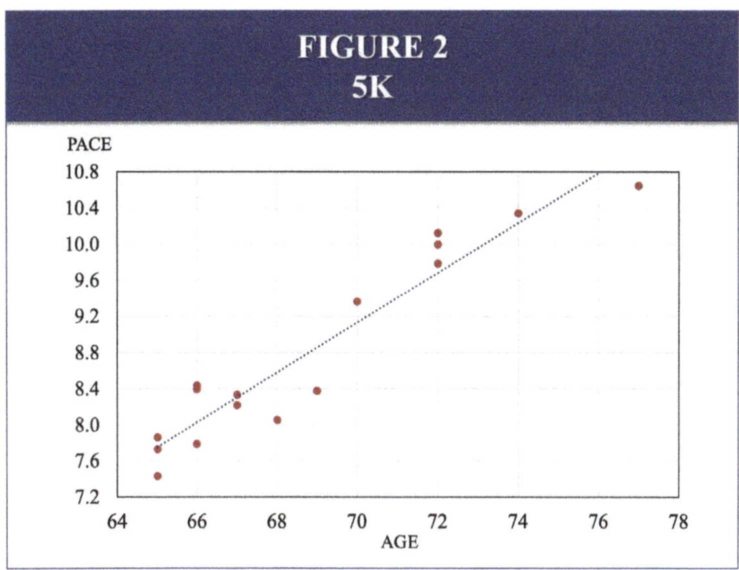

The coefficient for Age in Table 1 is 0.28, a statistic that represents the 0.28 of a minute (17 seconds) average increase in pace for every increase in age of one year. The R-squared value of 0.91 means that 91 percent of all the variation in all my 5K races after 65 is explained by the Age variable. That, in turn, suggests that only about 9 percent of the variation in my 5K paces is explained by other factors such as conditioning, weather, and the course.

TABLE 1
5K Regression Results

Dependent Variable: PACE
Sample (adjusted): 27 42 — Included observations: 16

Independent Variables:	Coefficient	Std. Error	t-Statistic	Prob.
Constant	-10.18	1.61	-6.32	0.00
AGE	0.28	0.02	11.80	0.00

R-Squared	0.91	Mean Dependent var	8.80
Adjusted R-squared	0.90	S.D. dependent var	1.06
S.E. of regression	0.33	Akaike info criterion	0.74
Sum squared resid	1.53	Schwarz criterion	0.84
Log likelihood	-3.94	Hannan-Quinn criterion	0.75
F-statistic	139.26	Durbin-Watson stat	1.43

Half Marathons

Figure 3, is a scatter diagram that shows the relationship between my age and paces for the 61 half marathons I've run.

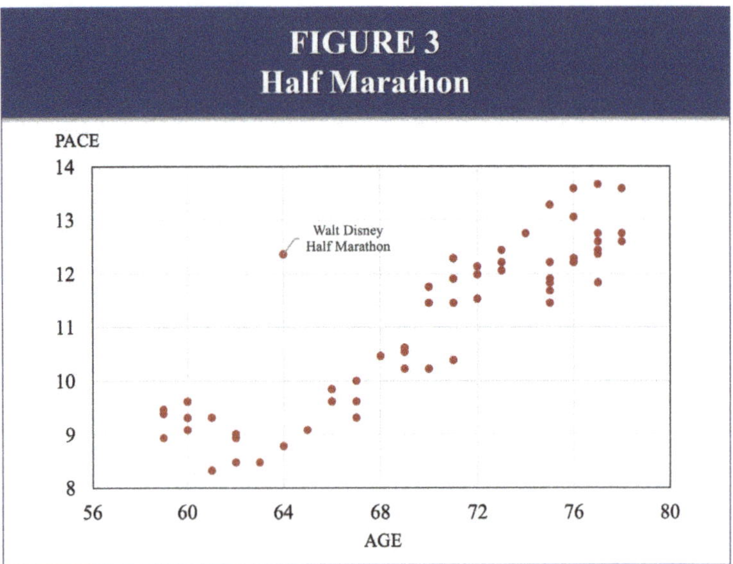

Similar to my 5K paces, Figure 3 suggests that there was no clear pattern between age and pace for my half marathons until I was 65 years old, after which my pace generally increased. In fact, before I hit 65, it seems my half-marathon pace was on the decline, except for an outlier pace of 12.70 that I ran when I was 64 at the Walt Disney World Half Marathon. That anomalous

The coveted Disney-Mickey Medal

result occurred because I deliberately ran that race slowly to save energy for the Walt Disney Marathon I ran the following day. My motivation for running the back-to-back half and full marathons was that runners who completed both races received a special medal that had the likeness of Mickey Mouse and Walt Disney on it. I simply had to have that medal. (Maybe it's that kind of obsession that explains why some people think distance runners are a bit bonkers.)

Figure 4, clearly shows the linear upward trend in my half-marathon pace times after the age of 65.

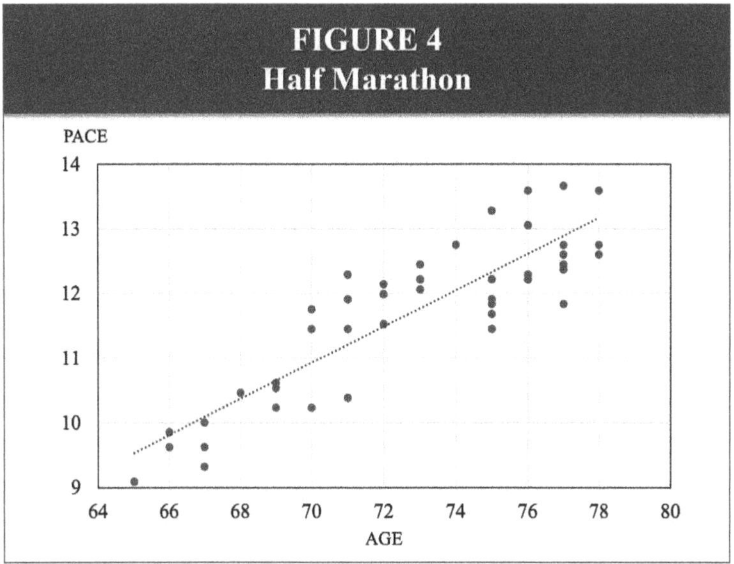

This trendline suggests that every year, on average, my half-marathon pace increased by 0.28 of a minute (17 seconds), the same as the increase in my 5K pace times over the same age period.

Table 2 presents the regression results.

As in Table 1, the coefficient of 0.28 represents the constant linear increase of 0.28 of a minute (17 seconds) for the annual increase in average pace for the half marathons I ran after the age of 65. The R-squared value of 0.79 indicates that 79 percent of all the variation in my half-marathon pace after age 65 is explained by advancing age. The fact that age explains 79 percent of the variation in half marathons versus a higher 91 percent for 5Ks, is likely the result of non-age-related factors like conditioning, weather, and course having a greater relative impact on pace over longer runs.

Dependent Variable: PACE				
Sample (adjusted): 15 61		Included observations: 47		
Independent Variables:	Coefficient	Std. Error	t-Statistic	Prob.
Constant	-8.66	1.58	-5.47	0.00
AGE	0.28	0.02	12.87	0.00
R-Squared	0.79	Mean Dependent var		11.68
Adjusted R-squared	0.78	S.D. dependent var		1.22
S.E. of regression	0.57	Akaike info criterion		1.75
Sum squared resid	14.57	Schwarz criterion		1.83
Log likelihood	-39.17	Hannan-Quinn criterion		1.78
F-statistic	165.51	Durbin-Watson stat		1.90

TABLE 2
Half Marathon Regression Results

Marathons

Figure 5 is a scatter diagram that shows the relationship between my age and pace for the 60 full marathons I've run.

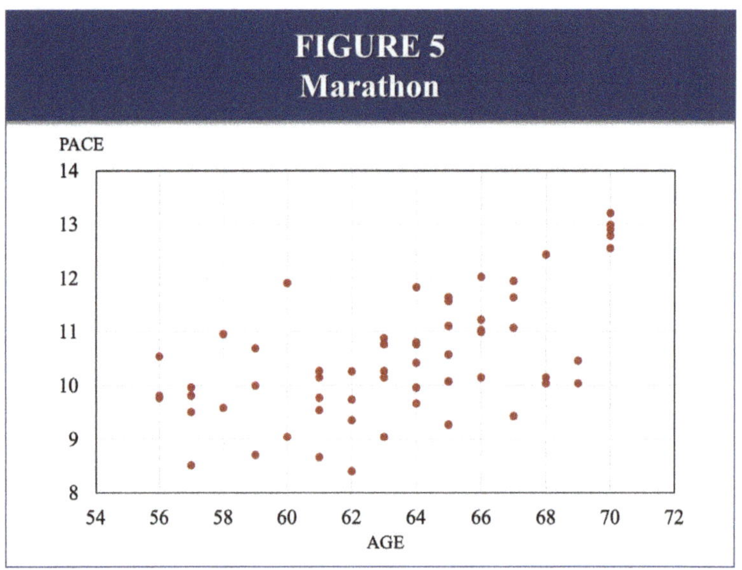

Unlike my 5Ks and half marathons, where linear upward trends in pace occurred at age 65, Figure 5 shows the upward trend for running full marathons started earlier for me at the age of 62. Before age 62, no relationship between age and pace is observed. It should be noted that, unlike 5Ks and half marathons that I'm still running, my last official marathon was the Boston Marathon that I ran at a pace of 12.55 eight years ago when I was 70 years old.

Nonetheless, from age 62 to 70, an upward linear trend in my pace times is clearly present. This can be seen in Figure 6, where the linear trendline suggests that every year, on average, my marathon pace increased by 0.29 of a minute (17 seconds), about the same as the annual increase of 0.28 of a minute in my 5K and half-marathon pace times.

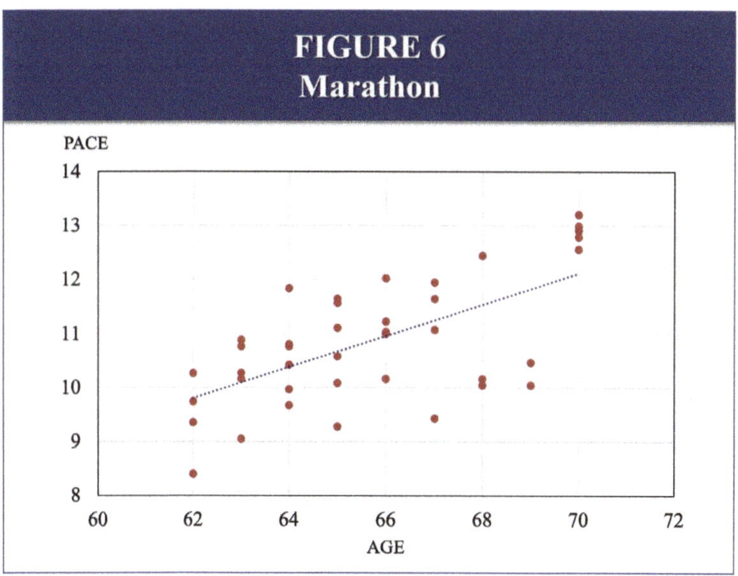

Table 3 shows the regression results for the 41 marathons I ran from age 62 to age 70 when I "retired" from running full marathons.

TABLE 3
Marathon Regression Results

Dependent Variable: PACE

Sample (adjusted): 20 60   Included observations: 41

Independent Variables:	Coefficient	Std. Error	t-Statistic	Prob.
Constant	-8.14	3.70	-2.20	0.03
AGE	0.29	0.06	5.13	0.00

R-Squared	0.40	Mean Dependent var	10.84
Adjusted R-squared	0.39	S.D. dependent var	1.15
S.E. of regression	0.90	Akaike info criterion	2.68
Sum squared resid	31.68	Schwarz criterion	2.76
Log likelihood	-52.89	Hannan-Quinn criterion	2.71
F-statistic	26.36	Durbin-Watson stat	2.05

The coefficient of 0.29 represents the constant linear increase of 0.29 of a minute (17 seconds) for the annual increase in average pace for my full marathon runs after the age of 62. The R-squared value of 0.40 indicates that only 40 percent of the variation in my marathon pace after 62 is explained by age, a result much lower than the 91 percent explained by age in my 5Ks and 78 percent explained in my half marathons. The greater variation in full marathons is reflected in Figure 6 by the greater deviation of the actual pace times from the predicted pace as shown by the linear trendline. Not surprisingly, running 26.2 miles versus 3.1 miles for a 5K and 13.1 miles for a half marathon allows for variables like conditioning, climate, and course to have a greater impact than those factors would have in a shorter race. For example, a temperature of 80 degrees will negatively affect a half-marathon pace more than a 5K and a full marathon more than a half-marathon.

The Relationship between Age and Pace
Figure 7 shows the relationship between age and pace times at the beginning and end of the three linear trend lines for my 5Ks, half, and full marathons. Although my pace times are higher for races of longer distance, the slopes of the curves are approximately the same. That finding for the relationship between my age and pace reflects the 17-second increase in pace times each year for 5Ks, half, and full marathons.

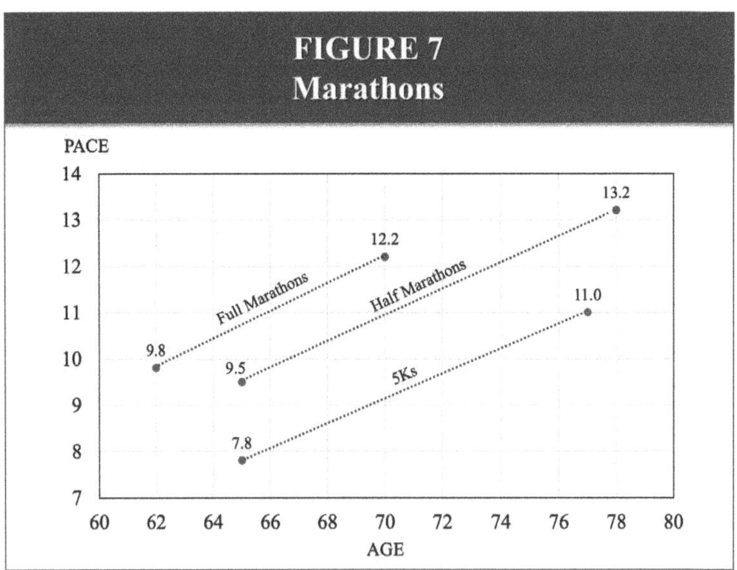

I'm not sure how the relationship between age and pace for me compares to that of other senior runners. Obviously, the sample of runners would have to be significantly increased to make interval estimates for population estimates around the sample results. Such a test, I believe, would be interesting and useful. I'd be particularly interested in seeing if the results using larger samples result in pace times that increase in a linear pattern for all three types of races, as they did in mine.

Although the analysis presented in this study relates specifically to the impact of age on my average pace and not to other senior runners, my empirical results are useful in a number of ways. Rather than getting discouraged about age-related pace creep, I realize it's a fact of life. That, I believe, has helped me to continue my long-distance running.

For example, I completed my most recent Orange County Half Marathon at age 78 (almost 79) at a pace of 12.60. That's a lot slower than my pace of 9.31 the first time I ran the Orange County Half Marathon at age 67. The fact that my pace increased from 9.31 to 12.60 means that in only eleven years, it took me on average about 3.3 minutes longer to run every mile in that race. It's that kind of diminished performance that might lead someone to give it all up and bronze their favorite running shoes.

Not me! Armed with a clearer picture of how age, on average, has affected my half-marathon time, I come away encouraged rather than disheartened by my recent performance at the Orange County Half. This can be seen in Figure 8, where my recent Orange County Half Marathon pace at age 78 was 12.60. The trendline, which shows the expected average increase in pace due to aging, as shown in Figure 8, is a pace of 13.18. So instead of being depressed about how much slower my 12.60 pace compared to my earlier half marathons, I was

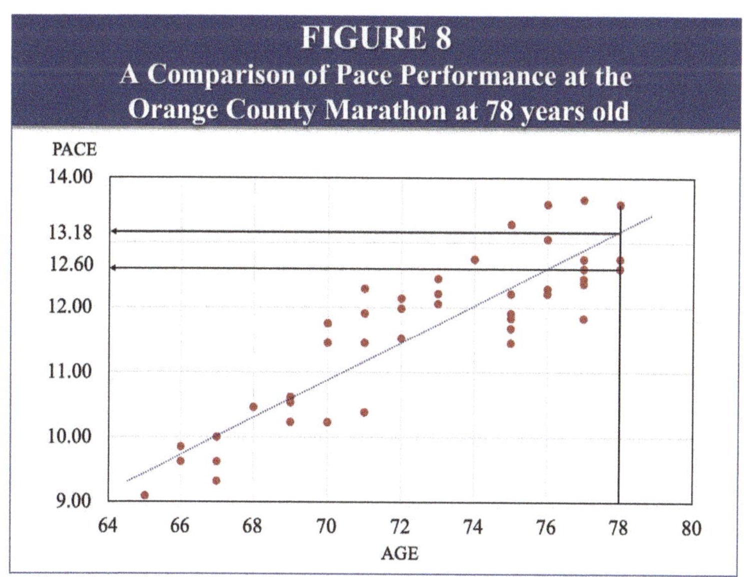

pleased to beat my expected or forecasted pace by 0.58 minutes (13.18 less 12.60 = 0.58) or 35 seconds.

Another example of how I use these empirical results relates to a recent thought I've had. Recall I "retired" from running full marathons when I ran my 60th at Boston at age 70 at a pace of 12.56 (12 minutes and 34 seconds). Lately, I've been thinking about ramping up my training so that I could run a full marathon at age 80. How cool would that be?

Not very. As shown in Figure 9, extending the average marathon trend line to age 80 results in a forecasted marathon pace of 15.00.

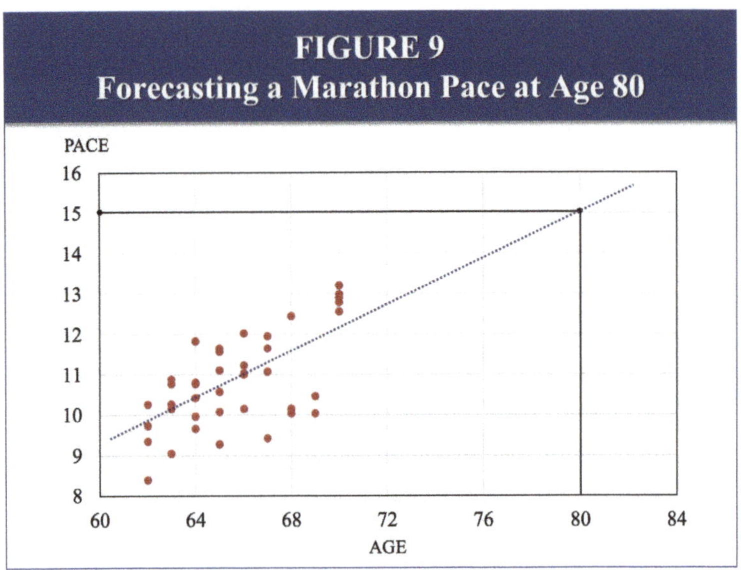

An average pace of 15.00 is more akin to walking rather than running. Even worse, at a pace of 15.00, it would take 6.55 hours (6 hours and 33 minutes) to complete this imagined marathon. After reflecting on that for a bit, I've decided to keep thoughts of returning to marathon glory strictly hypothetical.

Staying in the Game

The fact that I've accepted rather than fought the effects of aging on pace times has had a salutary effect on me. Instead of training harder to fight the relentless effects of aging, I've learned to not only accept the slower paces but be grateful that I'm still in the game. As Haruki Murakami reflects in his memoir:

> *I'll be happy if running and I can grow old together. There may not seem much logic to it, but it's the life I've chosen for myself. Not that, at this late date, I have other options.*

Three-peating at the Napa-Sonoma Wine County Half-Marathon

The upside to being a senior distance runner is that I'm increasingly finding myself in the top 3 of runners in my age cohort – something I never did in my earlier years. This year, for example, I'll be going for my fourth first-place win in the 75-79 age cohort in the Napa-Sonoma Wine Country Half Marathon. The fact that I've been either alone or among only a few runners in that age cohort does not diminish for me the pleasure of three-peating. As I attempt a fourth consecutive win in my 75-79 cohort this year, my fear is that some 75-year-old whipper snapper will take my place at the winner's circle. But if that happens, I won't dwell on it. I'll just shift my focus on how sweet it will be when I move into the 80-84 bracket as the newest spring chicken on the block.

If I'm lucky enough to run in that 80-84 age cohort, I know my pace-setting goals will change. That's okay. In my mind, being able to set those goals, whatever they may be, explains the joy of running. As Haruki Murakami describes it:

Most runners run not because they want to live longer, but because they want to live life to the fullest. If you're going to while away the years, it's better to live them with clear goals and be fully alive than in a fog, and I believe running helps you do that.

About the Authors

JIM DOTI is President Emeritus and holds the Rick Muth Family Chair in Economics at the George Argyros College of Business & Economics, Chapman University. He earned his M.A. and Ph.D. degrees from the University of Chicago. Between 1991-2016, Dr. Doti served as President of Chapman University. Jim started running in 2002 as training for mountaineering. His running helped him successfully summit five of the world's famed Seven Summits, along with his son, Adam. He has completed 60 full marathons, including ten runnings of the famed Boston Marathon. He is shown here rappelling in Point Dume in Malibu.

LYNNE P. DOTI, Emeritus Professor of Economics at Chapman University, is the author of four books and over twenty-five articles on banking. She served as a director of several companies and was an organizing director of Plaza Bank. She is currently on the Board of Directors of Anivive, an animal pharmaceutical company. A gym is her currently preferred exercise venue. Lynne is shown hiking in Park City, Utah.

ADAM DOTI is a lifelong adventurer, creative leader, and builder. He leads design teams at Salesforce as VP of Design Systems, where he brings a multidisciplinary background in Fine Art, Psychology, and Animation to crafting intuitive, human-centered experiences. An artist at heart and technologist by craft, Adam has been building and innovating for the web since 1992—working at the intersection of creativity and technology from his home base in San Francisco. Beyond the screen, Adam is an avid expedition racer and mountaineer. He has climbed five of the world's Seven Summits alongside his father, and countless other peaks across the western U.S.—transforming challenge into a shared legacy. A dedicated member of the Burning Man community since 1999, Adam serves on the Board of Directors for the Temple Builders Guild and has played strategic, leadership, and community roles on the Temple Build Crew since 2000. In this photo, Adam is pictured in Nevada's Black Rock Desert—a place of profound meaning in his life, where stillness, creativity, and wild beauty converge.

SCOTT CHAPMAN is a theoretical nuclear physicist turned tech entrepreneur. He earned his B.S. from Yale University and a Ph.D. in Physics from UC Berkeley. Following postdoctoral research at Universität Regensburg and Los Alamos National Laboratory, Scott transitioned into business in the late 1990s. He began at McKinsey & Company before founding two cloud-focused companies, including Project Hosts, where he currently serves as CEO. Throughout his business career, Scott has remained active in theoretical physics, focusing on areas such as Quantum Chromodynamics (QCD), BRST Quantization of Gauge Theories, and Supersymmetry. He also serves as Secretary of the Board of Trustees of Chapman University. Mountaineering and rock climbing have been lifelong passions for Scott, especially when he is able to join Jim Doti on an expedition. He is shown here on the "Nose" route on El Capitan in Yosemite.

RYAN DAHLEM is Head of School at The Rivers School, a leading independent school in Boston serving students in grades 6-12 and home of The Rivers School Conservatory, an elite music program. Ryan earned his A.B. from Stanford University and Ed.M. from the Harvard Graduate School of Education. Ryan and his father, Dr. John Dahlem, also a lifelong educator, pursued climbing expeditions around the world and completed the storied Seven Summits, the highest peak on each of the seven continents. When they reached the summit of Mt. Everest, they were the oldest father-son climbing duo to stand on top of the world. Ryan is pictured here with his father on their Mt. Everest expedition.

DANIELE STRUPPA is President Emeritus of Chapman University and holds the Donald Bren Presidential Chair in Mathematics. He earned his Ph.D. from the University of Maryland in 1981 and is the author of more than 200 peer-reviewed publications in several areas of mathematics, including more than 10 full-length books. He has summited three of the Seven Summits and twice Kilimanjaro (the second time 25 years after his first summit). He has run, with pitiful times, several marathons but has also completed a few ultramarathons and two 24-hour races with his son Alessandro. He is shown here on a winter climb of the Baldy Bowl in Southern California.

DAN TEMIANKA was one of the founding partners of the HealthCare Partners Medical Group, where he practiced primary-care internal medicine and served as quality medical director. He became a triathlete in 1992 and completed over 40 endurance sports events, including three ironman triathlons and eight ultra-marathons. His extensive travels have included the North Pole, Antarctica, and Patagonia. He established a Professorship, Scholarship, and Archives at Chapman University in the name of his late father, the great violinist, conductor, and educator Henri Temianka. He has copyrighted 20 books, including *The Witches' Brew, a novel*; a dictionary, *The Jack Vance Lexicon*; and an anthology of his father's articles on string playing and teaching. He is an accomplished woodworker and has crafted hundreds of wind chimes, bowls, and other specialty pieces. He is shown here throwing the ceremonial first pitch at Dodger Stadium in August 2018.